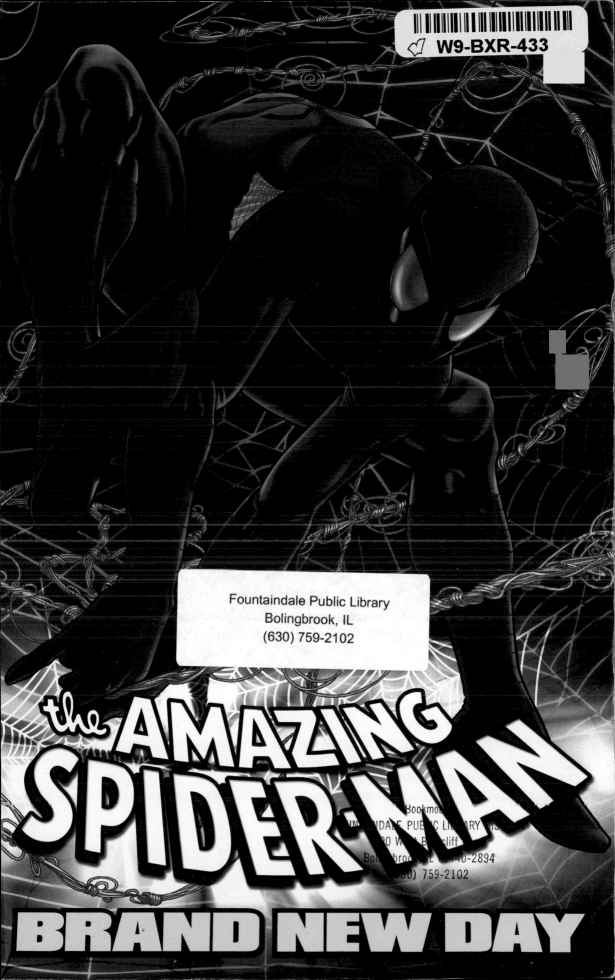

the AMAZING SPIDER-MAN

BRAND NEW DAY

the AMAZING SPIDER-MAN

BRAND NEW DAY

AMAZING SPIDER-MAN #559-561
Writer: **DAN SLOTT** · Art: **MARCOS MARTIN**
Colorist: **JAVIER RODRIGUEZ** · Covers, #560-561: **MARCOS MARTIN**
Cover, #559: **ED MCGUINNESS** & **MORRY HOLLOWELL**

AMAZING SPIDER-MAN #562-563
Writer: **BOB GALE** · Pencils: **MIKE MCKONE**
Inkers: **ANDY LANNING** and **MARLO ALQUIZA**
Colorists: **JEROMY COX** & **STUDIO F'S ANTONIO FABELA**
Covers: **MIKE MCKONE, ANDY LANNING** & **JEROMY COX**

Letters: **VC'S CORY PETIT**
Spidey's Braintrust: **BOB GALE, MARC GUGGENHEIM,**
DAN SLOTT & **ZEB WELLS**
Assistant Editor: **TOM BRENNAN**
Editor: **STEPHEN WACKER**
Executive Editor: **TOM BREVOORT**

Collection Editor: **JENNIFER GRÜNWALD**
Editorial Assistant: **ALEX STARBUCK**
Assistant Editors: **CORY LEVINE** & **JOHN DENNING**
Editor, Special Projects: **MARK D. BEAZLEY**
Senior Editor, Special Projects: **JEFF YOUNGQUIST**
Senior Vice President of Sales: **DAVID GABRIEL**
Book Designer: **RODOLFO MURAGUCHI**

Editor in Chief: **JOE QUESADA**
Publisher: **DAN BUCKLEY**

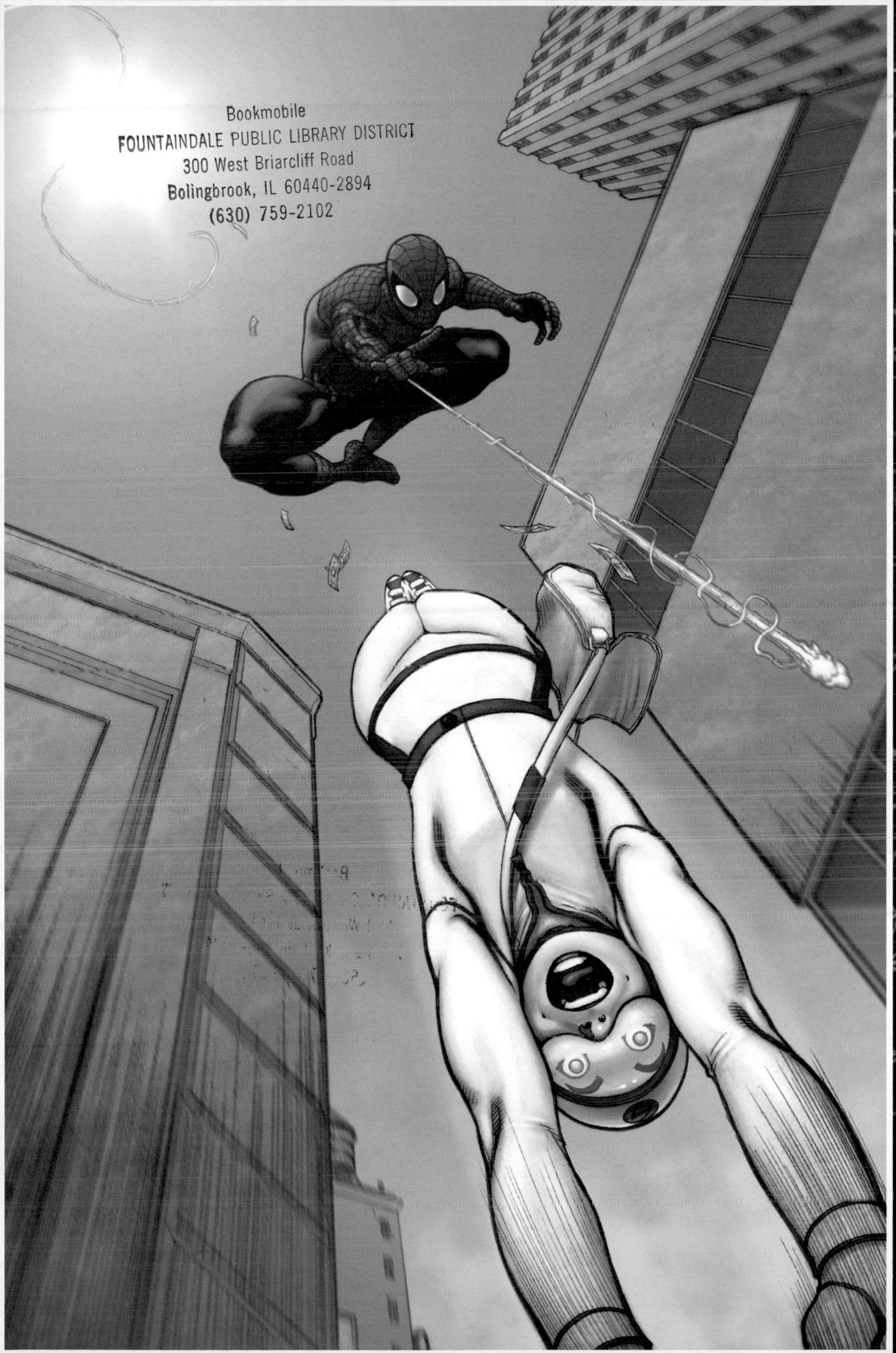

AMAZING SPIDER-MAN #559

THE OFFICIAL NEWSPAPER OF SPIDER-MAN

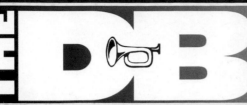

THE DB

COLD DAYS AND HOT NIGHTS – HOLLISTER'S DAUGHTER PARTIES ALL NIGHT WHILE CITY DIGS OUT ALL DAY. ALSO, WITNESSES SEE LEAPING LARCENER COMMITTING HOPPING HEISTS ACROSS MANHATTAN. IS SHE IN CAHOOTS WITH SPIDER-MAN? – MORE ON PAGE D12

MAY 14, 2008 • WEDNESDAY

FREAKSHOW'S OVER!

VISIT THE SPIDEY-BLOG!
www.marvel.com/blogs/spider-office

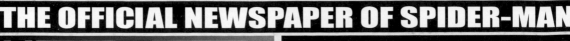

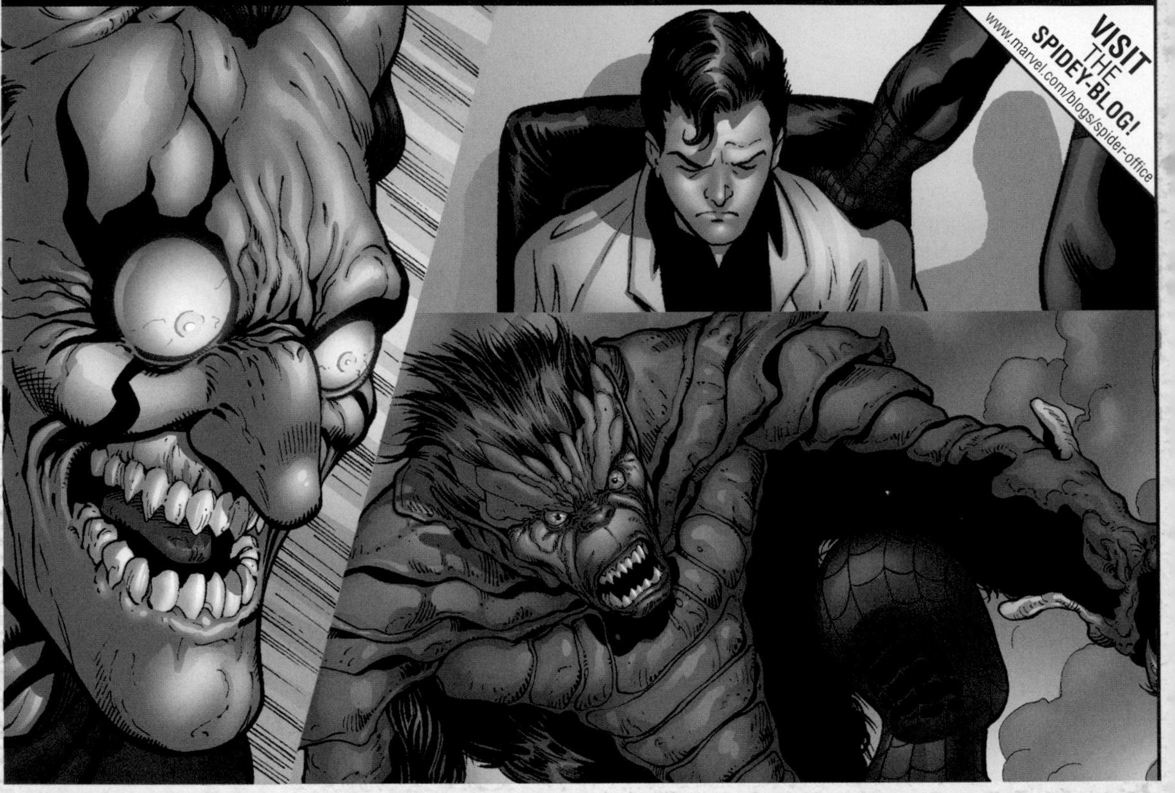

Spidey's drug-abusing beastly foe, Freak, resurfaced after New York's blizzard finally came to an end. With the help of Dr. Curt Connors, Freak was subdued and taken away – by Oscorp. Things ain't too much easier for Spidey, though – Menace raises his ugly jowls at a Hollister campaign rally, threatening Hollister and his family – including daughter, Lily. But some things are looking up – Pete's found a roommate in police officer (and Spider-Man foe) Vin Gonzales. Y'know, maybe things ARE looking up for Spidey. With the change of weather, maybe it's time for a walk across town. Or a dash. Or a high-speed chase…

POLICE TIE SPIDER-MAN TO RECENT MURDERS!

EXCLUSIVE TO THE DB!

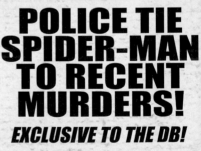

In off-the-record conversations with DB staffers, police have confirmed that Spider-Man is the key suspect in the string of recent murders that has shocked this city. Although police have been reluctant to discuss the specifics of the murders, so-called "Spider Tracers" have definitely been found on each victim, leaving no doubt as to the involvement of Spider-Man. Spider-Man is already wanted for violations of…

CONTINUED ON A2

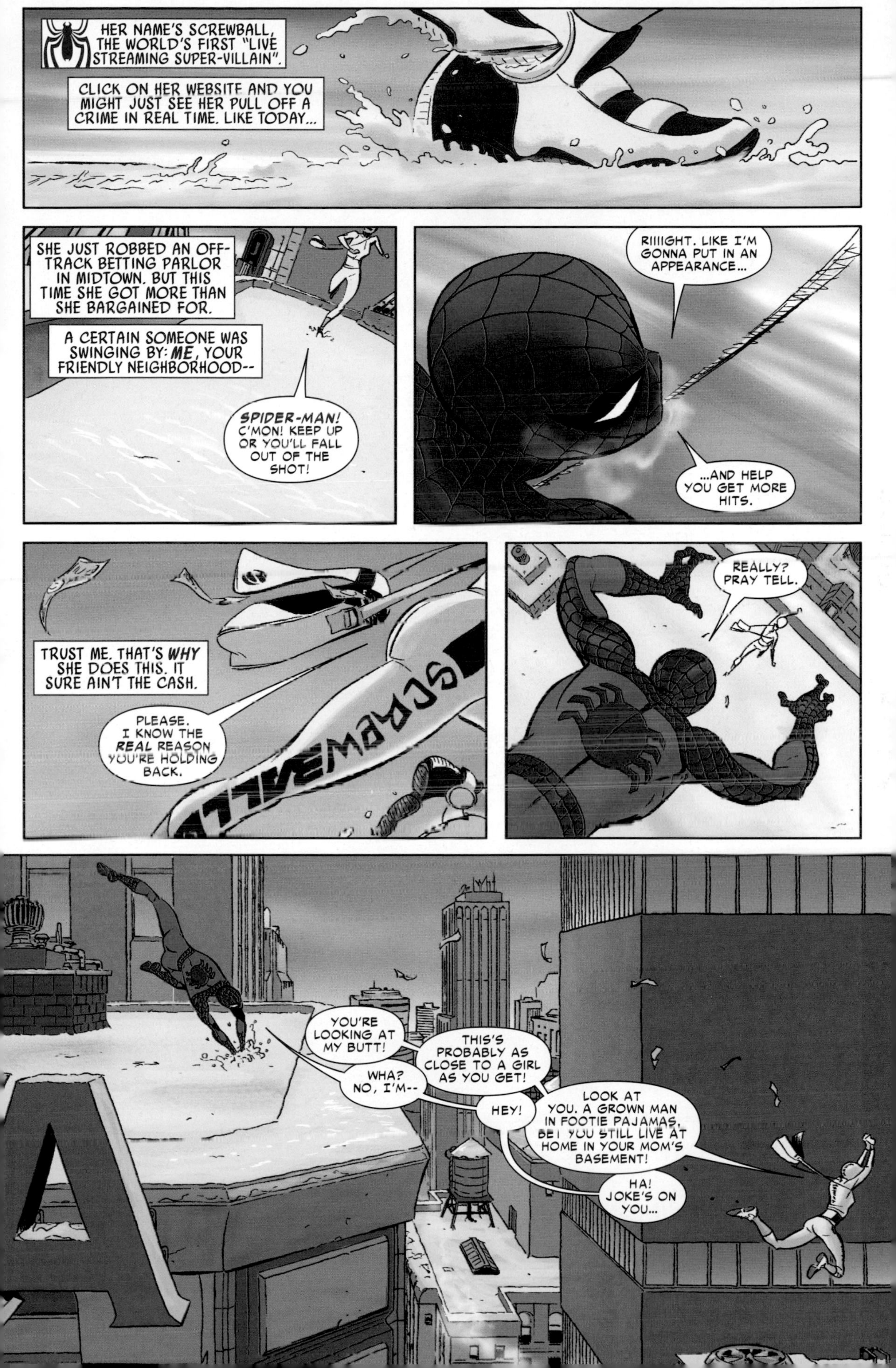
HER NAME'S SCREWBALL, THE WORLD'S FIRST "LIVE STREAMING SUPER-VILLAIN".
CLICK ON HER WEBSITE AND YOU MIGHT JUST SEE HER PULL OFF A CRIME IN REAL TIME. LIKE TODAY...
SHE JUST ROBBED AN OFF-TRACK BETTING PARLOR IN MIDTOWN. BUT THIS TIME SHE GOT MORE THAN SHE BARGAINED FOR.
A CERTAIN SOMEONE WAS SWINGING BY: ME, YOUR FRIENDLY NEIGHBORHOOD--
SPIDER-MAN! C'MON! KEEP UP OR YOU'LL FALL OUT OF THE SHOT!
RIIIGHT. LIKE I'M GONNA PUT IN AN APPEARANCE...
...AND HELP YOU GET MORE HITS.
TRUST ME. THAT'S WHY SHE DOES THIS. IT SURE AIN'T THE CASH.
PLEASE. I KNOW THE REAL REASON YOU'RE HOLDING BACK.
SCREWBALL
REALLY? PRAY TELL.
YOU'RE LOOKING AT MY BUTT!
THIS'S PROBABLY AS CLOSE TO A GIRL AS YOU GET!
WHA? NO, I'M--
HEY!
LOOK AT YOU. A GROWN MAN IN FOOTIE PAJAMAS. BET YOU STILL LIVE AT HOME IN YOUR MOM'S BASEMENT!
HA! JOKE'S ON YOU...

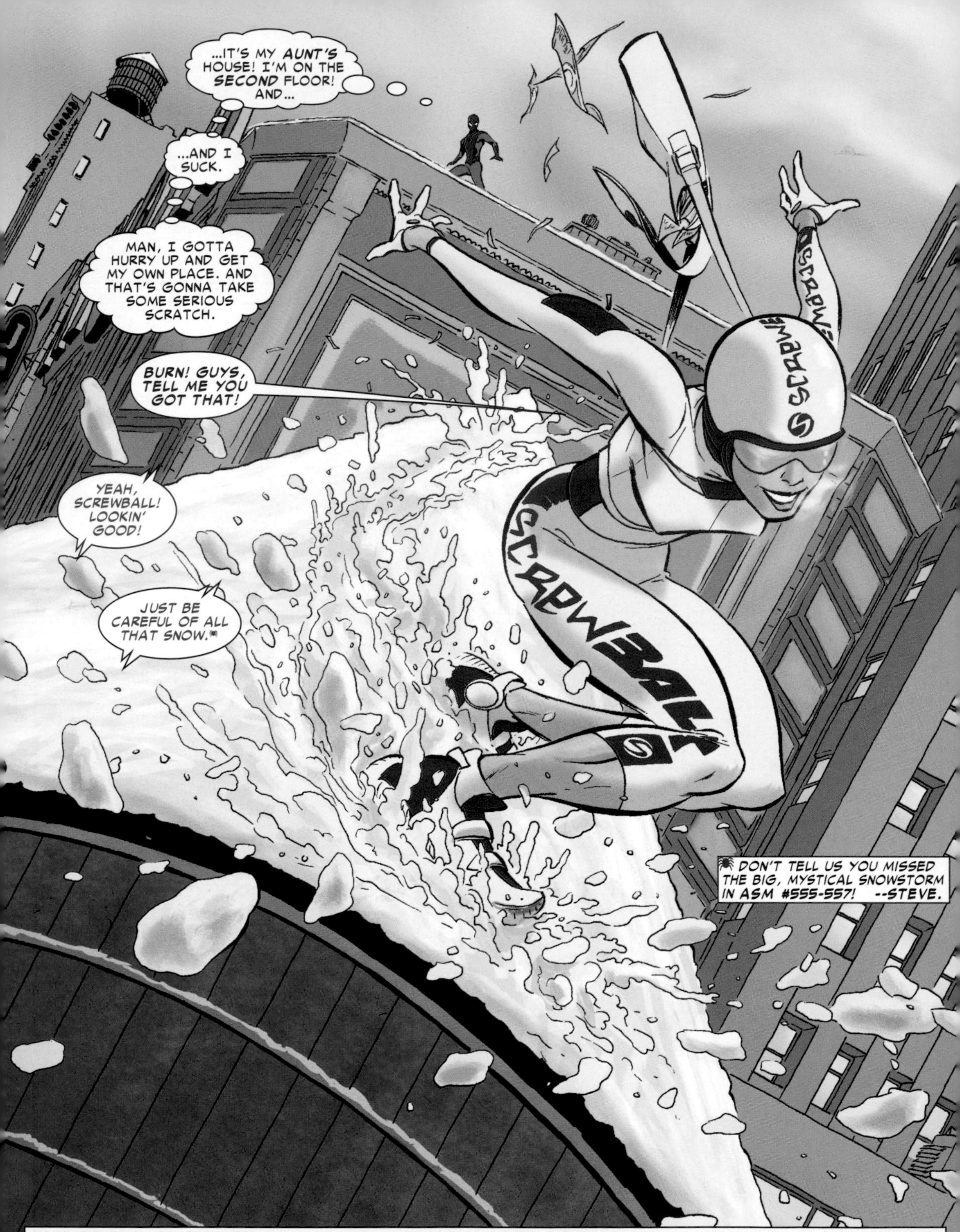
...IT'S MY AUNT'S HOUSE! I'M ON THE SECOND FLOOR! AND...
...AND I SUCK.
MAN, I GOTTA HURRY UP AND GET MY OWN PLACE. AND THAT'S GONNA TAKE SOME SERIOUS SCRATCH.
BURN! GUYS, TELL ME YOU GOT THAT!
YEAH, SCREWBALL! LOOKIN' GOOD!
JUST BE CAREFUL OF ALL THAT SNOW.*
SCREWBALL
* DON'T TELL US YOU MISSED THE BIG, MYSTICAL SNOWSTORM IN ASM #555-557! --STEVE.

WHILE ATTENDING A DEMONSTRATION IN RADIOLOGY, HIGH SCHOOL STUDENT **PETER PARKER** WAS BITTEN BY A SPIDER WHICH HAD ACCIDENTALLY BEEN EXPOSED TO **RADIOACTIVE RAYS.** THROUGH A MIRACLE OF SCIENCE, PETER SOON FOUND THAT HE HAD **GAINED** THE SPIDER'S POWERS...AND HAD, IN EFFECT, BECOME A HUMAN SPIDER! FROM THAT DAY ON HE WAS...

THE AMAZING SPIDER-MAN™

PETER PARKER, PAPARAZZI Part One THE MONEY $HOT

DAN SLOTT	MARCOS MARTIN	JAVIER RODRIGUEZ	VC'S CORY PETIT	TOM BRENNAN	STEPHEN WACKER	TOM BREVOORT	JOE QUESADA	DAN BUCKLEY
WRITER	ART	COLORS	LETTERS	ASST. EDITOR	OUTSOURCED	EXECUTIVE EDITOR	EDITOR IN CHIEF	PUBLISHER

GALE, GUGGENHEIM, SLOTT & WELLS SPIDEY'S BRAINTRUST

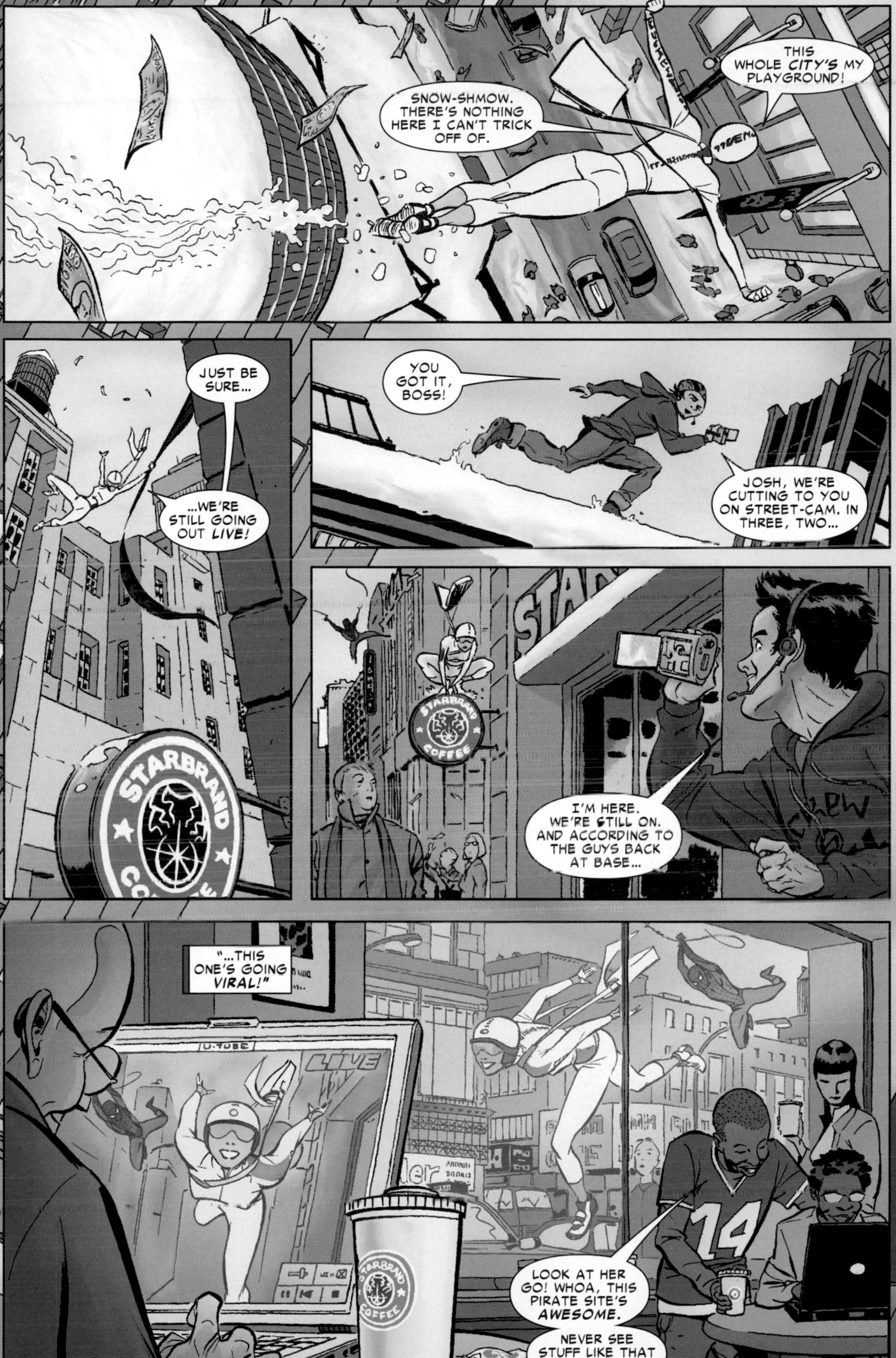
SNOW-SHMOW. THERE'S NOTHING HERE I CAN'T TRICK OFF OF.
THIS WHOLE CITY'S MY PLAYGROUND!
JUST BE SURE...
...WE'RE STILL GOING OUT LIVE!
YOU GOT IT, BOSS!
JOSH, WE'RE CUTTING TO YOU ON STREET-CAM. IN THREE, TWO...
STARBRAND COFFEE
I'M HERE. WE'RE STILL ON. AND ACCORDING TO THE GUYS BACK AT BASE...
"...THIS ONE'S GOING VIRAL!"
LIVE
STARBRAND COFFEE
LOOK AT HER GO! WHOA, THIS PIRATE SITE'S AWESOME.
NEVER SEE STUFF LIKE THAT AROUND HERE!

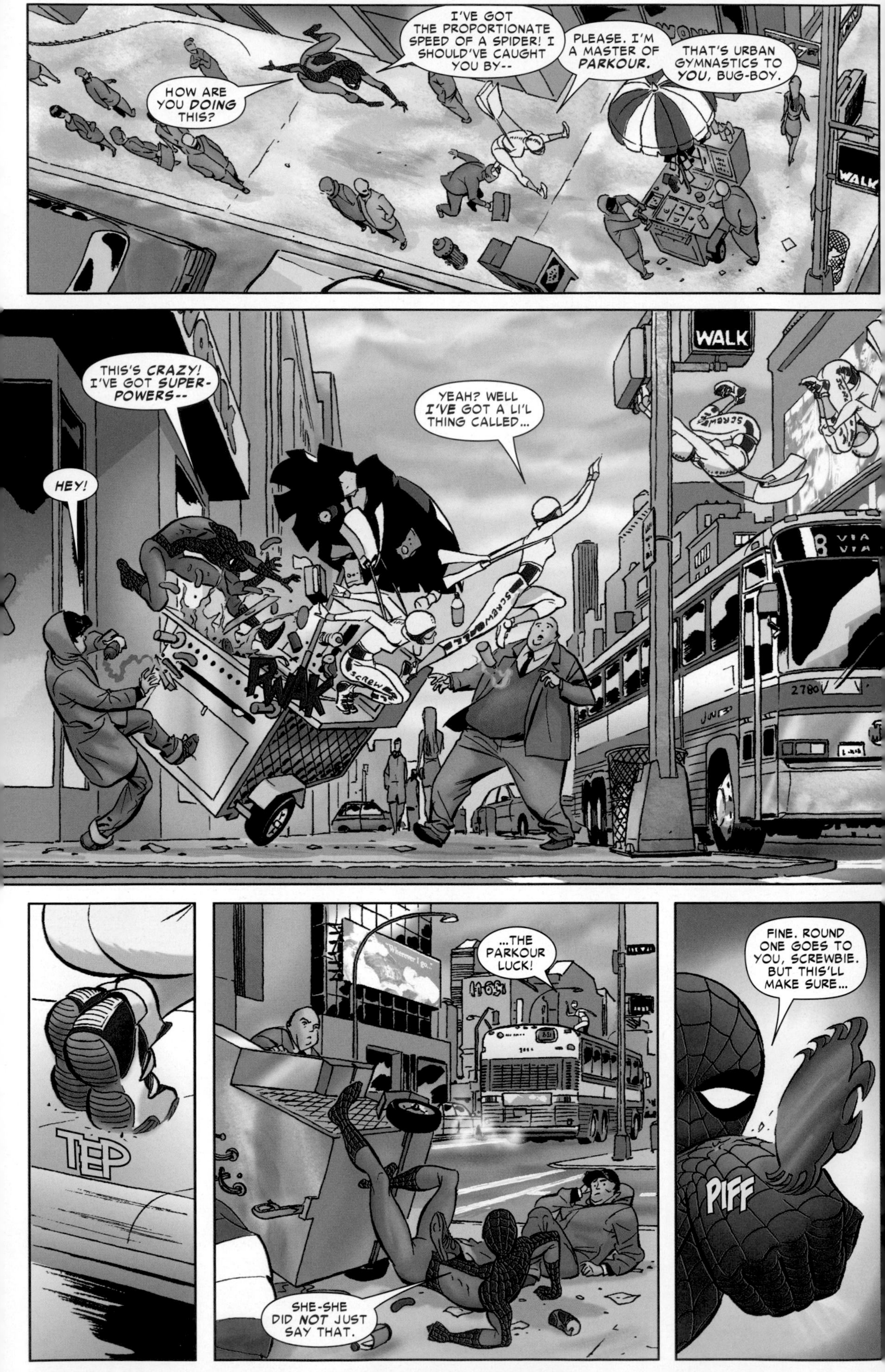
HOW ARE YOU DOING THIS?
I'VE GOT THE PROPORTIONATE SPEED OF A SPIDER! I SHOULD'VE CAUGHT YOU BY--
PLEASE. I'M A MASTER OF PARKOUR.
THAT'S URBAN GYMNASTICS TO YOU, BUG-BOY.
WALK
THIS'S CRAZY! I'VE GOT SUPER-POWERS--
YEAH? WELL I'VE GOT A LI'L THING CALLED...
WALK
HEY!
PWAK
TEP
...THE PARKOUR LUCK!
SHE-SHE DID NOT JUST SAY THAT.
FINE. ROUND ONE GOES TO YOU, SCREWBIE. BUT THIS'LL MAKE SURE...
PIFF

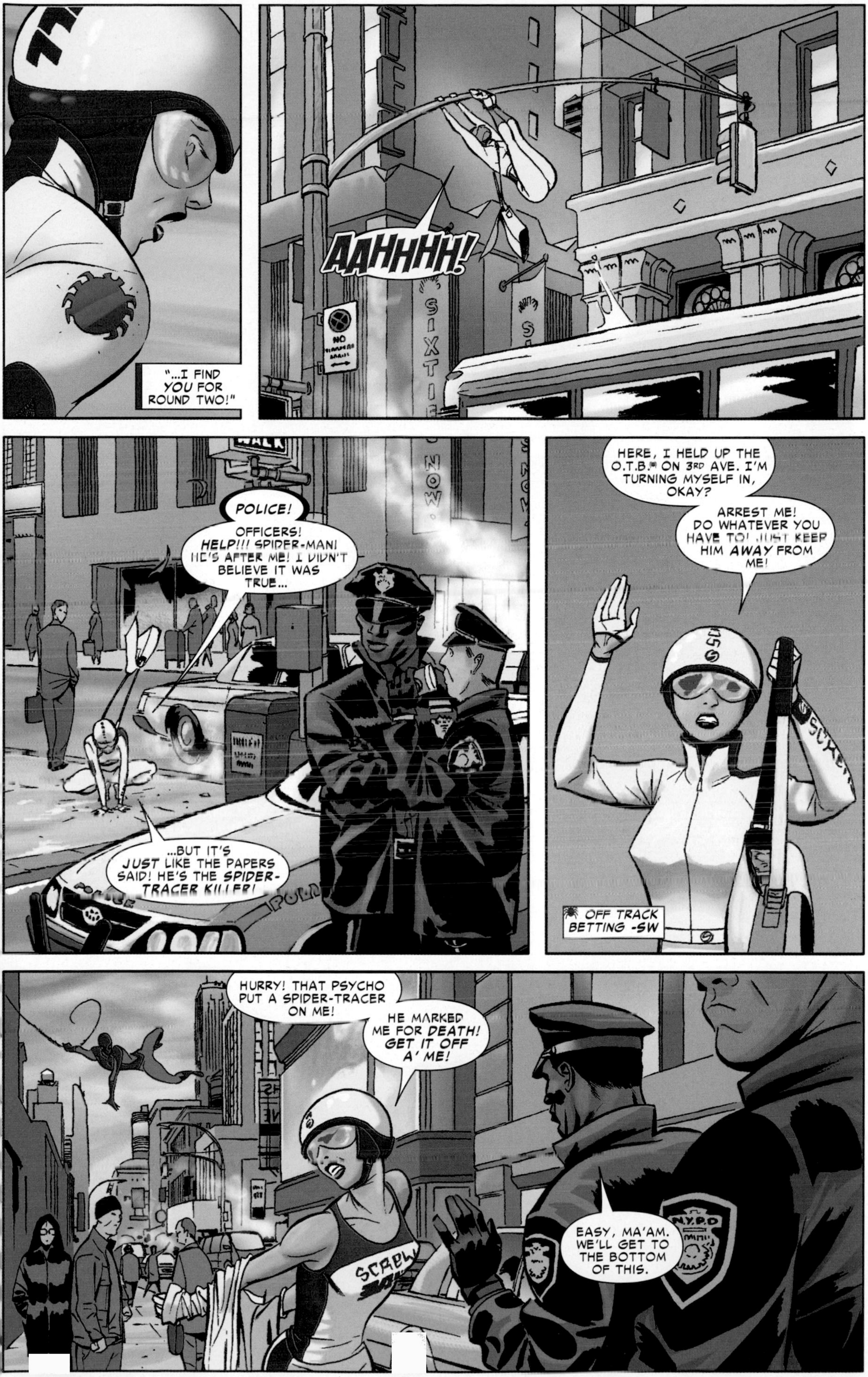
"...I FIND YOU FOR ROUND TWO!"
AAHHHH!
POLICE!
OFFICERS! HELP!!! SPIDER-MAN! HE'S AFTER ME! I DIDN'T BELIEVE IT WAS TRUE...
...BUT IT'S JUST LIKE THE PAPERS SAID! HE'S THE SPIDER-TRACER KILLER!
HERE, I HELD UP THE O.T.B.* ON 3RD AVE. I'M TURNING MYSELF IN, OKAY?
ARREST ME! DO WHATEVER YOU HAVE TO! JUST KEEP HIM AWAY FROM ME!
*OFF TRACK BETTING -SW
HURRY! THAT PSYCHO PUT A SPIDER-TRACER ON ME!
HE MARKED ME FOR DEATH! GET IT OFF A' ME!
EASY, MA'AM. WE'LL GET TO THE BOTTOM OF THIS.

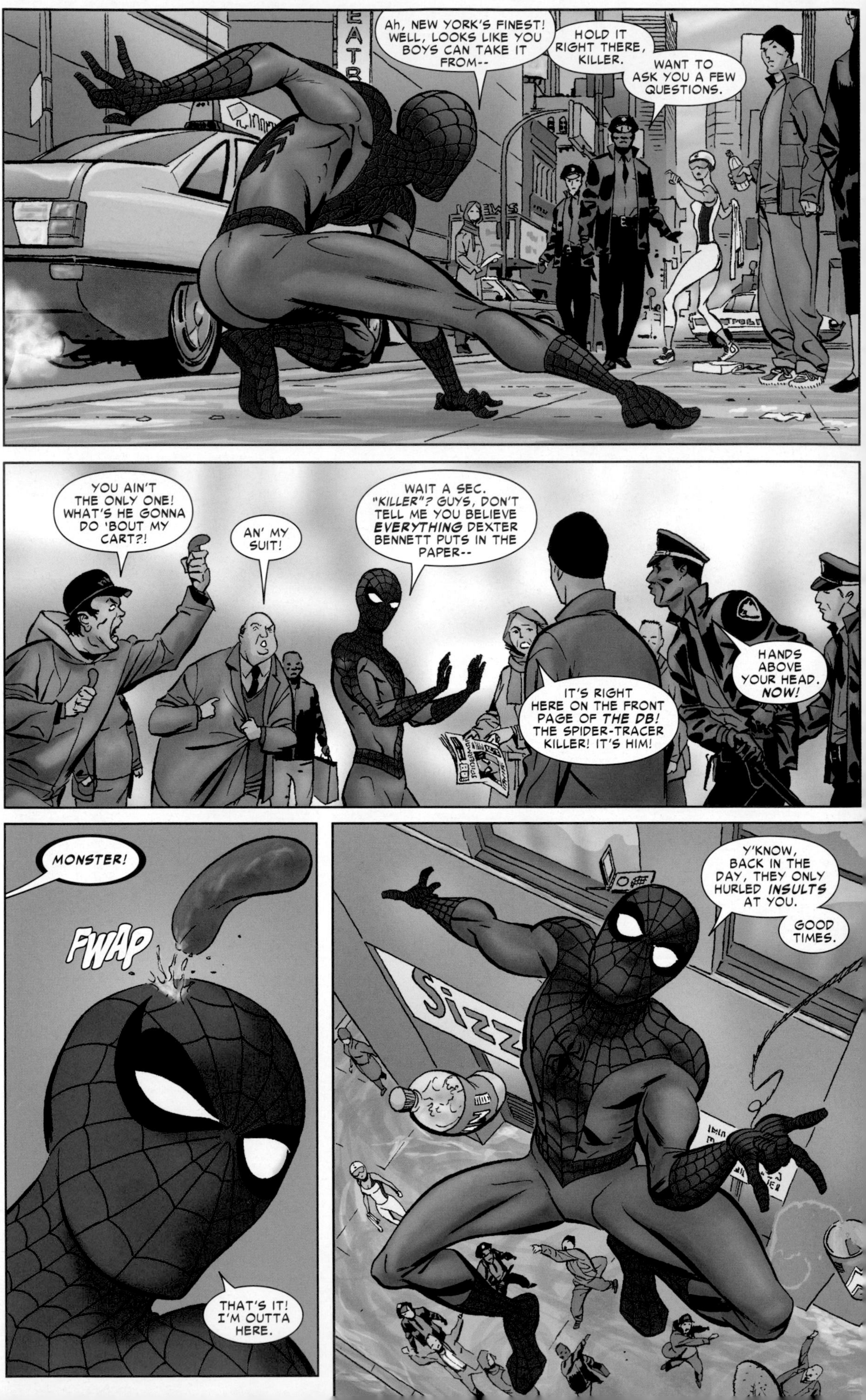

Ah, NEW YORK'S FINEST! WELL, LOOKS LIKE YOU BOYS CAN TAKE IT FROM--
HOLD IT RIGHT THERE, KILLER.
WANT TO ASK YOU A FEW QUESTIONS.
YOU AIN'T THE ONLY ONE! WHAT'S HE GONNA DO 'BOUT MY CART?!
AN' MY SUIT!
WAIT A SEC. "KILLER"? GUYS, DON'T TELL ME YOU BELIEVE EVERYTHING DEXTER BENNETT PUTS IN THE PAPER--
HANDS ABOVE YOUR HEAD. NOW!
IT'S RIGHT HERE ON THE FRONT PAGE OF THE DB! THE SPIDER-TRACER KILLER! IT'S HIM!
MONSTER!
FWAP
THAT'S IT! I'M OUTTA HERE.
Y'KNOW, BACK IN THE DAY, THEY ONLY HURLED INSULTS AT YOU.
GOOD TIMES.

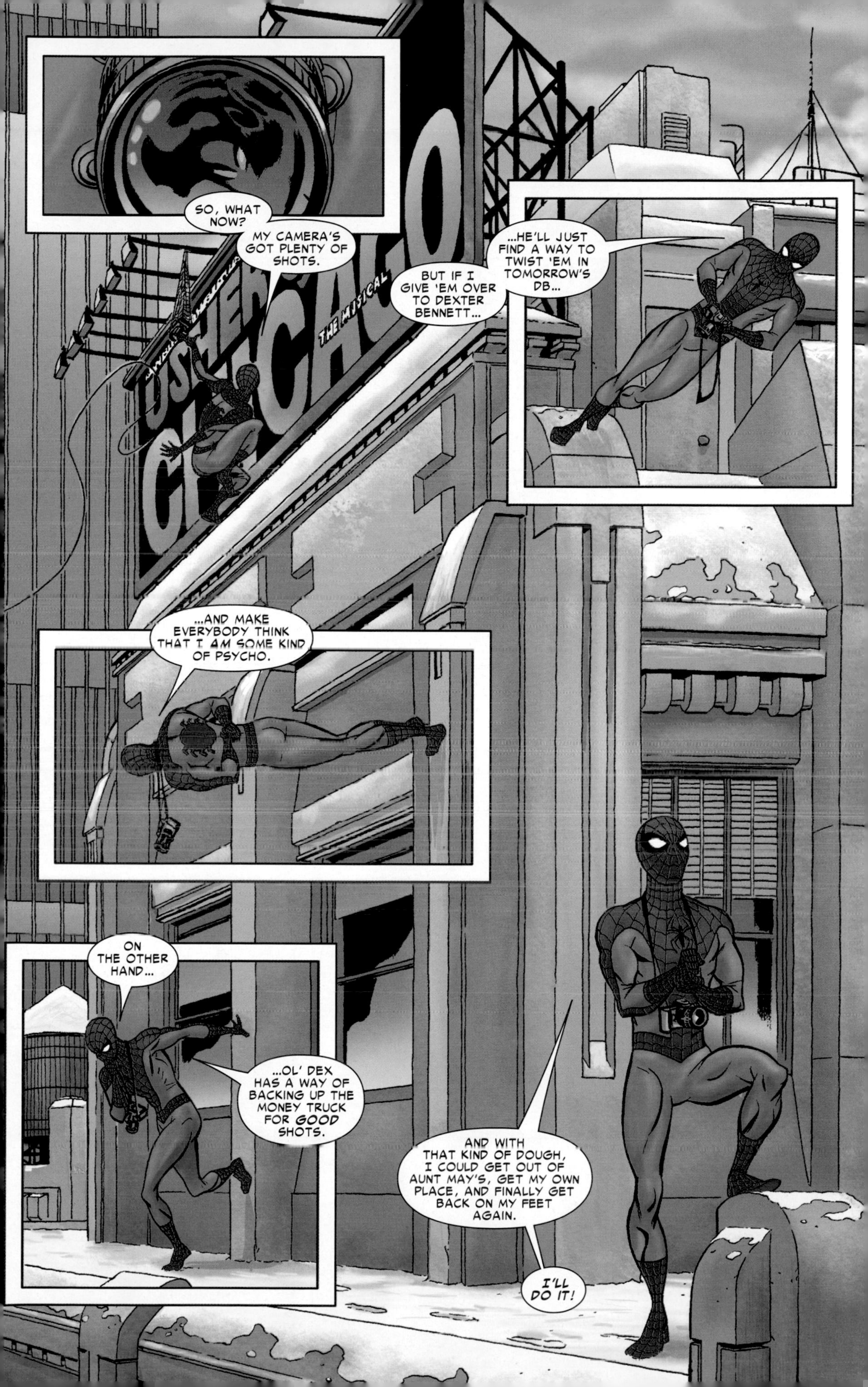
SO, WHAT NOW?
MY CAMERA'S GOT PLENTY OF SHOTS.
BUT IF I GIVE 'EM OVER TO DEXTER BENNETT...
...HE'LL JUST FIND A WAY TO TWIST 'EM IN TOMORROW'S DB...
...AND MAKE EVERYBODY THINK THAT I AM SOME KIND OF PSYCHO.
ON THE OTHER HAND...
...OL' DEX HAS A WAY OF BACKING UP THE MONEY TRUCK FOR GOOD SHOTS.
AND WITH THAT KIND OF DOUGH, I COULD GET OUT OF AUNT MAY'S, GET MY OWN PLACE, AND FINALLY GET BACK ON MY FEET AGAIN.
I'LL DO IT!
CHICAGO
THE MUSICAL

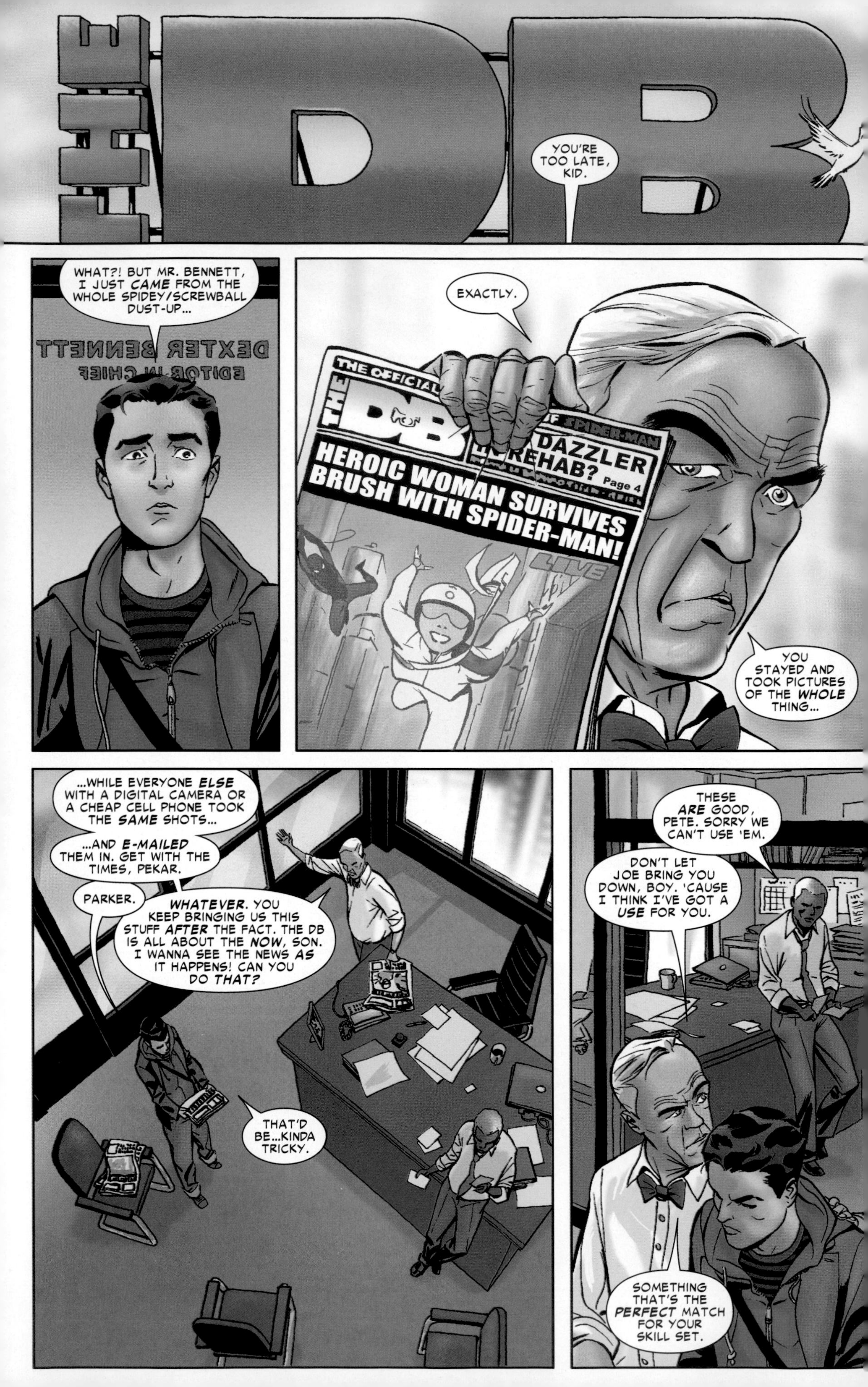
THE DB
YOU'RE TOO LATE, KID.
WHAT?! BUT MR. BENNETT, I JUST CAME FROM THE WHOLE SPIDEY/SCREWBALL DUST-UP...
DEXTER BENNETT
EDITOR-IN-CHIEF
EXACTLY.
THE OFFICIAL
THE DB
OF SPIDER-MAN
DAZZLER
REHAB? Page 4
HEROIC WOMAN SURVIVES BRUSH WITH SPIDER-MAN!
YOU STAYED AND TOOK PICTURES OF THE WHOLE THING...
...WHILE EVERYONE ELSE WITH A DIGITAL CAMERA OR A CHEAP CELL PHONE TOOK THE SAME SHOTS...
...AND E-MAILED THEM IN. GET WITH THE TIMES, PEKAR.
PARKER.
WHATEVER. YOU KEEP BRINGING US THIS STUFF AFTER THE FACT. THE DB IS ALL ABOUT THE NOW, SON. I WANNA SEE THE NEWS AS IT HAPPENS! CAN YOU DO THAT?
THAT'D BE...KINDA TRICKY.
THESE ARE GOOD, PETE. SORRY WE CAN'T USE 'EM.
DON'T LET JOE BRING YOU DOWN, BOY. 'CAUSE I THINK I'VE GOT A USE FOR YOU.
SOMETHING THAT'S THE PERFECT MATCH FOR YOUR SKILL SET.

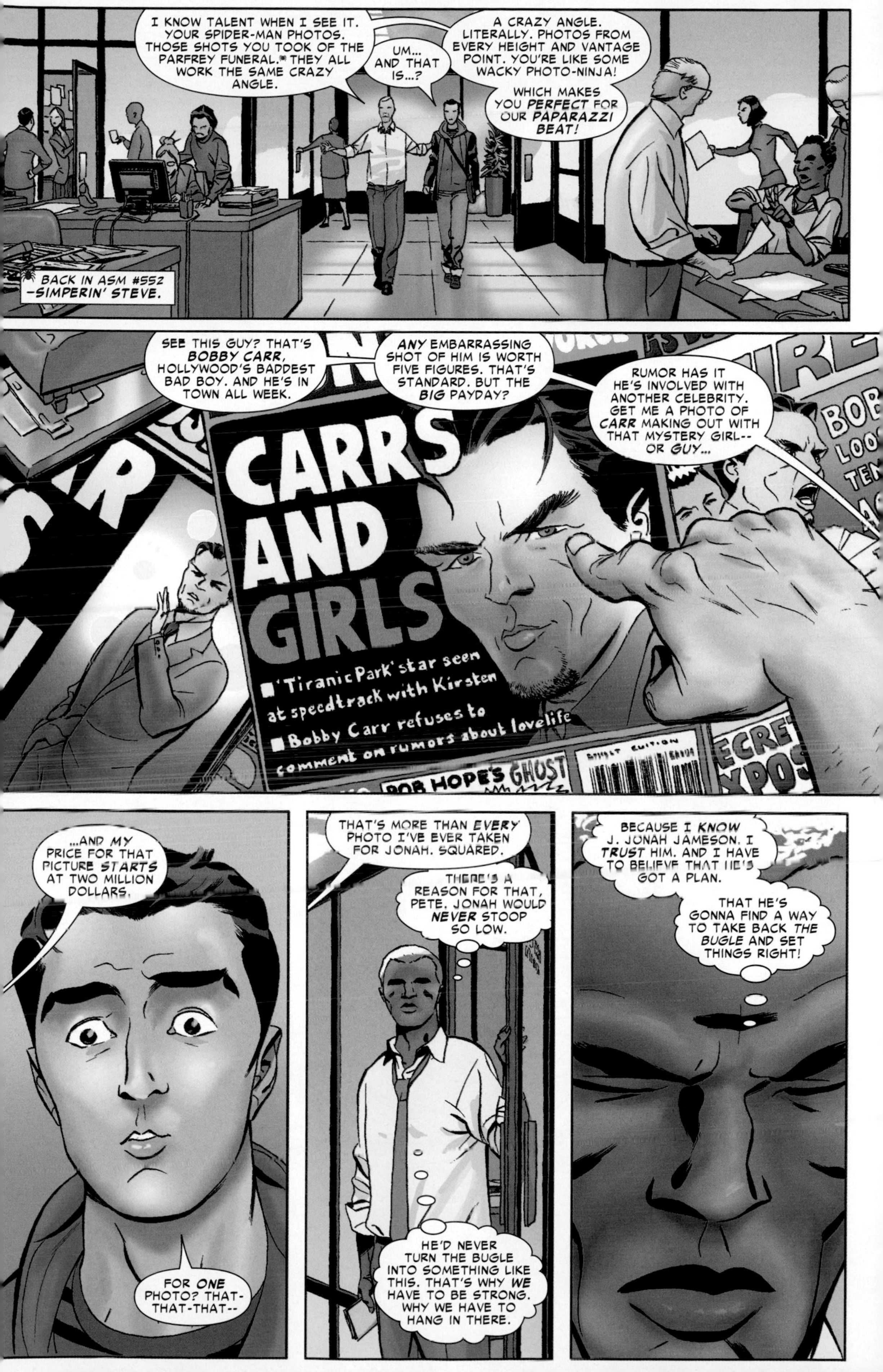

I KNOW TALENT WHEN I SEE IT. YOUR SPIDER-MAN PHOTOS. THOSE SHOTS YOU TOOK OF THE PARFREY FUNERAL.* THEY ALL WORK THE SAME CRAZY ANGLE.
UM... AND THAT IS...?
A CRAZY ANGLE. LITERALLY. PHOTOS FROM EVERY HEIGHT AND VANTAGE POINT. YOU'RE LIKE SOME WACKY PHOTO-NINJA!
WHICH MAKES YOU PERFECT FOR OUR PAPARAZZI BEAT!
*BACK IN ASM #552 —SIMPERIN' STEVE.
SEE THIS GUY? THAT'S BOBBY CARR, HOLLYWOOD'S BADDEST BAD BOY. AND HE'S IN TOWN ALL WEEK.
ANY EMBARRASSING SHOT OF HIM IS WORTH FIVE FIGURES. THAT'S STANDARD. BUT THE BIG PAYDAY?
RUMOR HAS IT HE'S INVOLVED WITH ANOTHER CELEBRITY. GET ME A PHOTO OF CARR MAKING OUT WITH THAT MYSTERY GIRL-- OR GUY...
CARRS AND GIRLS
'Tiranic Park' star seen at speedtrack with Kirsten
Bobby Carr refuses to comment on rumors about lovelife
BOB HOPE'S GHOST
...AND MY PRICE FOR THAT PICTURE STARTS AT TWO MILLION DOLLARS.
FOR ONE PHOTO? THAT-THAT-THAT--
THAT'S MORE THAN EVERY PHOTO I'VE EVER TAKEN FOR JONAH. SQUARED.
THERE'S A REASON FOR THAT, PETE. JONAH WOULD NEVER STOOP SO LOW.
HE'D NEVER TURN THE BUGLE INTO SOMETHING LIKE THIS. THAT'S WHY WE HAVE TO BE STRONG. WHY WE HAVE TO HANG IN THERE.
BECAUSE I KNOW J. JONAH JAMESON. I TRUST HIM. AND I HAVE TO BELIEVE THAT HE'S GOT A PLAN.
THAT HE'S GONNA FIND A WAY TO TAKE BACK THE BUGLE AND SET THINGS RIGHT!

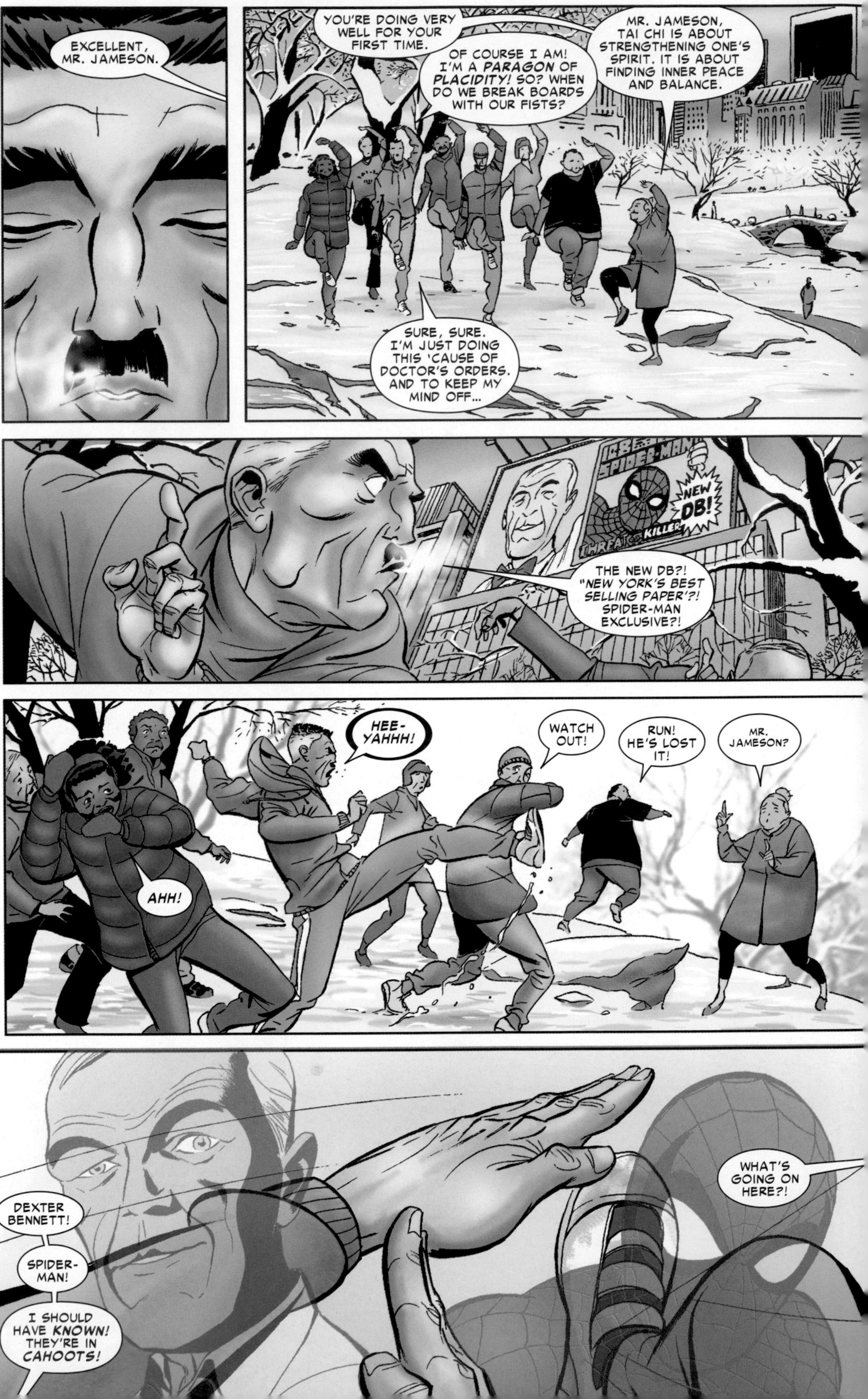
EXCELLENT, MR. JAMESON.
YOU'RE DOING VERY WELL FOR YOUR FIRST TIME.
OF COURSE I AM! I'M A PARAGON OF PLACIDITY! SO? WHEN DO WE BREAK BOARDS WITH OUR FISTS?
MR. JAMESON, TAI CHI IS ABOUT STRENGTHENING ONE'S SPIRIT. IT IS ABOUT FINDING INNER PEACE AND BALANCE.
SURE, SURE. I'M JUST DOING THIS 'CAUSE OF DOCTOR'S ORDERS. AND TO KEEP MY MIND OFF...
SPIDER-MAN
NEW DB!
KILLER
THE NEW DB?! "NEW YORK'S BEST SELLING PAPER"?! SPIDER-MAN EXCLUSIVE?!
HEE-YAHHH!
AHH!
WATCH OUT!
RUN! HE'S LOST IT!
MR. JAMESON?
DEXTER BENNETT!
SPIDER-MAN!
I SHOULD HAVE KNOWN! THEY'RE IN CAHOOTS!
WHAT'S GOING ON HERE?!

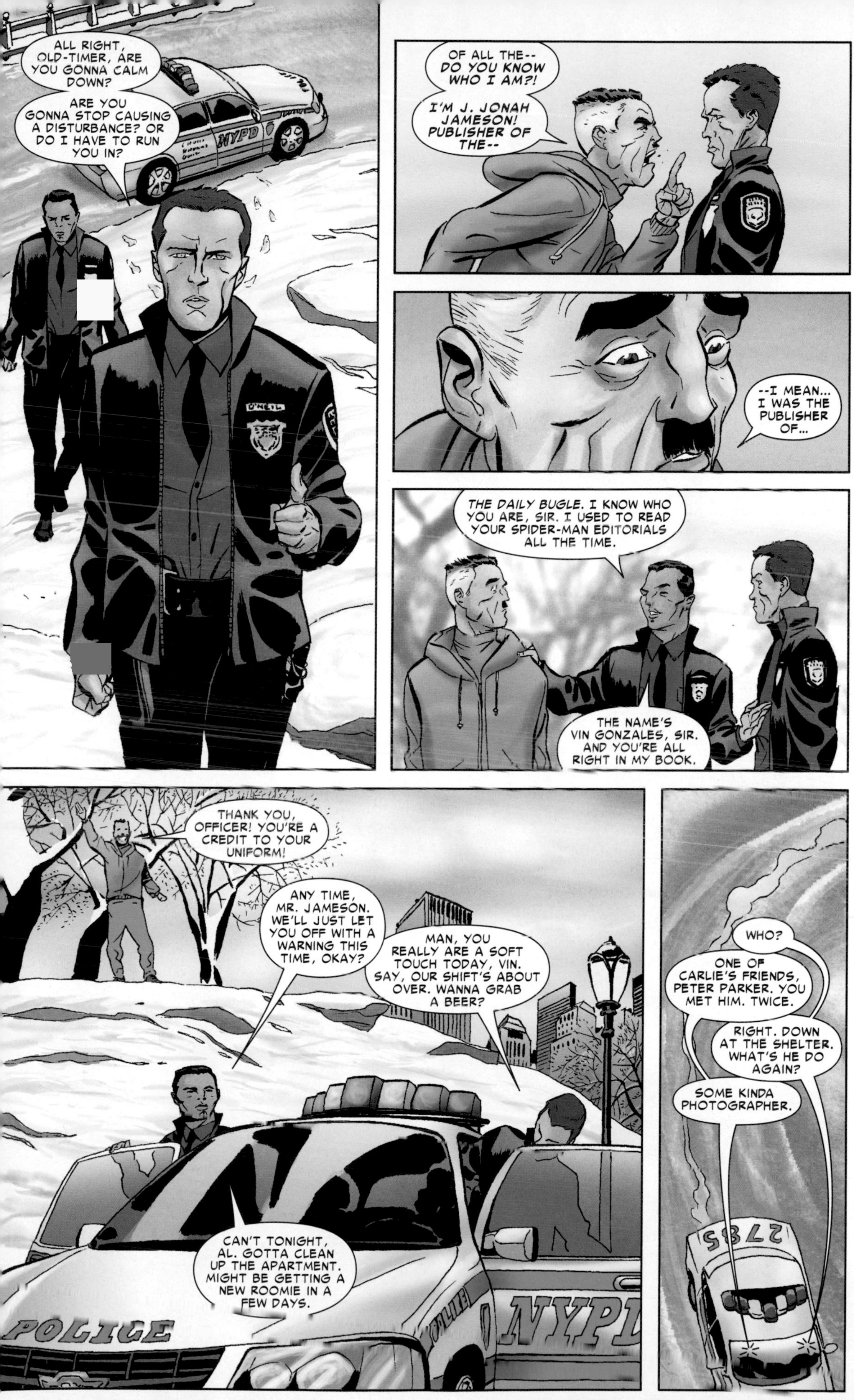
ALL RIGHT, OLD-TIMER, ARE YOU GONNA CALM DOWN?
ARE YOU GONNA STOP CAUSING A DISTURBANCE? OR DO I HAVE TO RUN YOU IN?
OF ALL THE-- DO YOU KNOW WHO I AM?!
I'M J. JONAH JAMESON! PUBLISHER OF THE--
--I MEAN... I WAS THE PUBLISHER OF...
THE DAILY BUGLE. I KNOW WHO YOU ARE, SIR. I USED TO READ YOUR SPIDER-MAN EDITORIALS ALL THE TIME.
THE NAME'S VIN GONZALES, SIR. AND YOU'RE ALL RIGHT IN MY BOOK.
THANK YOU, OFFICER! YOU'RE A CREDIT TO YOUR UNIFORM!
ANY TIME, MR. JAMESON. WE'LL JUST LET YOU OFF WITH A WARNING THIS TIME, OKAY?
MAN, YOU REALLY ARE A SOFT TOUCH TODAY, VIN. SAY, OUR SHIFT'S ABOUT OVER. WANNA GRAB A BEER?
CAN'T TONIGHT, AL. GOTTA CLEAN UP THE APARTMENT. MIGHT BE GETTING A NEW ROOMIE IN A FEW DAYS.
POLICE
NYPD
WHO?
ONE OF CARLIE'S FRIENDS, PETER PARKER. YOU MET HIM. TWICE.
RIGHT. DOWN AT THE SHELTER. WHAT'S HE DO AGAIN?
SOME KINDA PHOTOGRAPHER.

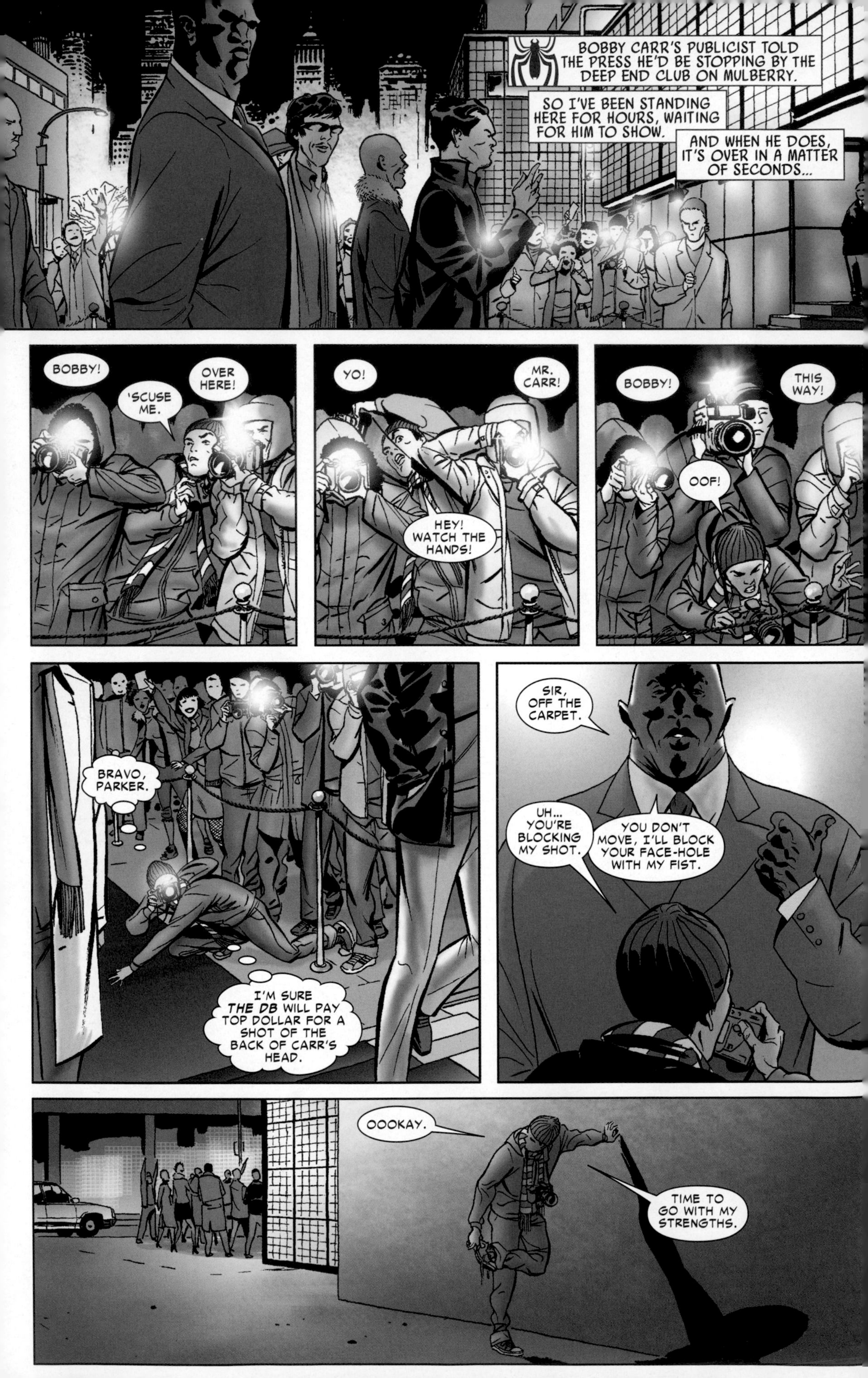
BOBBY CARR'S PUBLICIST TOLD THE PRESS HE'D BE STOPPING BY THE DEEP END CLUB ON MULBERRY.
SO I'VE BEEN STANDING HERE FOR HOURS, WAITING FOR HIM TO SHOW.
AND WHEN HE DOES, IT'S OVER IN A MATTER OF SECONDS...
BOBBY!
'SCUSE ME.
OVER HERE!
YO!
MR. CARR!
HEY! WATCH THE HANDS!
BOBBY!
THIS WAY!
OOF!
BRAVO, PARKER.
I'M SURE *THE DB* WILL PAY TOP DOLLAR FOR A SHOT OF THE BACK OF CARR'S HEAD.
SIR, OFF THE CARPET.
UH... YOU'RE BLOCKING MY SHOT.
YOU DON'T MOVE, I'LL BLOCK YOUR FACE-HOLE WITH MY FIST.
OOOKAY.
TIME TO GO WITH MY STRENGTHS.

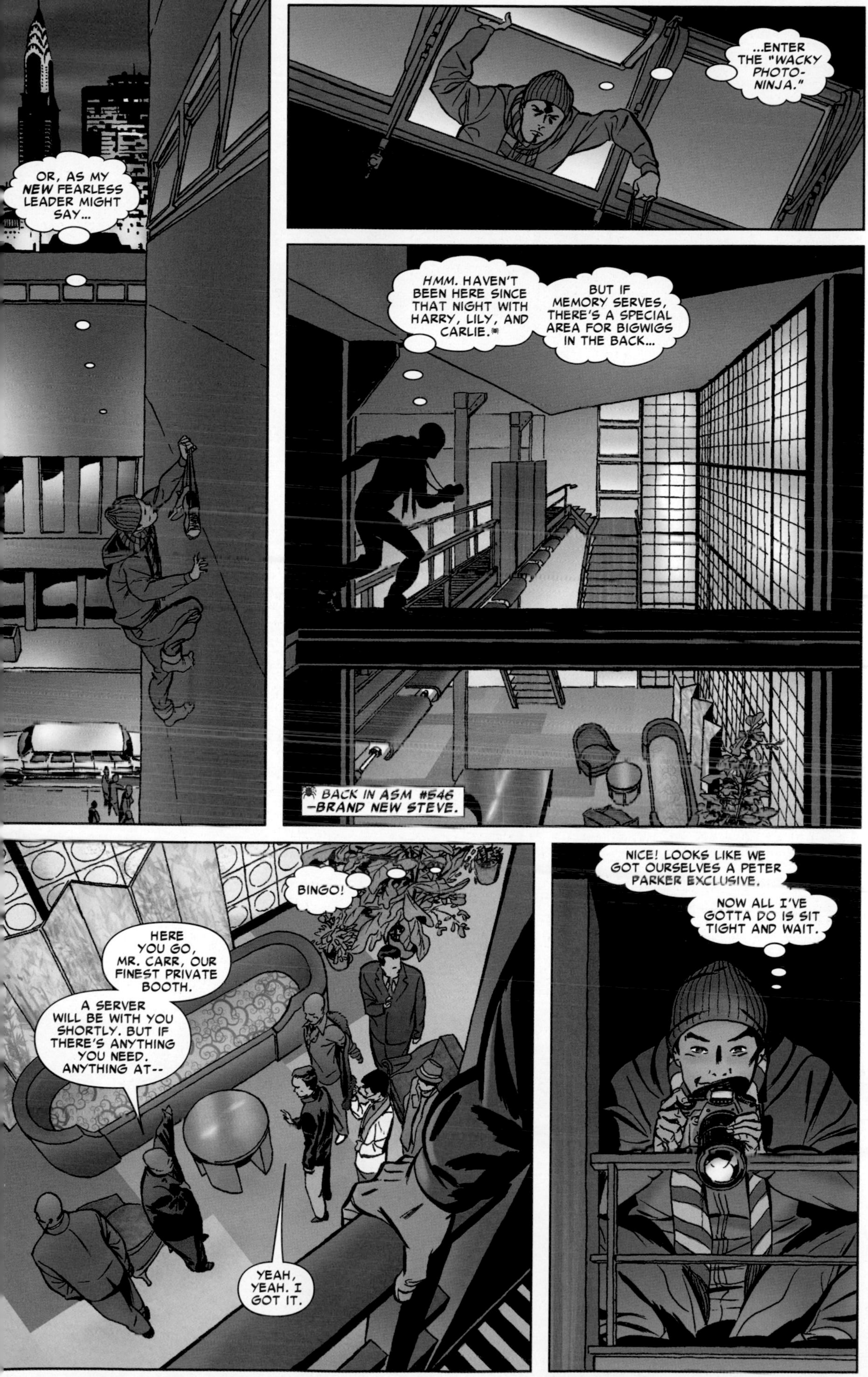
OR, AS MY NEW FEARLESS LEADER MIGHT SAY...
...ENTER THE "WACKY PHOTO-NINJA."
HMM. HAVEN'T BEEN HERE SINCE THAT NIGHT WITH HARRY, LILY, AND CARLIE.*
BUT IF MEMORY SERVES, THERE'S A SPECIAL AREA FOR BIGWIGS IN THE BACK...
*BACK IN ASM #546 —BRAND NEW STEVE.
BINGO!
HERE YOU GO, MR. CARR, OUR FINEST PRIVATE BOOTH.
A SERVER WILL BE WITH YOU SHORTLY. BUT IF THERE'S ANYTHING YOU NEED. ANYTHING AT--
YEAH, YEAH. I GOT IT.
NICE! LOOKS LIKE WE GOT OURSELVES A PETER PARKER EXCLUSIVE.
NOW ALL I'VE GOTTA DO IS SIT TIGHT AND WAIT.

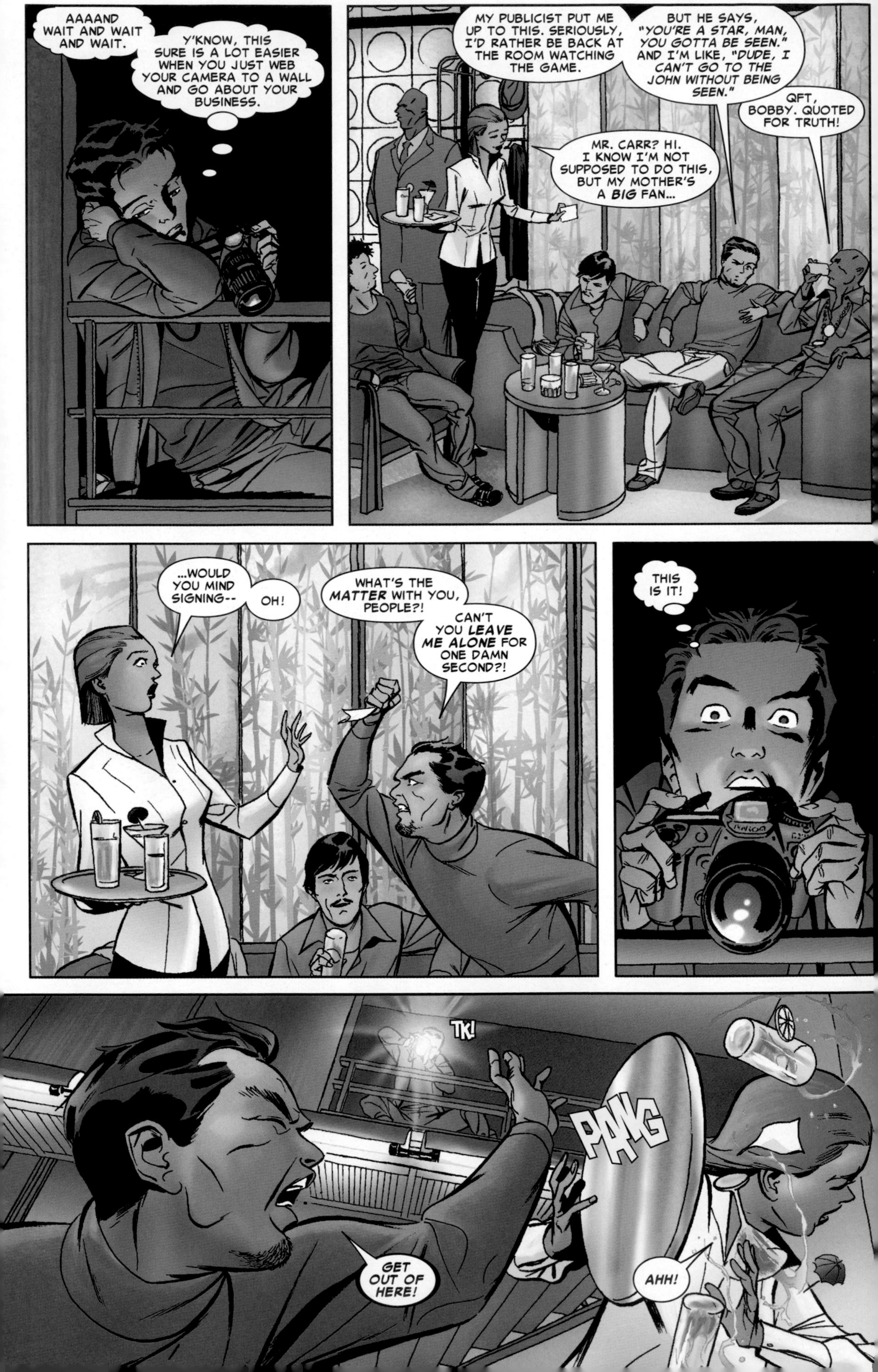
AAAAND WAIT AND WAIT AND WAIT.
Y'KNOW, THIS SURE IS A LOT EASIER WHEN YOU JUST WEB YOUR CAMERA TO A WALL AND GO ABOUT YOUR BUSINESS.
MY PUBLICIST PUT ME UP TO THIS. SERIOUSLY, I'D RATHER BE BACK AT THE ROOM WATCHING THE GAME.
BUT HE SAYS, "YOU'RE A STAR, MAN, YOU GOTTA BE SEEN." AND I'M LIKE, "DUDE, I CAN'T GO TO THE JOHN WITHOUT BEING SEEN."
QFT, BOBBY. QUOTED FOR TRUTH!
MR. CARR? HI. I KNOW I'M NOT SUPPOSED TO DO THIS, BUT MY MOTHER'S A BIG FAN...
...WOULD YOU MIND SIGNING--
OH!
WHAT'S THE MATTER WITH YOU, PEOPLE?!
CAN'T YOU LEAVE ME ALONE FOR ONE DAMN SECOND?!
THIS IS IT!
TK!
PANG
GET OUT OF HERE!
AHH!

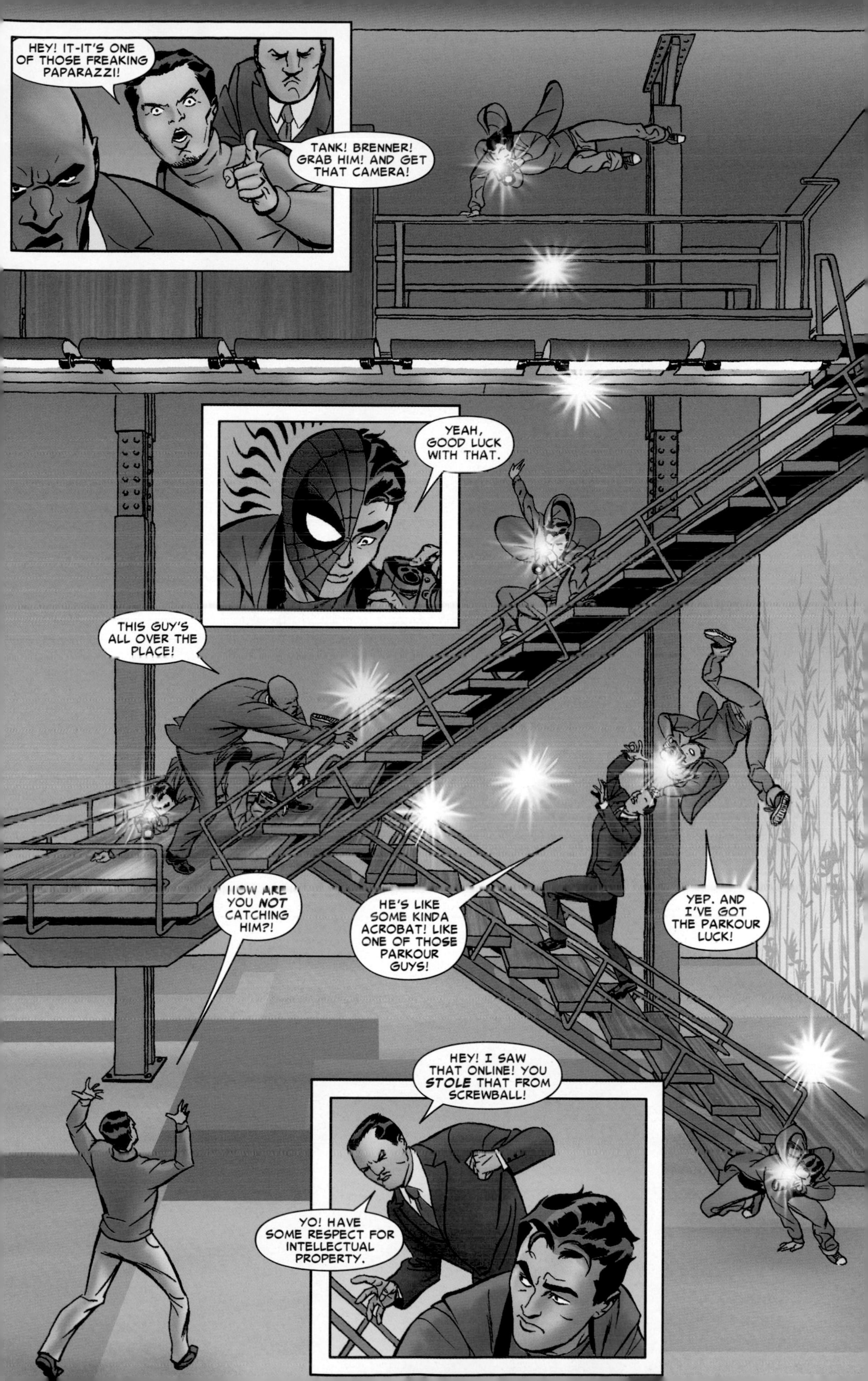
HEY! IT-IT'S ONE OF THOSE FREAKING PAPARAZZI!
TANK! BRENNER! GRAB HIM! AND GET THAT CAMERA!
YEAH, GOOD LUCK WITH THAT.
THIS GUY'S ALL OVER THE PLACE!
HOW ARE YOU NOT CATCHING HIM?!
HE'S LIKE SOME KINDA ACROBAT! LIKE ONE OF THOSE PARKOUR GUYS!
YEP. AND I'VE GOT THE PARKOUR LUCK!
HEY! I SAW THAT ONLINE! YOU STOLE THAT FROM SCREWBALL!
YO! HAVE SOME RESPECT FOR INTELLECTUAL PROPERTY.

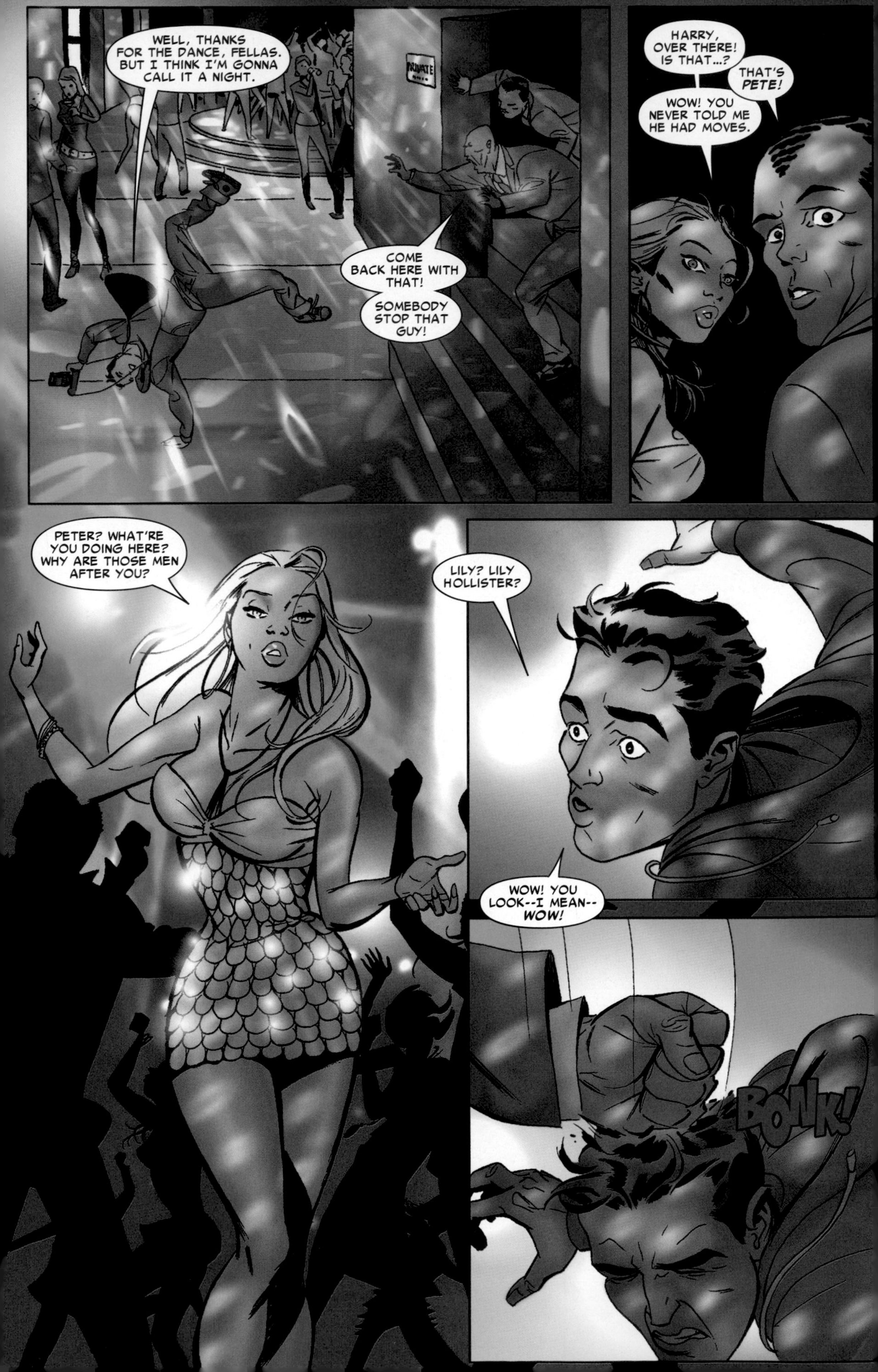
WELL, THANKS FOR THE DANCE, FELLAS. BUT I THINK I'M GONNA CALL IT A NIGHT.
PRIVATE
COME BACK HERE WITH THAT!
SOMEBODY STOP THAT GUY!
HARRY, OVER THERE! IS THAT...?
THAT'S *PETE!*
WOW! YOU NEVER TOLD ME HE HAD MOVES.
PETER? WHAT'RE YOU DOING HERE? WHY ARE THOSE MEN AFTER YOU?
LILY? LILY HOLLISTER?
WOW! YOU LOOK--I MEAN-- **WOW!**
BONK!

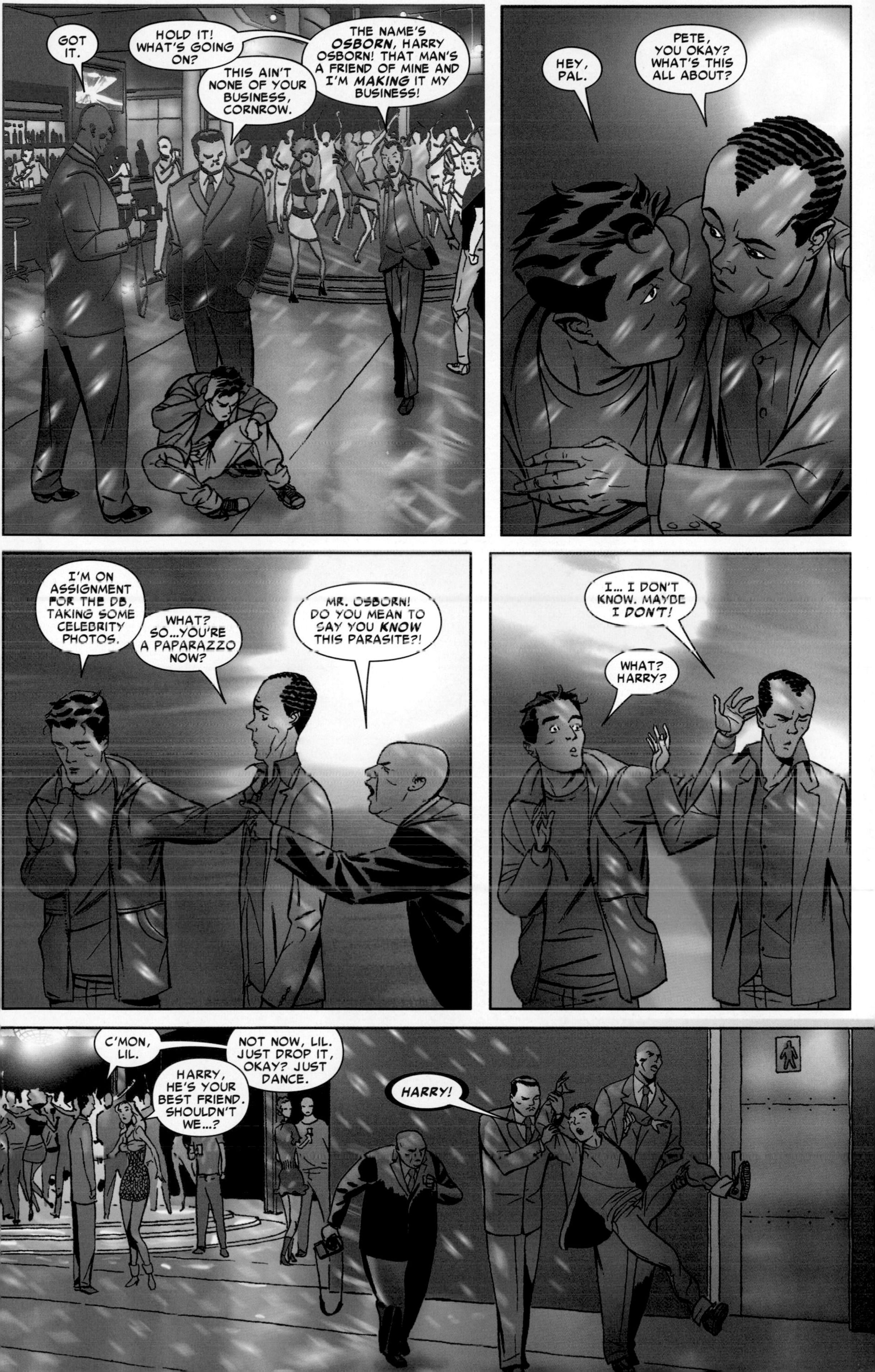
GOT IT.
HOLD IT! WHAT'S GOING ON?
THIS AIN'T NONE OF YOUR BUSINESS, CORNROW.
THE NAME'S OSBORN, HARRY OSBORN! THAT MAN'S A FRIEND OF MINE AND I'M MAKING IT MY BUSINESS!
HEY, PAL.
PETE, YOU OKAY? WHAT'S THIS ALL ABOUT?
I'M ON ASSIGNMENT FOR THE DB, TAKING SOME CELEBRITY PHOTOS.
WHAT? SO...YOU'RE A PAPARAZZO NOW?
MR. OSBORN! DO YOU MEAN TO SAY YOU KNOW THIS PARASITE?!
I... I DON'T KNOW. MAYBE I DON'T!
WHAT? HARRY?
C'MON, LIL.
HARRY, HE'S YOUR BEST FRIEND. SHOULDN'T WE...?
NOT NOW, LIL. JUST DROP IT, OKAY? JUST DANCE.
HARRY!

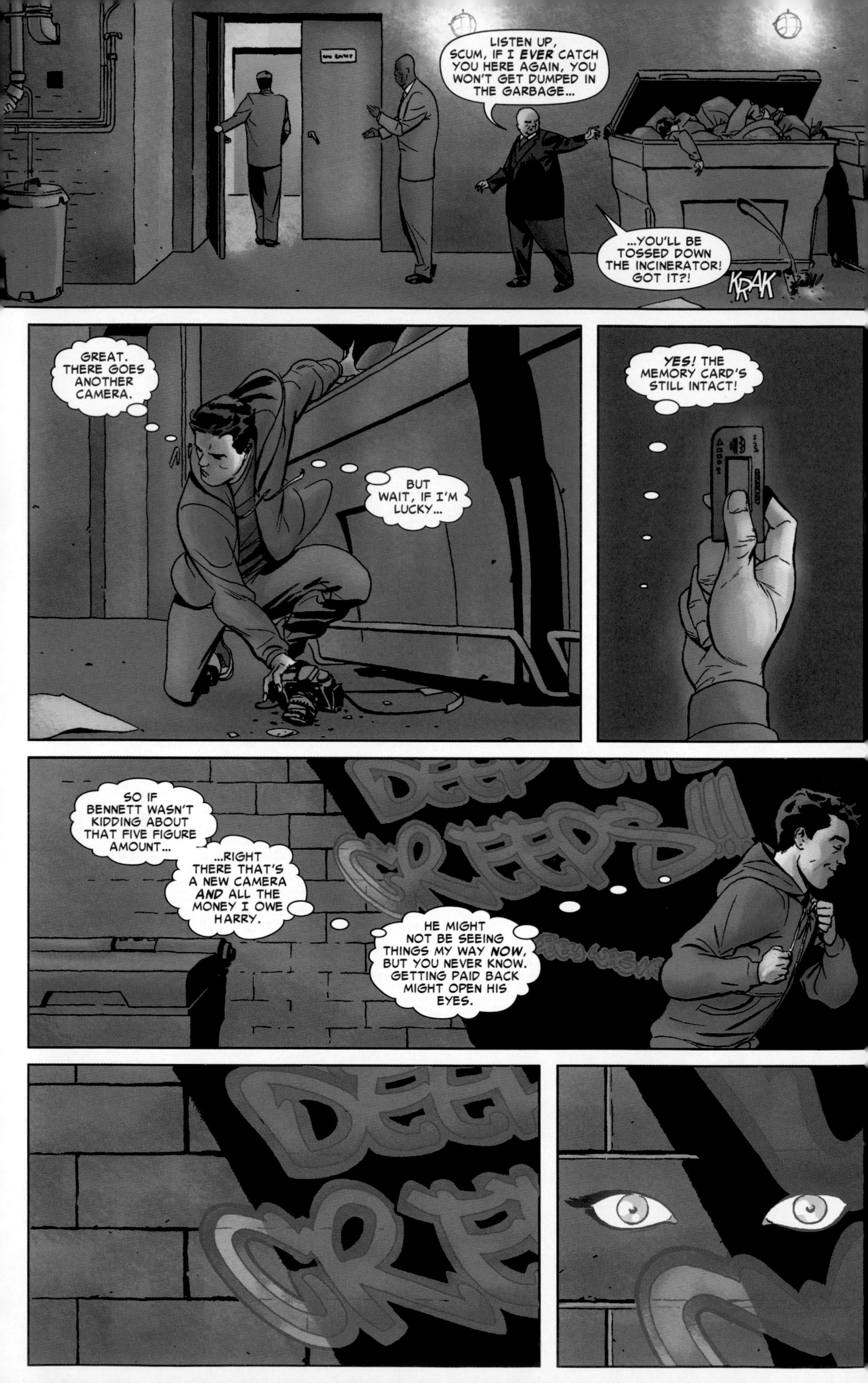
LISTEN UP, SCUM, IF I EVER CATCH YOU HERE AGAIN, YOU WON'T GET DUMPED IN THE GARBAGE...
...YOU'LL BE TOSSED DOWN THE INCINERATOR! GOT IT?!
KRAK
GREAT. THERE GOES ANOTHER CAMERA.
BUT WAIT, IF I'M LUCKY...
YES! THE MEMORY CARD'S STILL INTACT!
SO IF BENNETT WASN'T KIDDING ABOUT THAT FIVE FIGURE AMOUNT...
...RIGHT THERE THAT'S A NEW CAMERA AND ALL THE MONEY I OWE HARRY.
HE MIGHT NOT BE SEEING THINGS MY WAY NOW, BUT YOU NEVER KNOW. GETTING PAID BACK MIGHT OPEN HIS EYES.

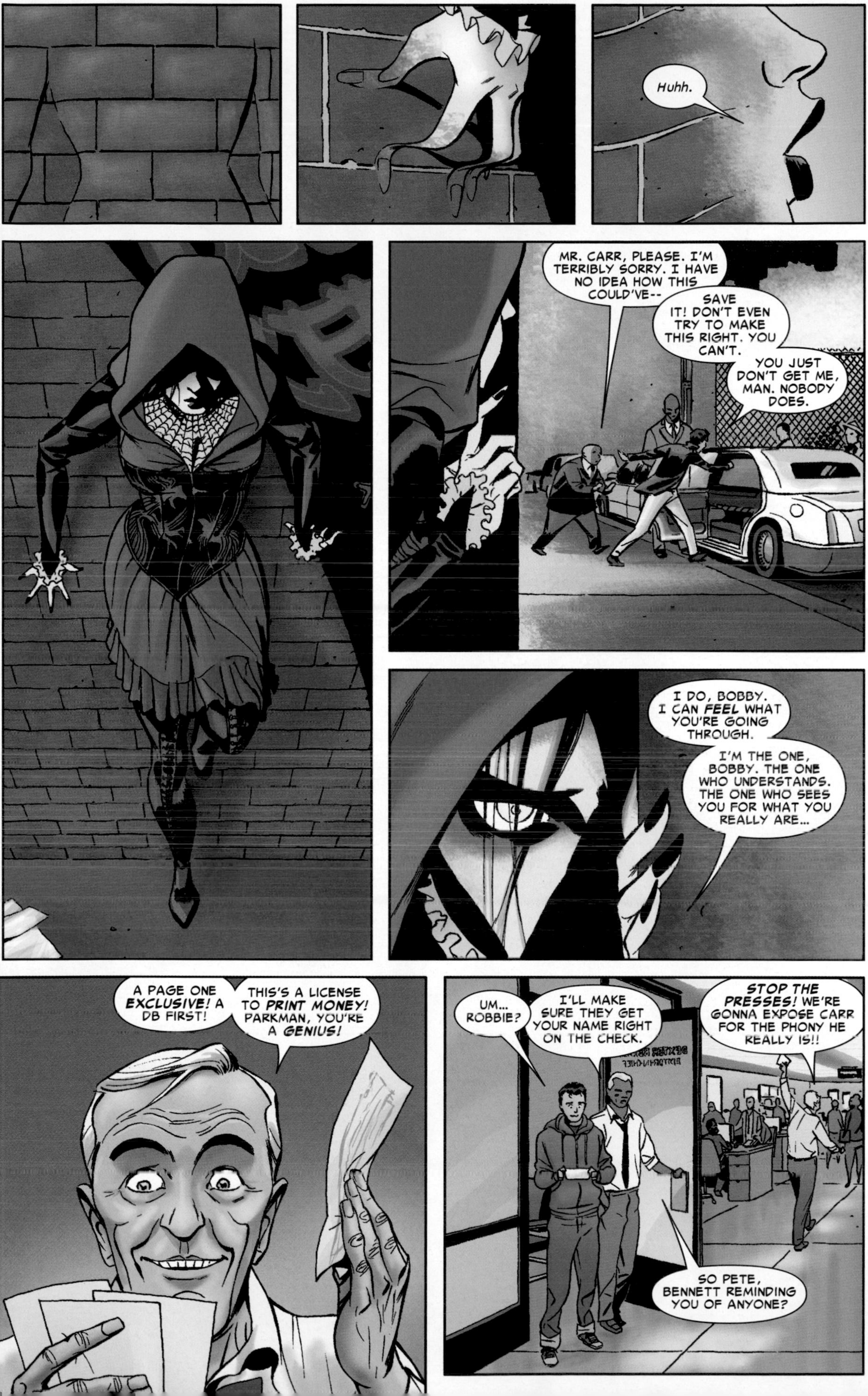
Huhh.
MR. CARR, PLEASE. I'M TERRIBLY SORRY. I HAVE NO IDEA HOW THIS COULD'VE--
SAVE IT! DON'T EVEN TRY TO MAKE THIS RIGHT. YOU CAN'T.
YOU JUST DON'T GET ME, MAN. NOBODY DOES.
I DO, BOBBY. I CAN FEEL WHAT YOU'RE GOING THROUGH.
I'M THE ONE, BOBBY. THE ONE WHO UNDERSTANDS. THE ONE WHO SEES YOU FOR WHAT YOU REALLY ARE...
A PAGE ONE EXCLUSIVE! A DB FIRST!
THIS'S A LICENSE TO PRINT MONEY! PARKMAN, YOU'RE A GENIUS!
UM... ROBBIE?
I'LL MAKE SURE THEY GET YOUR NAME RIGHT ON THE CHECK.
STOP THE PRESSES! WE'RE GONNA EXPOSE CARR FOR THE PHONY HE REALLY IS!!
SO PETE, BENNETT REMINDING YOU OF ANYONE?

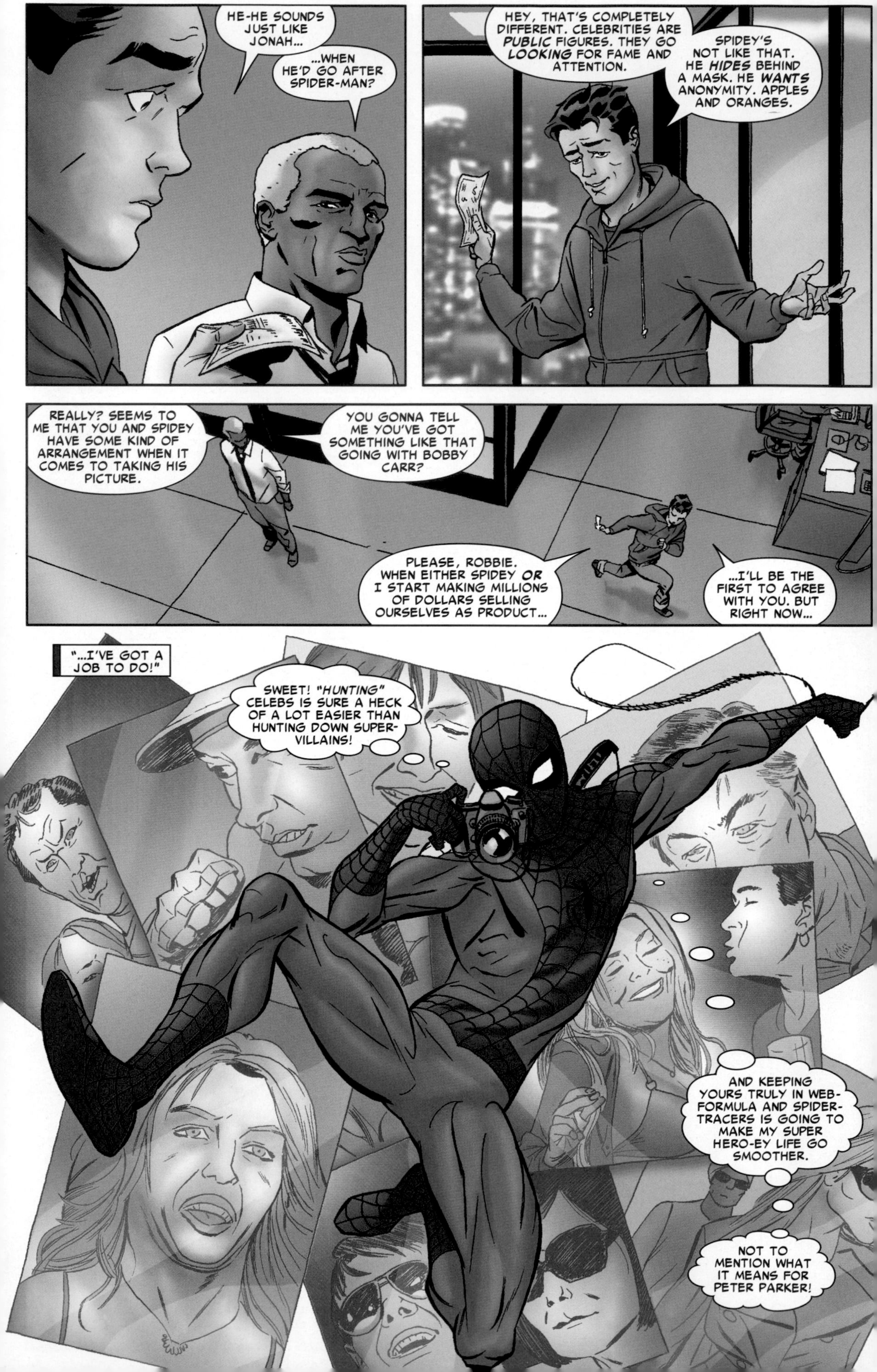
HE-HE SOUNDS JUST LIKE JONAH...
...WHEN HE'D GO AFTER SPIDER-MAN?
HEY, THAT'S COMPLETELY DIFFERENT. CELEBRITIES ARE PUBLIC FIGURES. THEY GO LOOKING FOR FAME AND ATTENTION.
SPIDEY'S NOT LIKE THAT. HE HIDES BEHIND A MASK. HE WANTS ANONYMITY. APPLES AND ORANGES.
REALLY? SEEMS TO ME THAT YOU AND SPIDEY HAVE SOME KIND OF ARRANGEMENT WHEN IT COMES TO TAKING HIS PICTURE.
YOU GONNA TELL ME YOU'VE GOT SOMETHING LIKE THAT GOING WITH BOBBY CARR?
PLEASE, ROBBIE. WHEN EITHER SPIDEY OR I START MAKING MILLIONS OF DOLLARS SELLING OURSELVES AS PRODUCT...
...I'LL BE THE FIRST TO AGREE WITH YOU. BUT RIGHT NOW...
"...I'VE GOT A JOB TO DO!"
SWEET! "HUNTING" CELEBS IS SURE A HECK OF A LOT EASIER THAN HUNTING DOWN SUPER-VILLAINS!
AND KEEPING YOURS TRULY IN WEB-FORMULA AND SPIDER-TRACERS IS GOING TO MAKE MY SUPER HERO-EY LIFE GO SMOOTHER.
NOT TO MENTION WHAT IT MEANS FOR PETER PARKER!

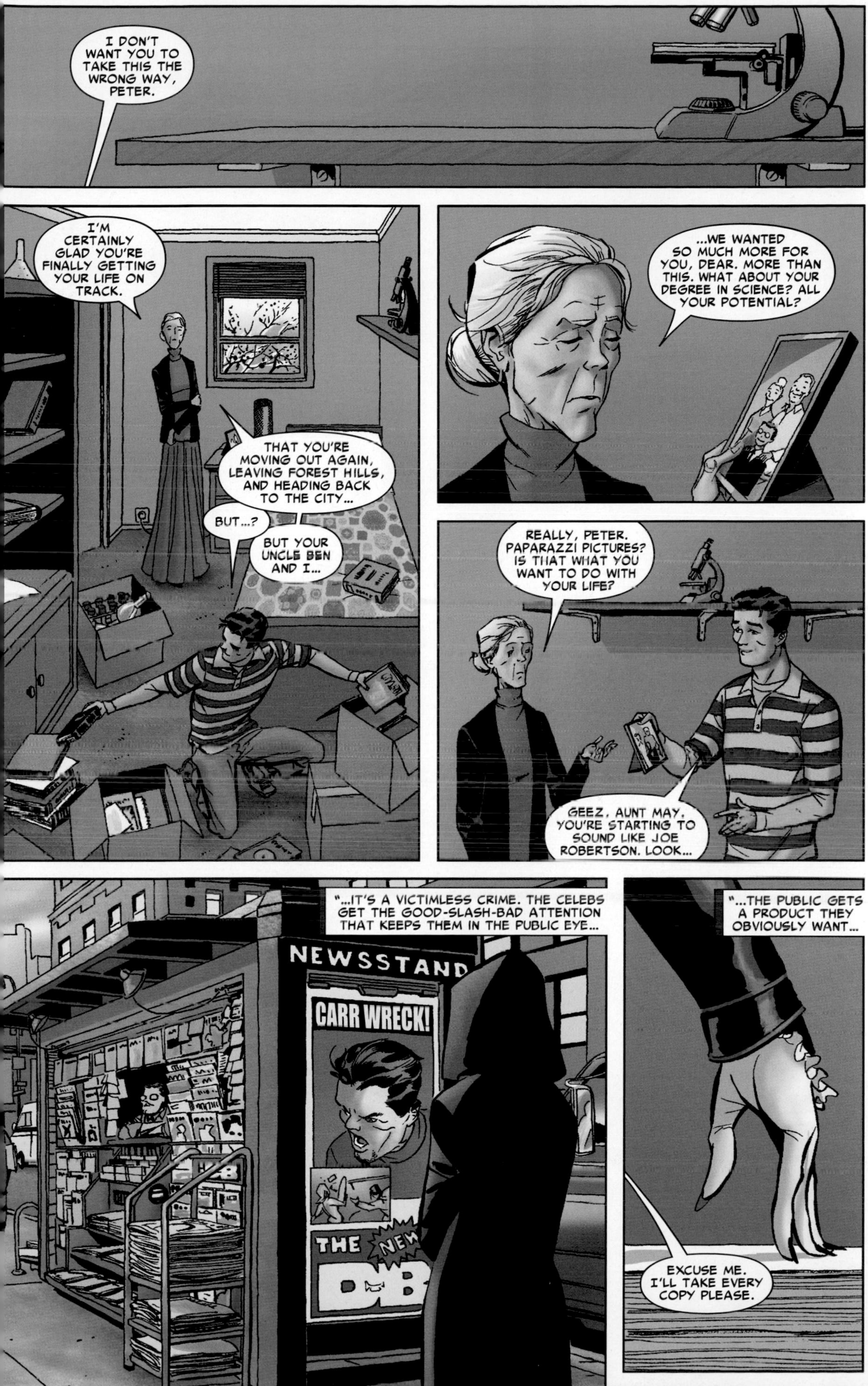
I DON'T WANT YOU TO TAKE THIS THE WRONG WAY, PETER.
I'M CERTAINLY GLAD YOU'RE FINALLY GETTING YOUR LIFE ON TRACK.
THAT YOU'RE MOVING OUT AGAIN, LEAVING FOREST HILLS, AND HEADING BACK TO THE CITY...
BUT...?
BUT YOUR UNCLE BEN AND I...
...WE WANTED SO MUCH MORE FOR YOU, DEAR. MORE THAN THIS. WHAT ABOUT YOUR DEGREE IN SCIENCE? ALL YOUR POTENTIAL?
REALLY, PETER. PAPARAZZI PICTURES? IS THAT WHAT YOU WANT TO DO WITH YOUR LIFE?
GEEZ, AUNT MAY. YOU'RE STARTING TO SOUND LIKE JOE ROBERTSON. LOOK...
"...IT'S A VICTIMLESS CRIME. THE CELEBS GET THE GOOD-SLASH-BAD ATTENTION THAT KEEPS THEM IN THE PUBLIC EYE...
NEWSSTAND
CARR WRECK!
THE NEW DB
"...THE PUBLIC GETS A PRODUCT THEY OBVIOUSLY WANT...
EXCUSE ME. I'LL TAKE EVERY COPY PLEASE.

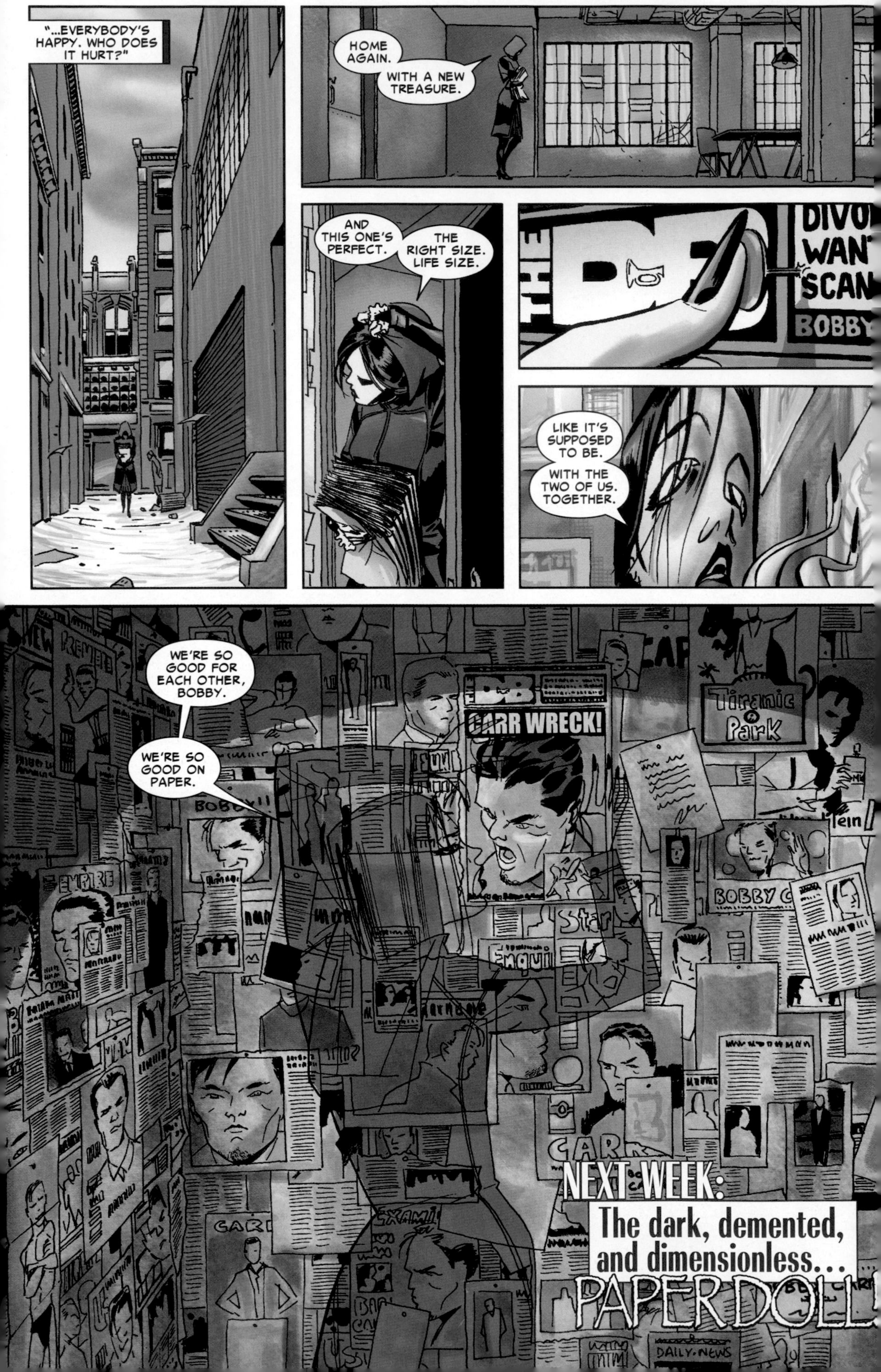
"...EVERYBODY'S HAPPY. WHO DOES IT HURT?"
HOME AGAIN.
WITH A NEW TREASURE.
AND THIS ONE'S PERFECT.
THE RIGHT SIZE. LIFE SIZE.
LIKE IT'S SUPPOSED TO BE.
WITH THE TWO OF US. TOGETHER.
WE'RE SO GOOD FOR EACH OTHER, BOBBY.
WE'RE SO GOOD ON PAPER.
CARR WRECK!
NEXT WEEK:
The dark, demented, and dimensionless...
PAPERDOLL!

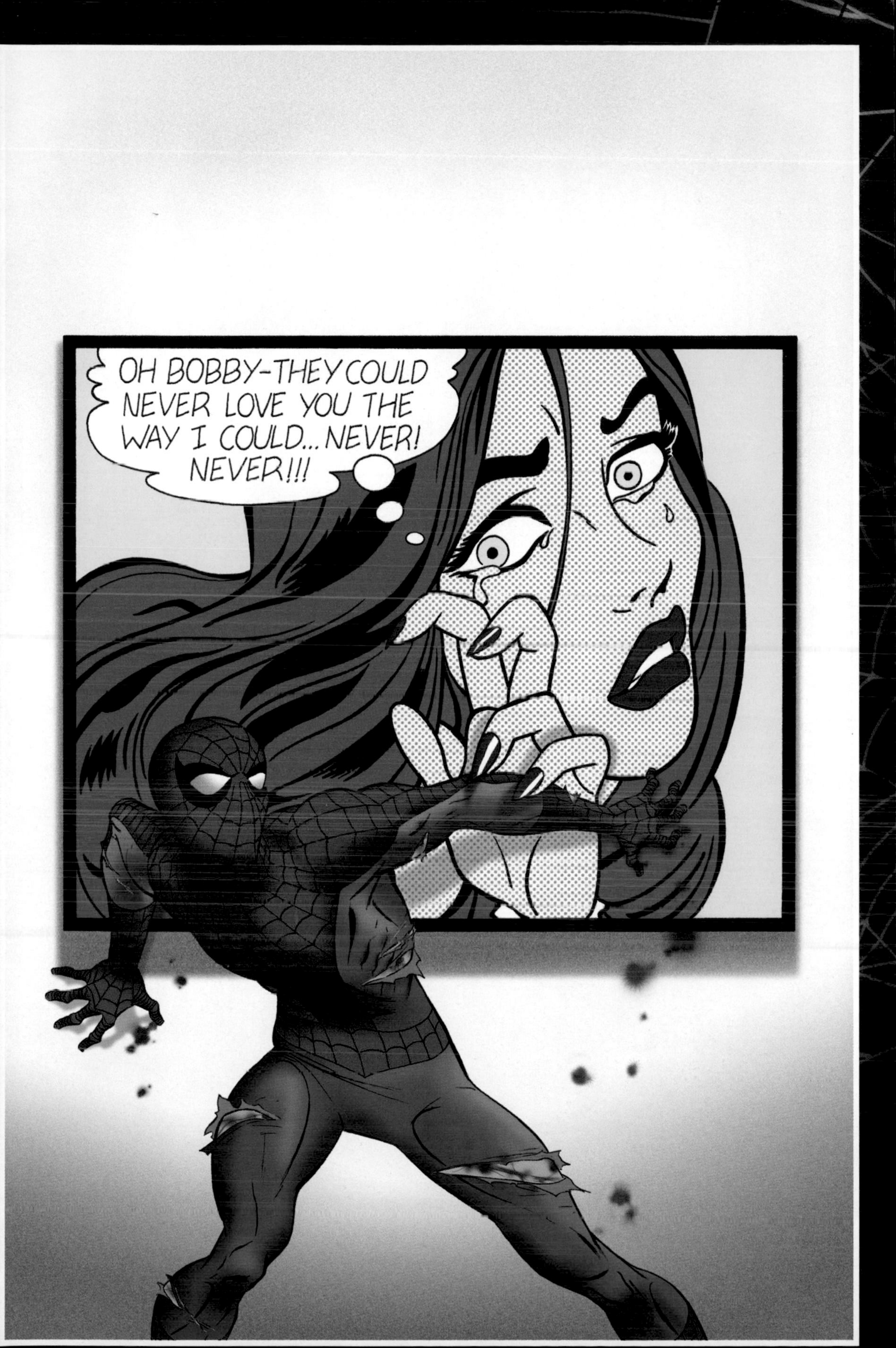
OH BOBBY-THEY COULD NEVER LOVE YOU THE WAY I COULD... NEVER! NEVER!!!

AMAZING SPIDER-MAN #560

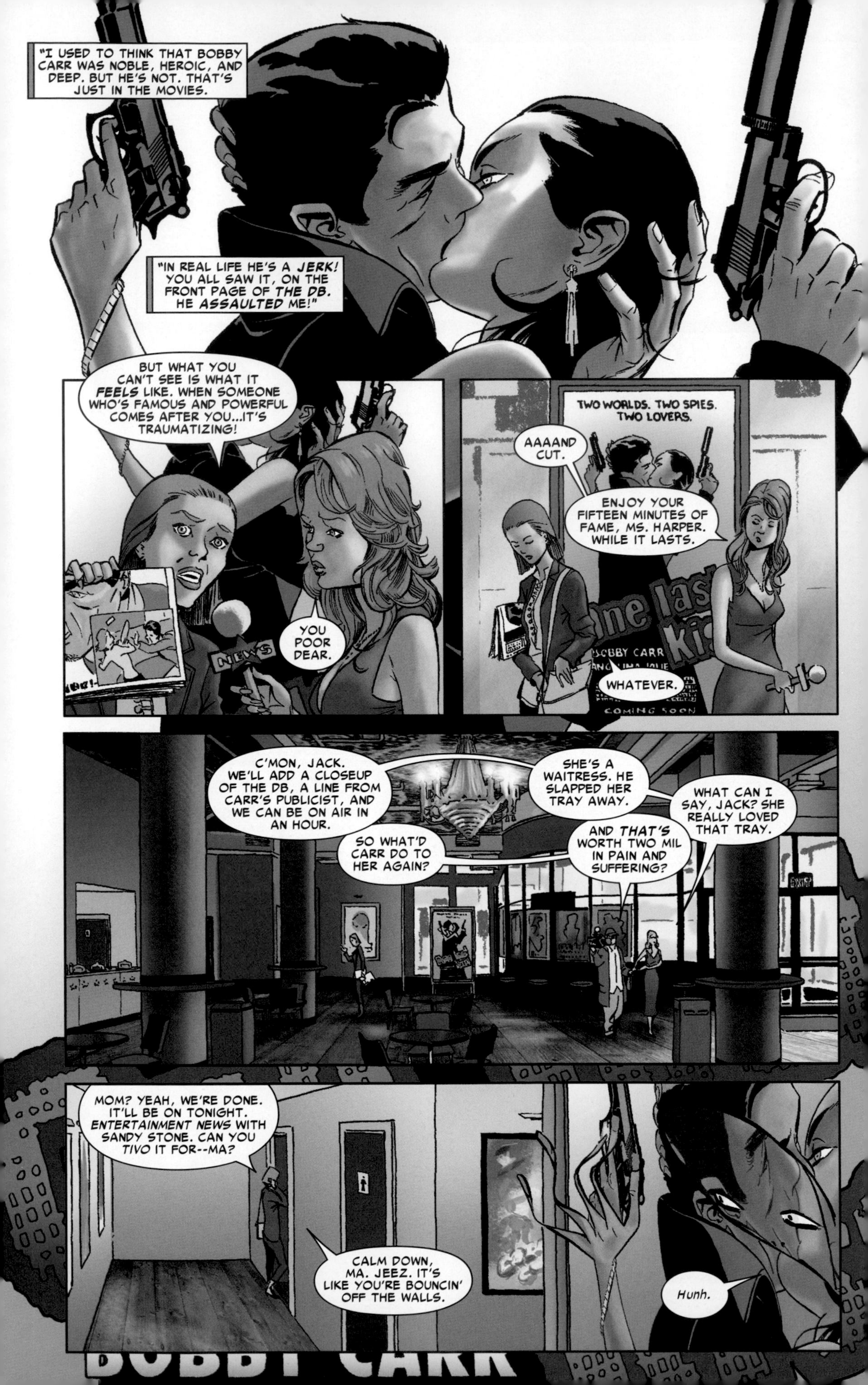
"I USED TO THINK THAT BOBBY CARR WAS NOBLE, HEROIC, AND DEEP. BUT HE'S NOT. THAT'S JUST IN THE MOVIES.
"IN REAL LIFE HE'S A JERK! YOU ALL SAW IT, ON THE FRONT PAGE OF THE DB. HE ASSAULTED ME!"
BUT WHAT YOU CAN'T SEE IS WHAT IT FEELS LIKE. WHEN SOMEONE WHO'S FAMOUS AND POWERFUL COMES AFTER YOU...IT'S TRAUMATIZING!
NEWS
YOU POOR DEAR.
TWO WORLDS. TWO SPIES. TWO LOVERS.
AAAAND CUT.
ENJOY YOUR FIFTEEN MINUTES OF FAME, MS. HARPER. WHILE IT LASTS.
One last kiss
BOBBY CARR
WHATEVER.
COMING SOON
C'MON, JACK. WE'LL ADD A CLOSEUP OF THE DB, A LINE FROM CARR'S PUBLICIST, AND WE CAN BE ON AIR IN AN HOUR.
SO WHAT'D CARR DO TO HER AGAIN?
SHE'S A WAITRESS. HE SLAPPED HER TRAY AWAY.
AND THAT'S WORTH TWO MIL IN PAIN AND SUFFERING?
WHAT CAN I SAY, JACK? SHE REALLY LOVED THAT TRAY.
EXIT
MOM? YEAH, WE'RE DONE. IT'LL BE ON TONIGHT. ENTERTAINMENT NEWS WITH SANDY STONE. CAN YOU TIVO IT FOR--MA?
CALM DOWN, MA. JEEZ. IT'S LIKE YOU'RE BOUNCIN' OFF THE WALLS.
Hunh.

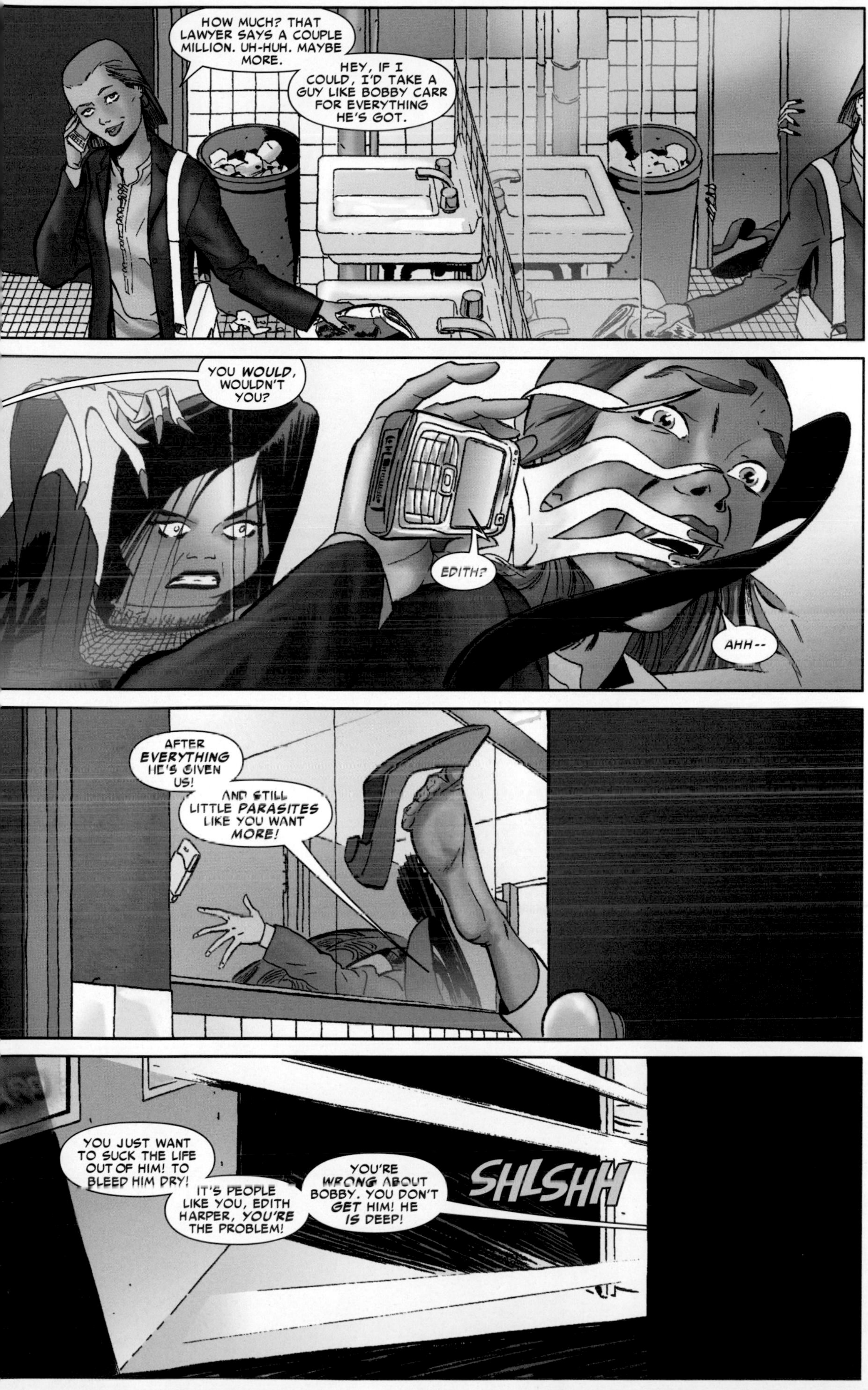
HOW MUCH? THAT LAWYER SAYS A COUPLE MILLION. UH-HUH. MAYBE MORE.
HEY, IF I COULD, I'D TAKE A GUY LIKE BOBBY CARR FOR EVERYTHING HE'S GOT.
YOU WOULD, WOULDN'T YOU?
EDITH?
AHH--
AFTER EVERYTHING HE'S GIVEN US!
AND STILL LITTLE PARASITES LIKE YOU WANT MORE!
YOU JUST WANT TO SUCK THE LIFE OUT OF HIM! TO BLEED HIM DRY!
IT'S PEOPLE LIKE YOU, EDITH HARPER, YOU'RE THE PROBLEM!
YOU'RE WRONG ABOUT BOBBY. YOU DON'T GET HIM! HE IS DEEP!
SHLSHH

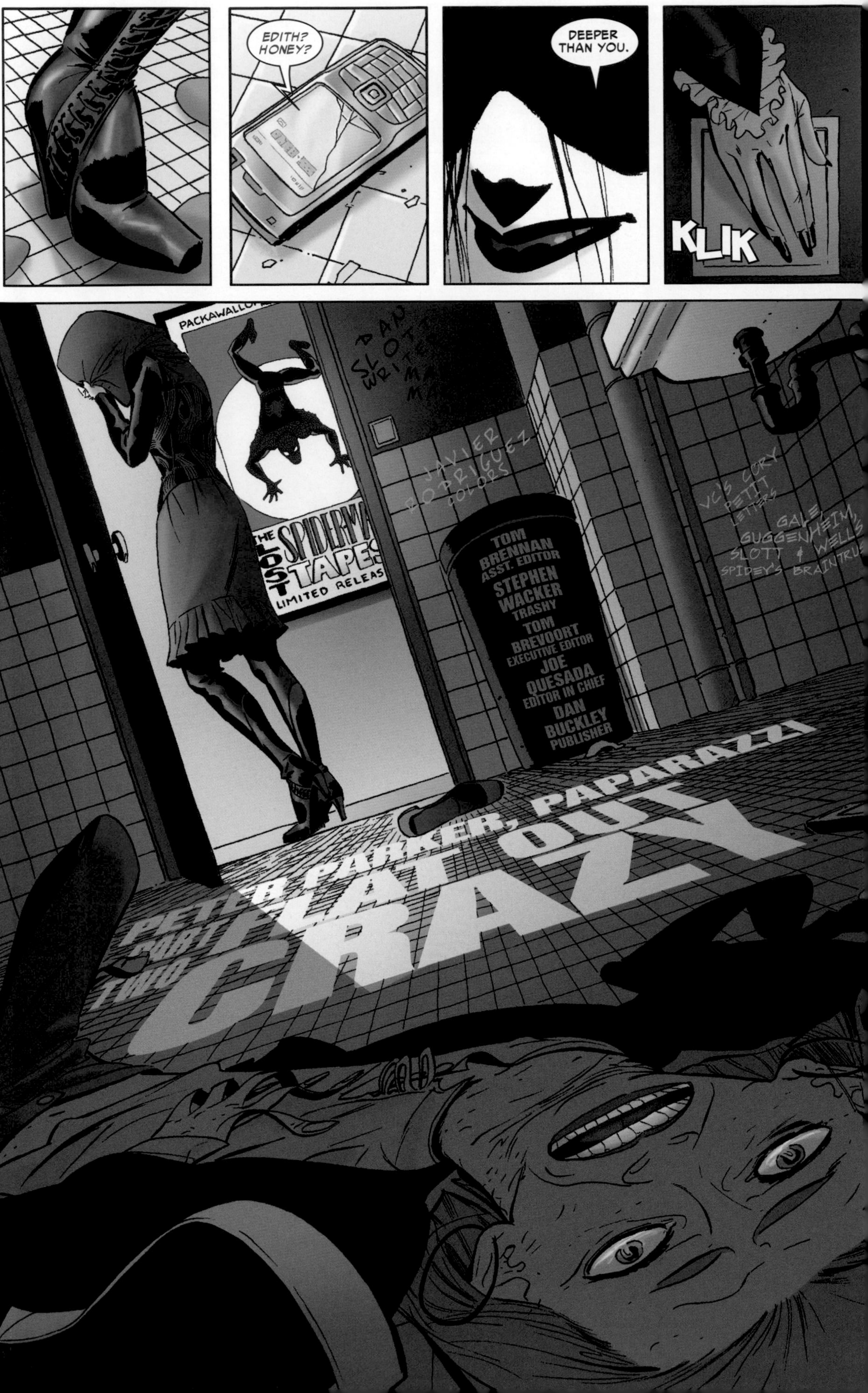
EDITH? HONEY?
DEEPER THAN YOU.
KLIK
PACKAWALLOP
THE LOST SPIDERMA TAPES
LIMITED RELEAS
DAN SLOTT WRITES
JAVIER RODRIGUEZ COLORS
VC'S CORY PETIT LETTERS
GALE, GUGGENHEIM, SLOTT & WELLS SPIDEY'S BRAINTRUS
TOM BRENNAN ASST. EDITOR
STEPHEN WACKER TRASHY
TOM BREVOORT EXECUTIVE EDITOR
JOE QUESADA EDITOR IN CHIEF
DAN BUCKLEY PUBLISHER
PARKER, PAPARAZZI
FLAT OUT CRAZY

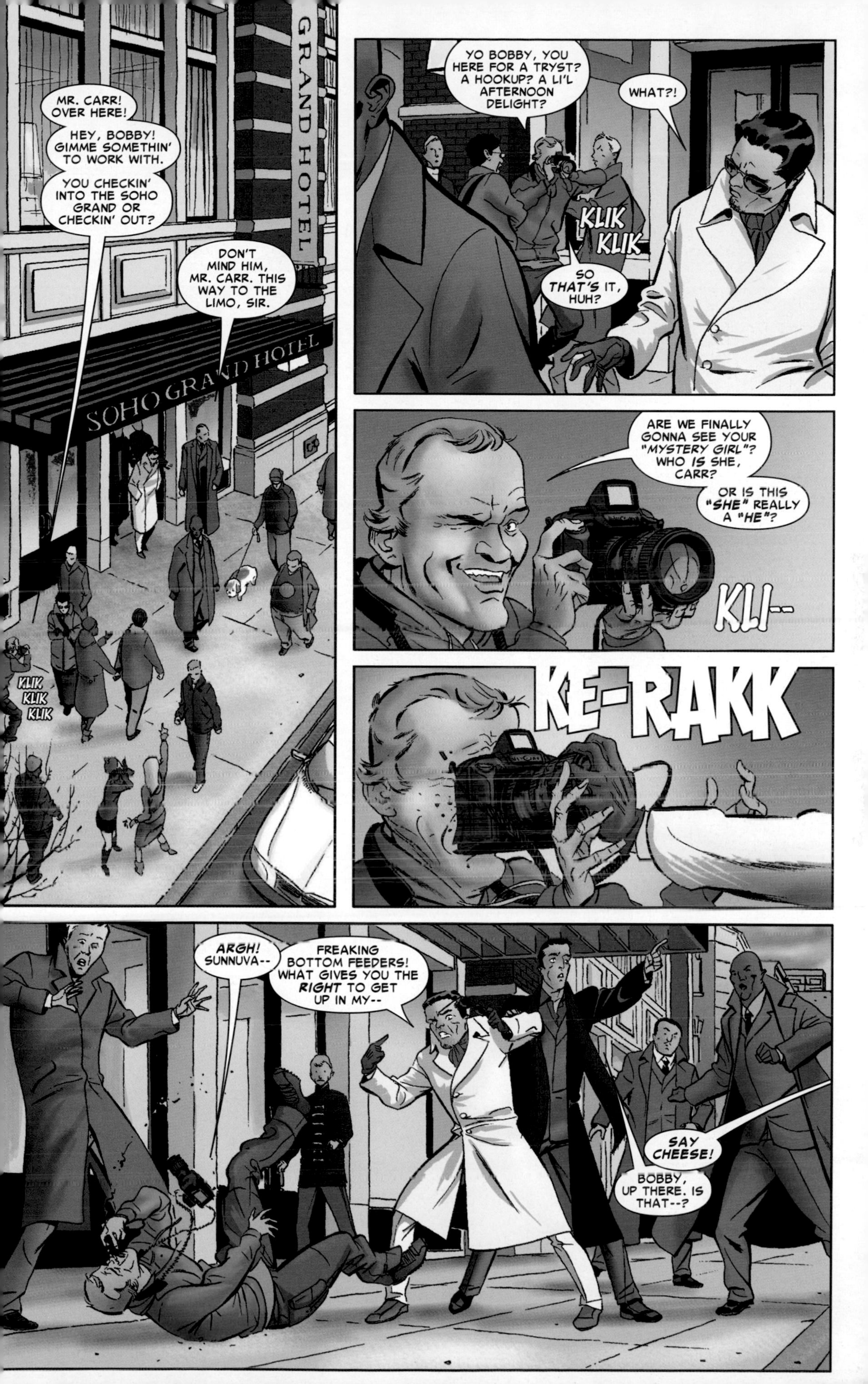

GRAND HOTEL
MR. CARR! OVER HERE!
HEY, BOBBY! GIMME SOMETHIN' TO WORK WITH.
YOU CHECKIN' INTO THE SOHO GRAND OR CHECKIN' OUT?
DON'T MIND HIM, MR. CARR. THIS WAY TO THE LIMO, SIR.
SOHO GRAND HOTEL
SOHO GRAND HOTEL
KLIK KLIK KLIK
YO BOBBY, YOU HERE FOR A TRYST? A HOOKUP? A LI'L AFTERNOON DELIGHT?
WHAT?!
KLIK KLIK
SO *THAT'S* IT, HUH?
ARE WE FINALLY GONNA SEE YOUR "*MYSTERY GIRL*"? WHO *IS* SHE, CARR?
OR IS THIS "*SHE*" REALLY A "*HE*"?
KLI--
KE-RAKK
ARGH! SUNNUVA--
FREAKING BOTTOM FEEDERS! WHAT GIVES YOU THE *RIGHT* TO GET UP IN MY--
SAY CHEESE!
BOBBY, UP THERE. IS THAT--?

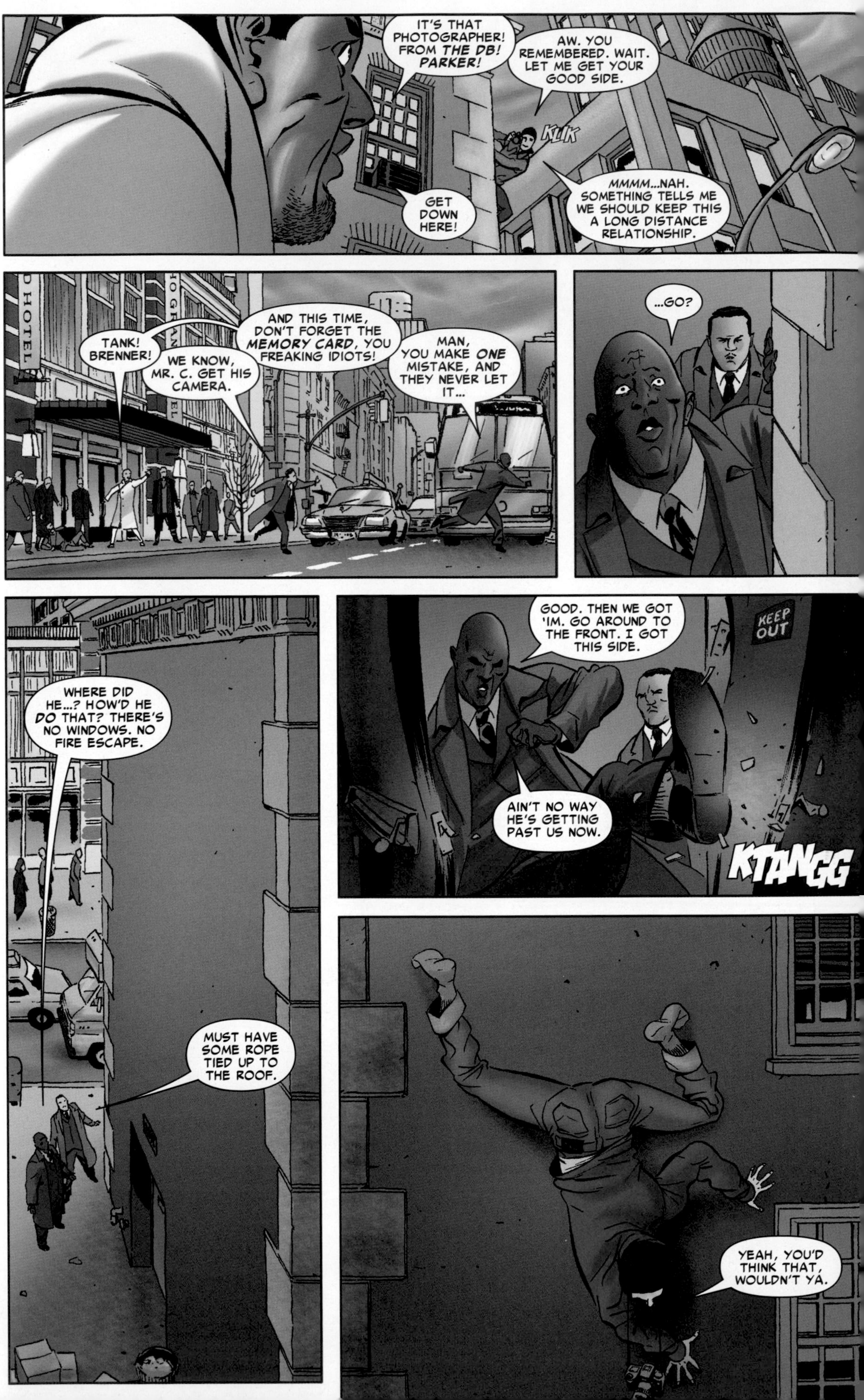
IT'S THAT PHOTOGRAPHER! FROM THE DB! PARKER!
AW. YOU REMEMBERED. WAIT. LET ME GET YOUR GOOD SIDE.
KLIK
GET DOWN HERE!
MMMM...NAH. SOMETHING TELLS ME WE SHOULD KEEP THIS A LONG DISTANCE RELATIONSHIP.
TANK! BRENNER!
AND THIS TIME, DON'T FORGET THE MEMORY CARD, YOU FREAKING IDIOTS!
WE KNOW, MR. C. GET HIS CAMERA.
MAN, YOU MAKE ONE MISTAKE, AND THEY NEVER LET IT...
...GO?
WHERE DID HE...? HOW'D HE DO THAT? THERE'S NO WINDOWS. NO FIRE ESCAPE.
MUST HAVE SOME ROPE TIED UP TO THE ROOF.
GOOD. THEN WE GOT 'IM. GO AROUND TO THE FRONT. I GOT THIS SIDE.
KEEP OUT
AIN'T NO WAY HE'S GETTING PAST US NOW.
KTANGG
YEAH, YOU'D THINK THAT, WOULDN'T YA.

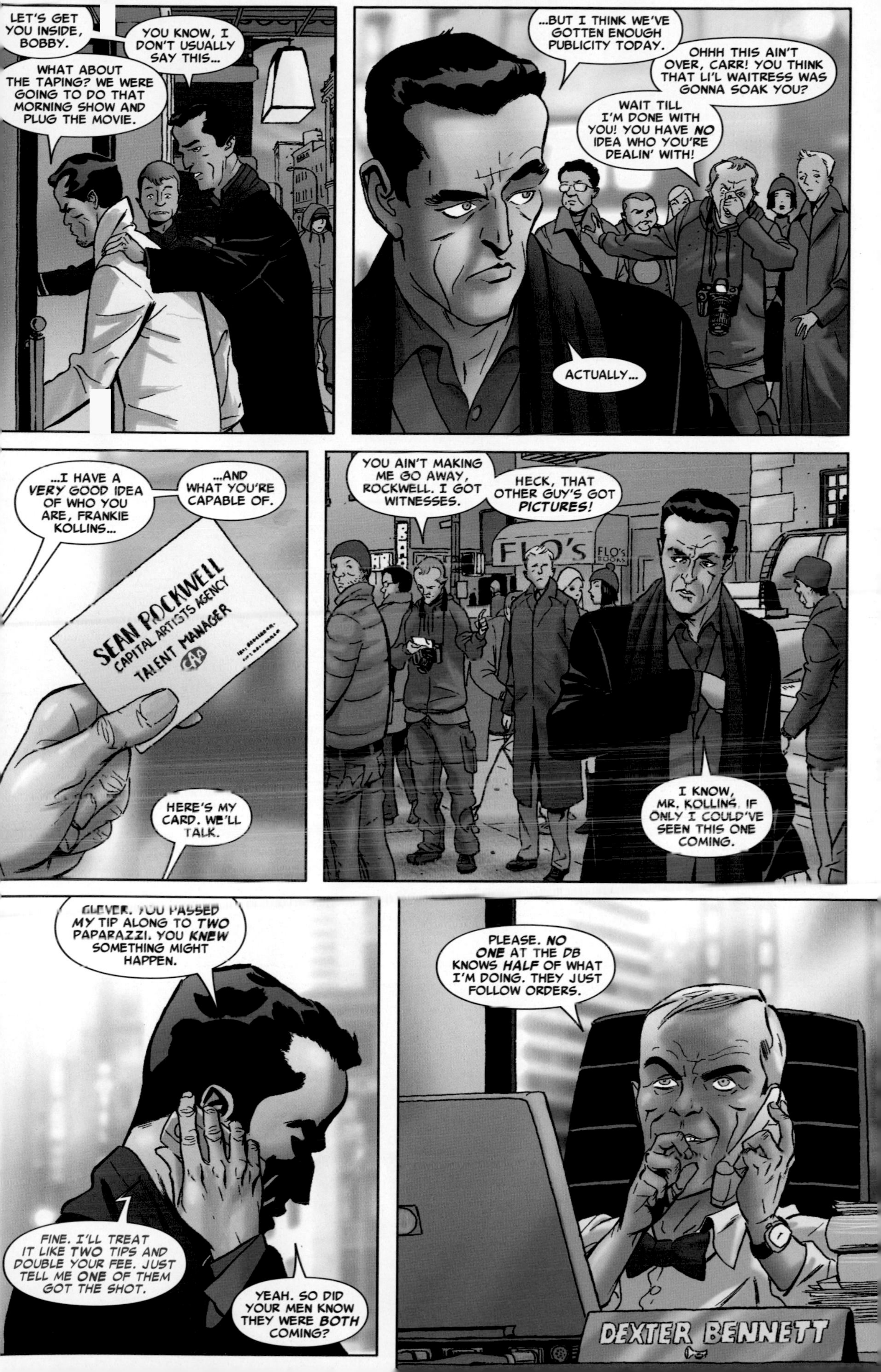
LET'S GET YOU INSIDE, BOBBY.
YOU KNOW, I DON'T USUALLY SAY THIS...
WHAT ABOUT THE TAPING? WE WERE GOING TO DO THAT MORNING SHOW AND PLUG THE MOVIE.
...BUT I THINK WE'VE GOTTEN ENOUGH PUBLICITY TODAY.
OHHH THIS AIN'T OVER, CARR! YOU THINK THAT LI'L WAITRESS WAS GONNA SOAK YOU?
WAIT TILL I'M DONE WITH YOU! YOU HAVE NO IDEA WHO YOU'RE DEALIN' WITH!
ACTUALLY...
...I HAVE A VERY GOOD IDEA OF WHO YOU ARE, FRANKIE KOLLINS...
...AND WHAT YOU'RE CAPABLE OF.
SEAN ROCKWELL
CAPITAL ARTISTS AGENCY
TALENT MANAGER
CAA
HERE'S MY CARD. WE'LL TALK.
YOU AIN'T MAKING ME GO AWAY, ROCKWELL. I GOT WITNESSES.
HECK, THAT OTHER GUY'S GOT PICTURES!
FLO'S
FLO'S BOOKS
I KNOW, MR. KOLLINS. IF ONLY I COULD'VE SEEN THIS ONE COMING.
CLEVER. YOU PASSED MY TIP ALONG TO TWO PAPARAZZI. YOU KNEW SOMETHING MIGHT HAPPEN.
FINE. I'LL TREAT IT LIKE TWO TIPS AND DOUBLE YOUR FEE. JUST TELL ME ONE OF THEM GOT THE SHOT.
YEAH. SO DID YOUR MEN KNOW THEY WERE BOTH COMING?
PLEASE. NO ONE AT THE DB KNOWS HALF OF WHAT I'M DOING. THEY JUST FOLLOW ORDERS.
DEXTER BENNETT

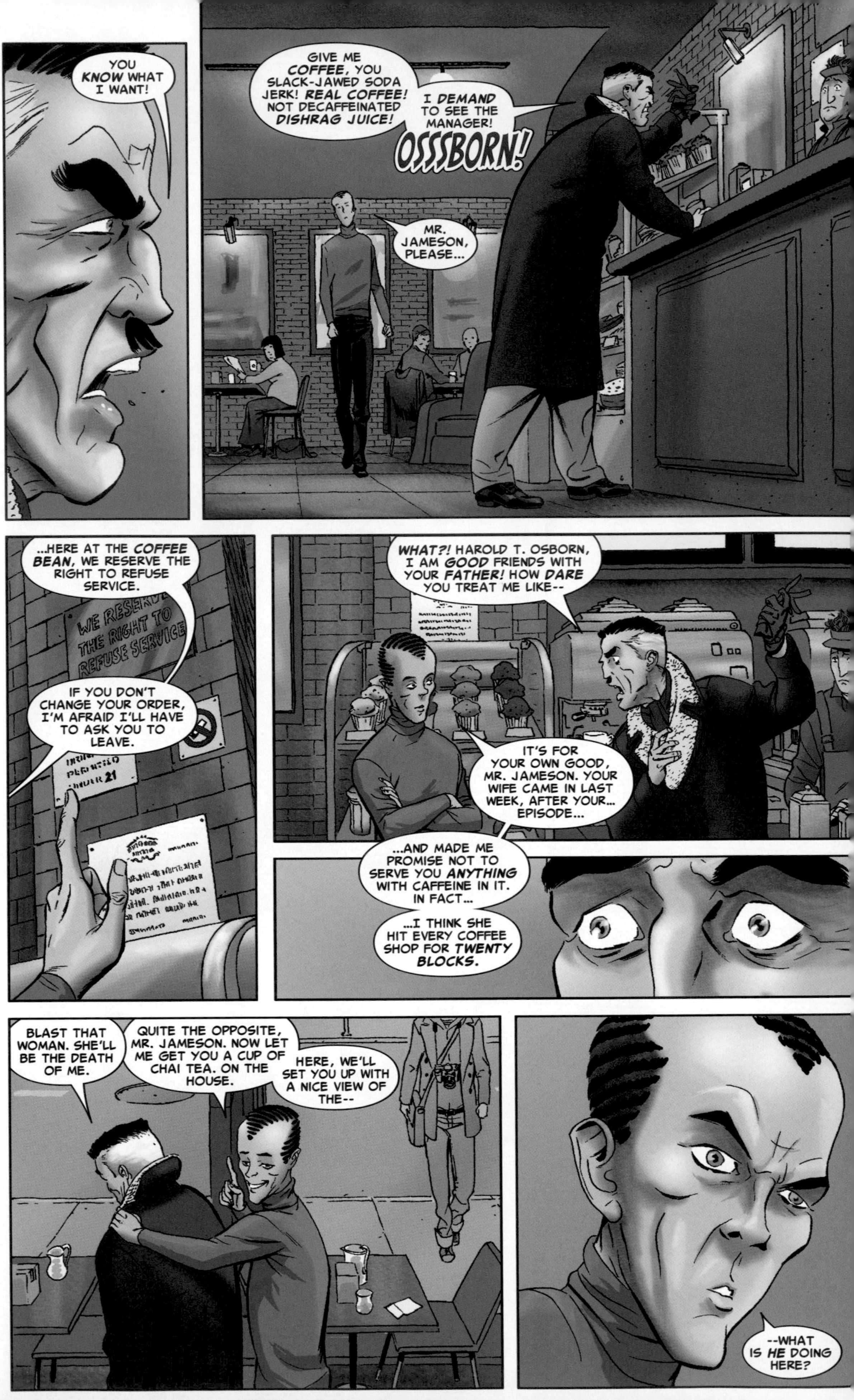
YOU KNOW WHAT I WANT!
GIVE ME COFFEE, YOU SLACK-JAWED SODA JERK! REAL COFFEE! NOT DECAFFEINATED DISHRAG JUICE!
I DEMAND TO SEE THE MANAGER!
OSSSBORN!
MR. JAMESON, PLEASE...
...HERE AT THE COFFEE BEAN, WE RESERVE THE RIGHT TO REFUSE SERVICE.
WE RESERVE THE RIGHT TO REFUSE SERVICE
IF YOU DON'T CHANGE YOUR ORDER, I'M AFRAID I'LL HAVE TO ASK YOU TO LEAVE.
WHAT?! HAROLD T. OSBORN, I AM GOOD FRIENDS WITH YOUR FATHER! HOW DARE YOU TREAT ME LIKE--
IT'S FOR YOUR OWN GOOD, MR. JAMESON. YOUR WIFE CAME IN LAST WEEK, AFTER YOUR... EPISODE...
...AND MADE ME PROMISE NOT TO SERVE YOU ANYTHING WITH CAFFEINE IN IT. IN FACT...
...I THINK SHE HIT EVERY COFFEE SHOP FOR TWENTY BLOCKS.
BLAST THAT WOMAN. SHE'LL BE THE DEATH OF ME.
QUITE THE OPPOSITE, MR. JAMESON. NOW LET ME GET YOU A CUP OF CHAI TEA. ON THE HOUSE.
HERE, WE'LL SET YOU UP WITH A NICE VIEW OF THE--
--WHAT IS HE DOING HERE?

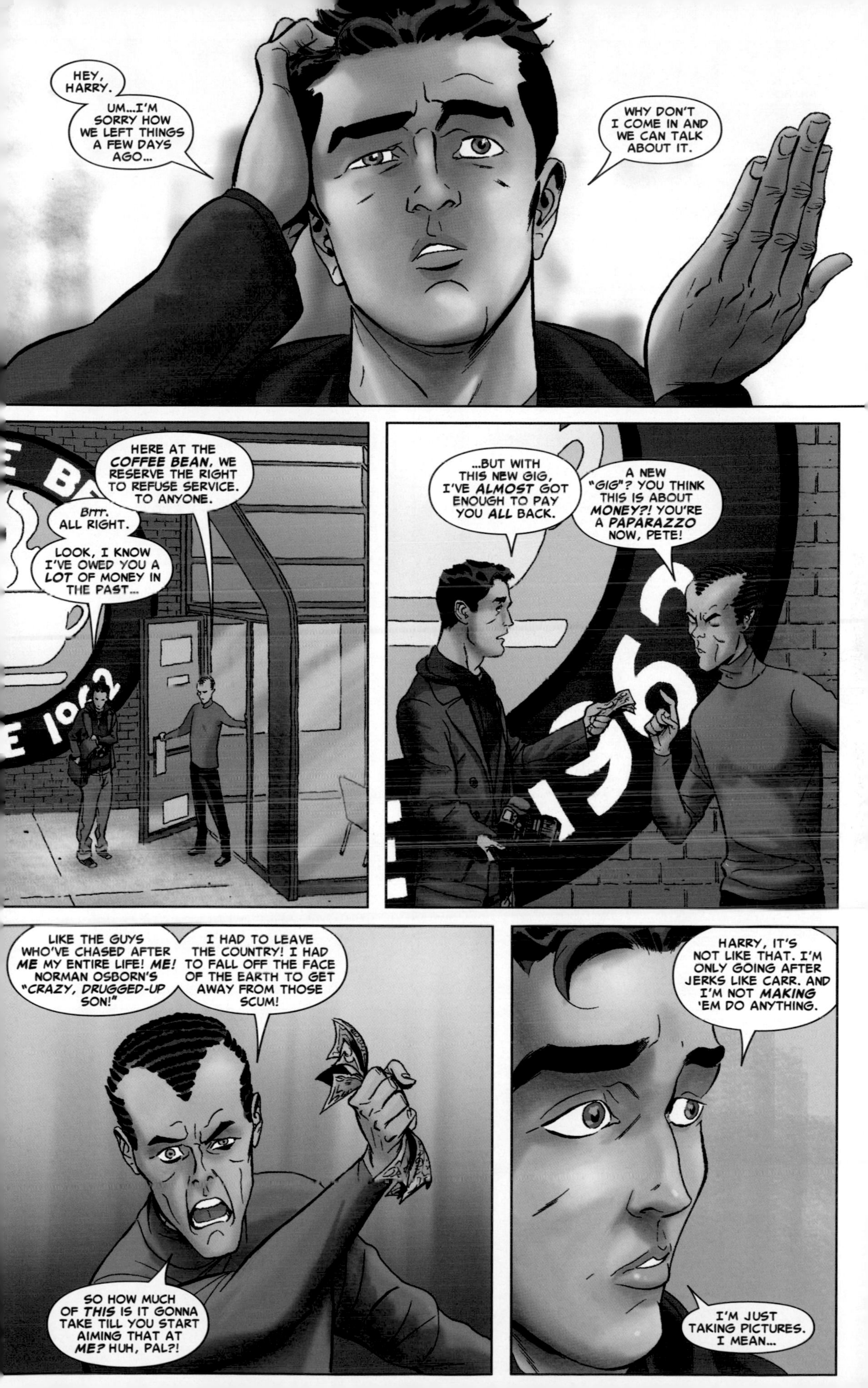
HEY, HARRY.
UM...I'M SORRY HOW WE LEFT THINGS A FEW DAYS AGO...
WHY DON'T I COME IN AND WE CAN TALK ABOUT IT.
HERE AT THE COFFEE BEAN, WE RESERVE THE RIGHT TO REFUSE SERVICE. TO ANYONE.
Brrr. ALL RIGHT.
LOOK, I KNOW I'VE OWED YOU A LOT OF MONEY IN THE PAST...
...BUT WITH THIS NEW GIG, I'VE ALMOST GOT ENOUGH TO PAY YOU ALL BACK.
A NEW "GIG"? YOU THINK THIS IS ABOUT MONEY?! YOU'RE A PAPARAZZO NOW, PETE!
LIKE THE GUYS WHO'VE CHASED AFTER ME MY ENTIRE LIFE! ME! NORMAN OSBORN'S "CRAZY, DRUGGED-UP SON!"
I HAD TO LEAVE THE COUNTRY! I HAD TO FALL OFF THE FACE OF THE EARTH TO GET AWAY FROM THOSE SCUM!
SO HOW MUCH OF THIS IS IT GONNA TAKE TILL YOU START AIMING THAT AT ME? HUH, PAL?!
HARRY, IT'S NOT LIKE THAT. I'M ONLY GOING AFTER JERKS LIKE CARR. AND I'M NOT MAKING 'EM DO ANYTHING.
I'M JUST TAKING PICTURES. I MEAN...

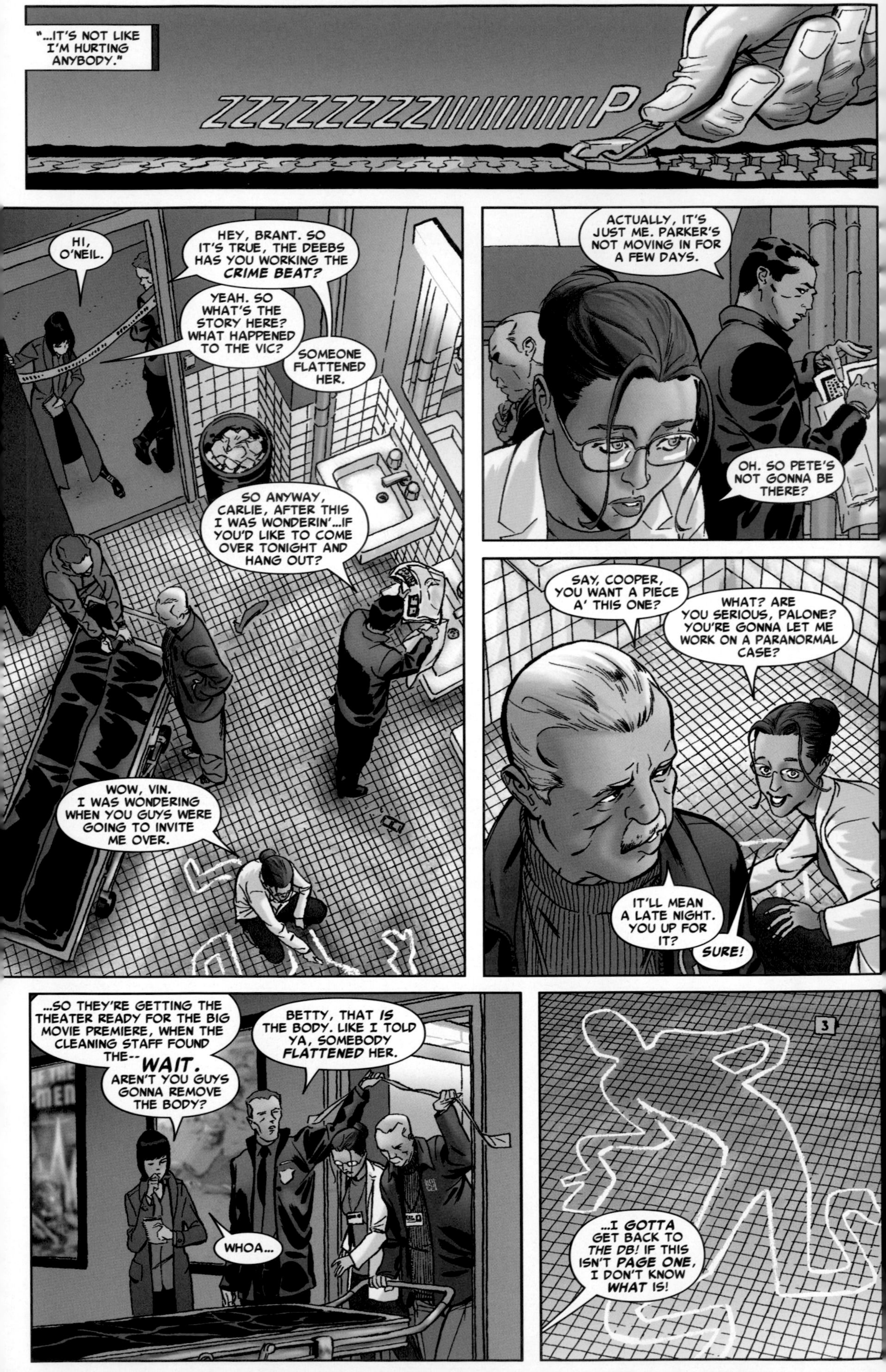
"...IT'S NOT LIKE I'M HURTING ANYBODY."
ZZZZZZZZZIIIIIIIIIIIIIP
HI, O'NEIL.
HEY, BRANT. SO IT'S TRUE, THE DEEBS HAS YOU WORKING THE CRIME BEAT?
YEAH. SO WHAT'S THE STORY HERE? WHAT HAPPENED TO THE VIC?
SOMEONE FLATTENED HER.
SO ANYWAY, CARLIE, AFTER THIS I WAS WONDERIN'...IF YOU'D LIKE TO COME OVER TONIGHT AND HANG OUT?
WOW, VIN. I WAS WONDERING WHEN YOU GUYS WERE GOING TO INVITE ME OVER.
ACTUALLY, IT'S JUST ME. PARKER'S NOT MOVING IN FOR A FEW DAYS.
OH. SO PETE'S NOT GONNA BE THERE?
SAY, COOPER, YOU WANT A PIECE A' THIS ONE?
WHAT? ARE YOU SERIOUS, PALONE? YOU'RE GONNA LET ME WORK ON A PARANORMAL CASE?
IT'LL MEAN A LATE NIGHT. YOU UP FOR IT?
SURE!
...SO THEY'RE GETTING THE THEATER READY FOR THE BIG MOVIE PREMIERE, WHEN THE CLEANING STAFF FOUND THE-- WAIT. AREN'T YOU GUYS GONNA REMOVE THE BODY?
BETTY, THAT IS THE BODY. LIKE I TOLD YA, SOMEBODY FLATTENED HER.
WHOA...
3
...I GOTTA GET BACK TO THE DB! IF THIS ISN'T PAGE ONE, I DON'T KNOW WHAT IS!

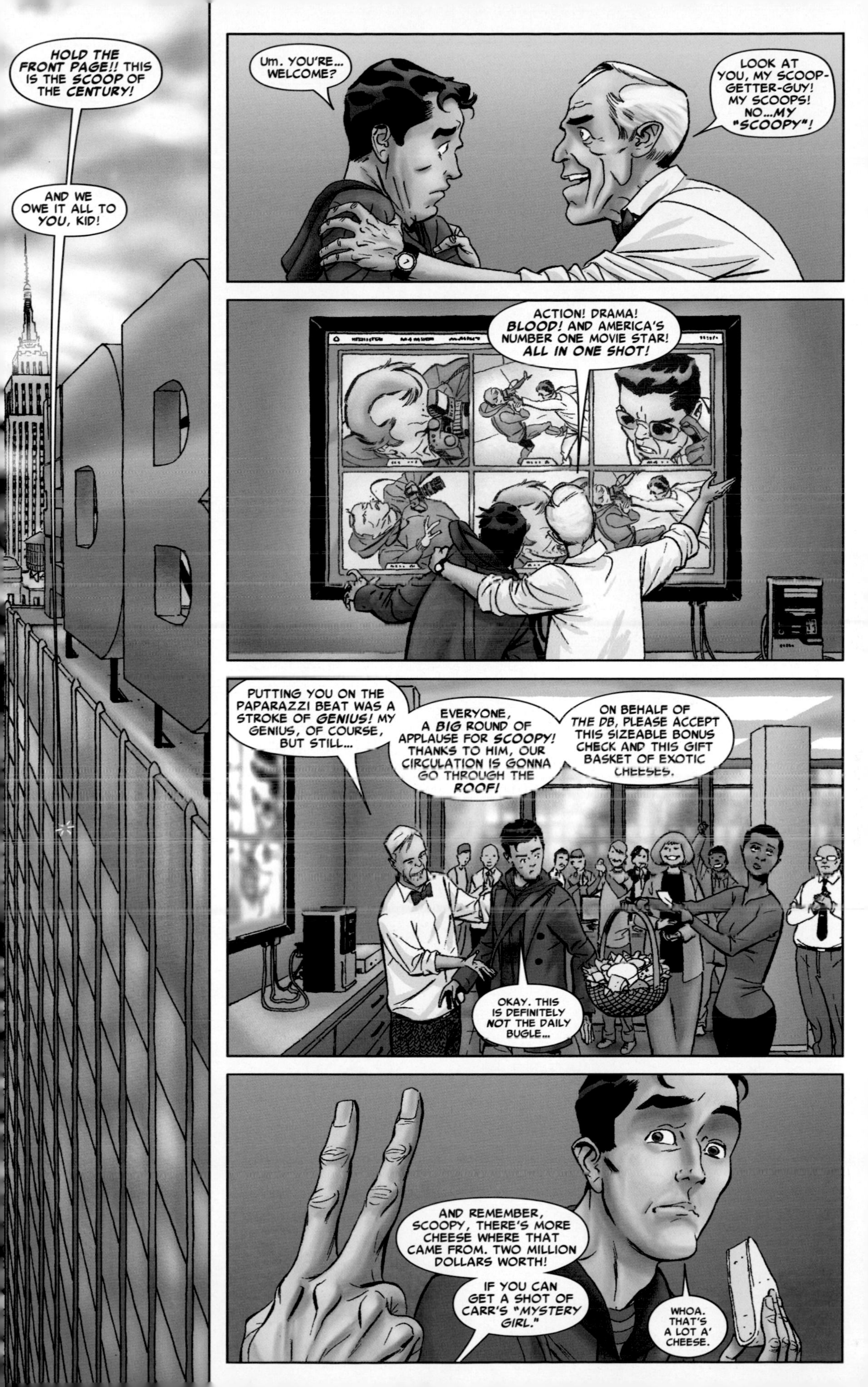
HOLD THE FRONT PAGE!! THIS IS THE SCOOP OF THE CENTURY!
AND WE OWE IT ALL TO YOU, KID!
Um. YOU'RE... WELCOME?
LOOK AT YOU, MY SCOOP-GETTER-GUY! MY SCOOPS! NO...MY "SCOOPY"!
ACTION! DRAMA! BLOOD! AND AMERICA'S NUMBER ONE MOVIE STAR! ALL IN ONE SHOT!
PUTTING YOU ON THE PAPARAZZI BEAT WAS A STROKE OF GENIUS! MY GENIUS, OF COURSE, BUT STILL...
EVERYONE, A BIG ROUND OF APPLAUSE FOR SCOOPY! THANKS TO HIM, OUR CIRCULATION IS GONNA GO THROUGH THE ROOF!
ON BEHALF OF THE DB, PLEASE ACCEPT THIS SIZEABLE BONUS CHECK AND THIS GIFT BASKET OF EXOTIC CHEESES.
OKAY. THIS IS DEFINITELY NOT THE DAILY BUGLE...
AND REMEMBER, SCOOPY, THERE'S MORE CHEESE WHERE THAT CAME FROM. TWO MILLION DOLLARS WORTH!
IF YOU CAN GET A SHOT OF CARR'S "MYSTERY GIRL."
WHOA. THAT'S A LOT A' CHEESE.

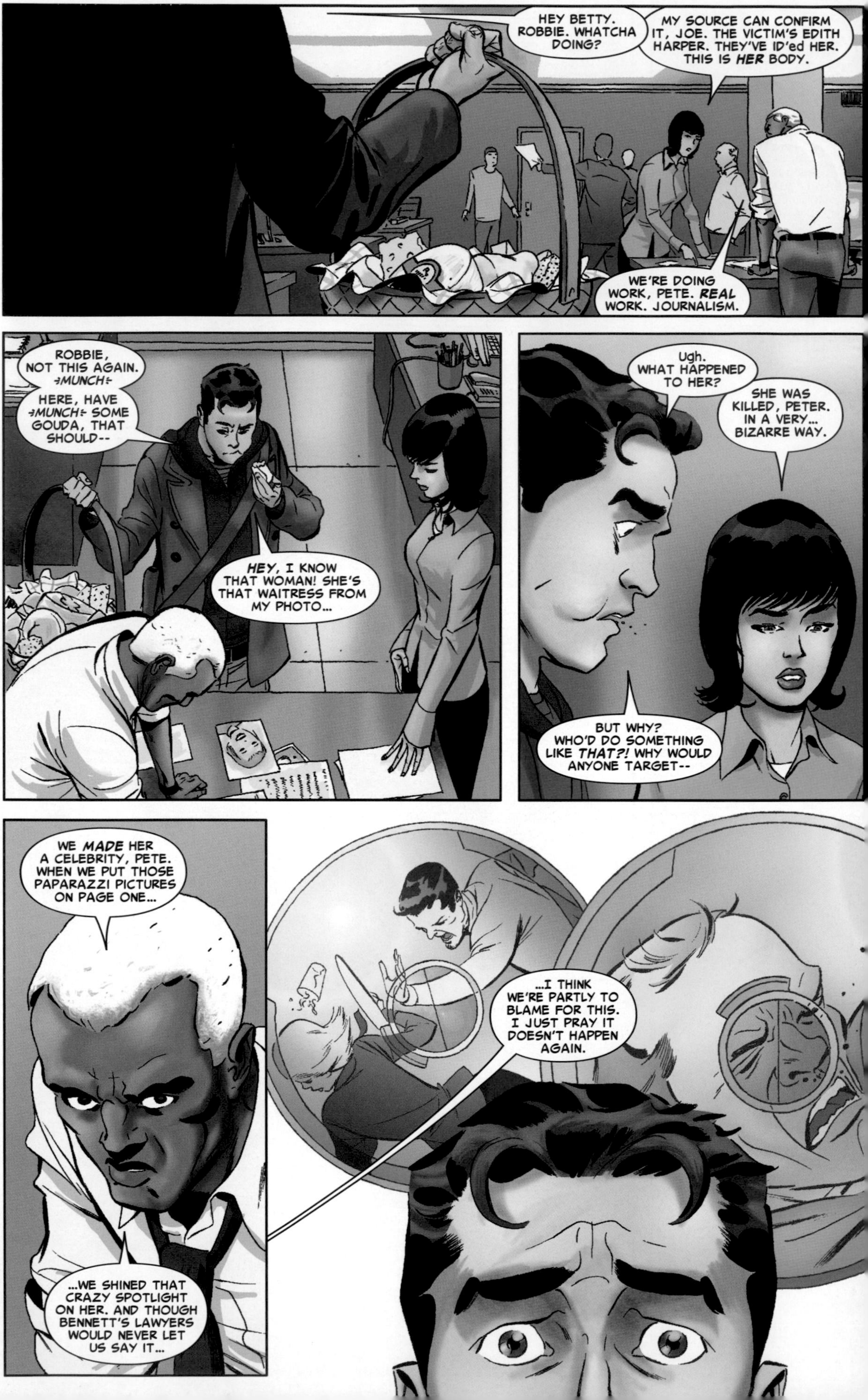
HEY BETTY. ROBBIE. WHATCHA DOING?
MY SOURCE CAN CONFIRM IT, JOE. THE VICTIM'S EDITH HARPER. THEY'VE ID'ed HER. THIS IS HER BODY.
WE'RE DOING WORK, PETE. REAL WORK. JOURNALISM.
ROBBIE, NOT THIS AGAIN. =MUNCH=
HERE, HAVE =MUNCH= SOME GOUDA, THAT SHOULD--
HEY, I KNOW THAT WOMAN! SHE'S THAT WAITRESS FROM MY PHOTO...
Ugh. WHAT HAPPENED TO HER?
SHE WAS KILLED, PETER. IN A VERY... BIZARRE WAY.
BUT WHY? WHO'D DO SOMETHING LIKE THAT?! WHY WOULD ANYONE TARGET--
WE MADE HER A CELEBRITY, PETE. WHEN WE PUT THOSE PAPARAZZI PICTURES ON PAGE ONE...
...WE SHINED THAT CRAZY SPOTLIGHT ON HER. AND THOUGH BENNETT'S LAWYERS WOULD NEVER LET US SAY IT...
...I THINK WE'RE PARTLY TO BLAME FOR THIS. I JUST PRAY IT DOESN'T HAPPEN AGAIN.

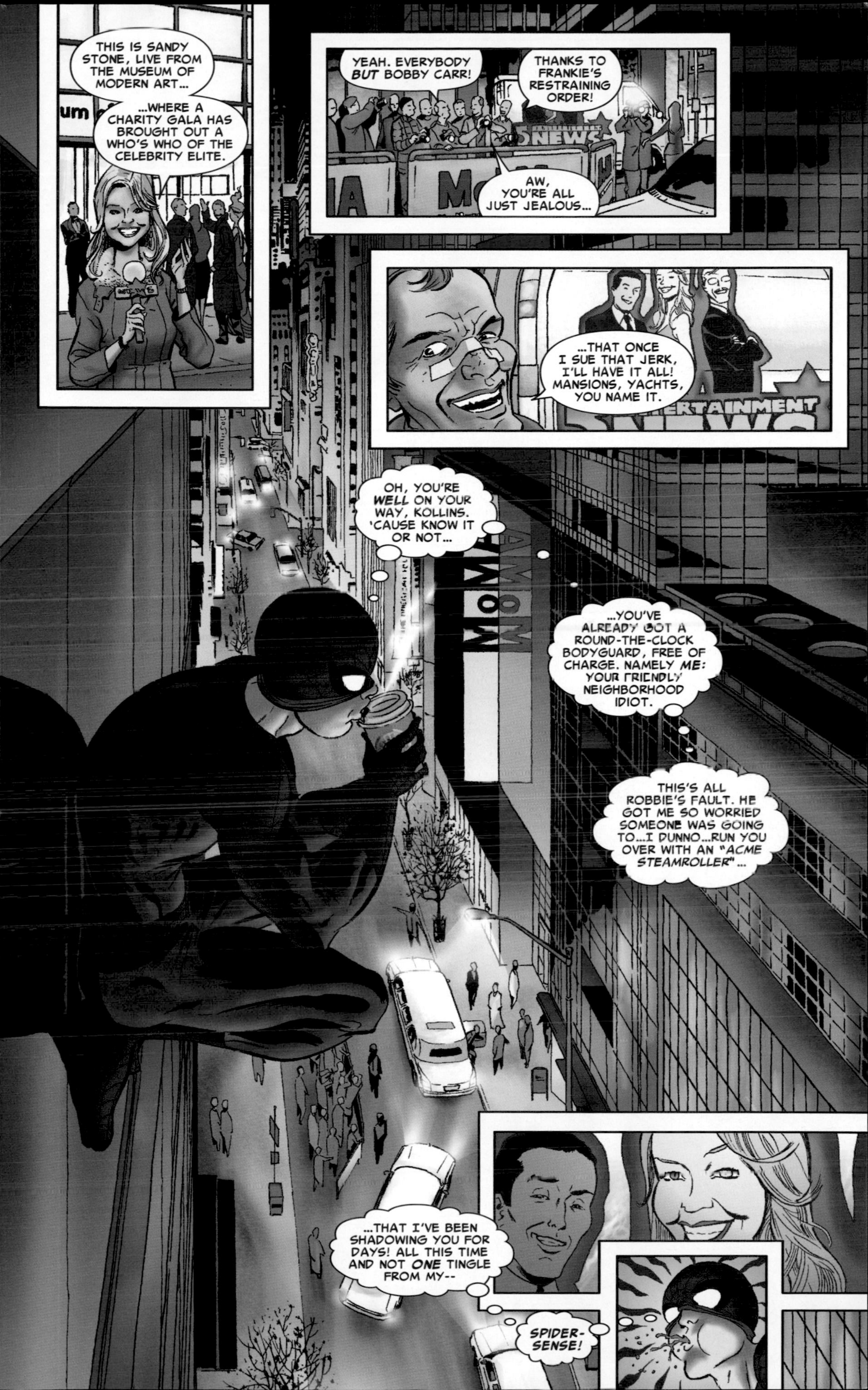
THIS IS SANDY STONE, LIVE FROM THE MUSEUM OF MODERN ART...
...WHERE A CHARITY GALA HAS BROUGHT OUT A WHO'S WHO OF THE CELEBRITY ELITE.
YEAH. EVERYBODY *BUT* BOBBY CARR!
THANKS TO FRANKIE'S RESTRAINING ORDER!
AW, YOU'RE ALL JUST JEALOUS...
...THAT ONCE I SUE THAT JERK, I'LL HAVE IT ALL! MANSIONS, YACHTS, YOU NAME IT.
OH, YOU'RE *WELL* ON YOUR WAY, KOLLINS. 'CAUSE KNOW IT OR NOT...
...YOU'VE ALREADY GOT A ROUND-THE-CLOCK BODYGUARD, FREE OF CHARGE. NAMELY *ME*: YOUR FRIENDLY NEIGHBORHOOD IDIOT.
THIS'S ALL ROBBIE'S FAULT. HE GOT ME SO WORRIED SOMEONE WAS GOING TO...I DUNNO...RUN YOU OVER WITH AN "*ACME STEAMROLLER*"...
...THAT I'VE BEEN SHADOWING YOU FOR DAYS! ALL THIS TIME AND NOT *ONE* TINGLE FROM MY--
SPIDER-SENSE!

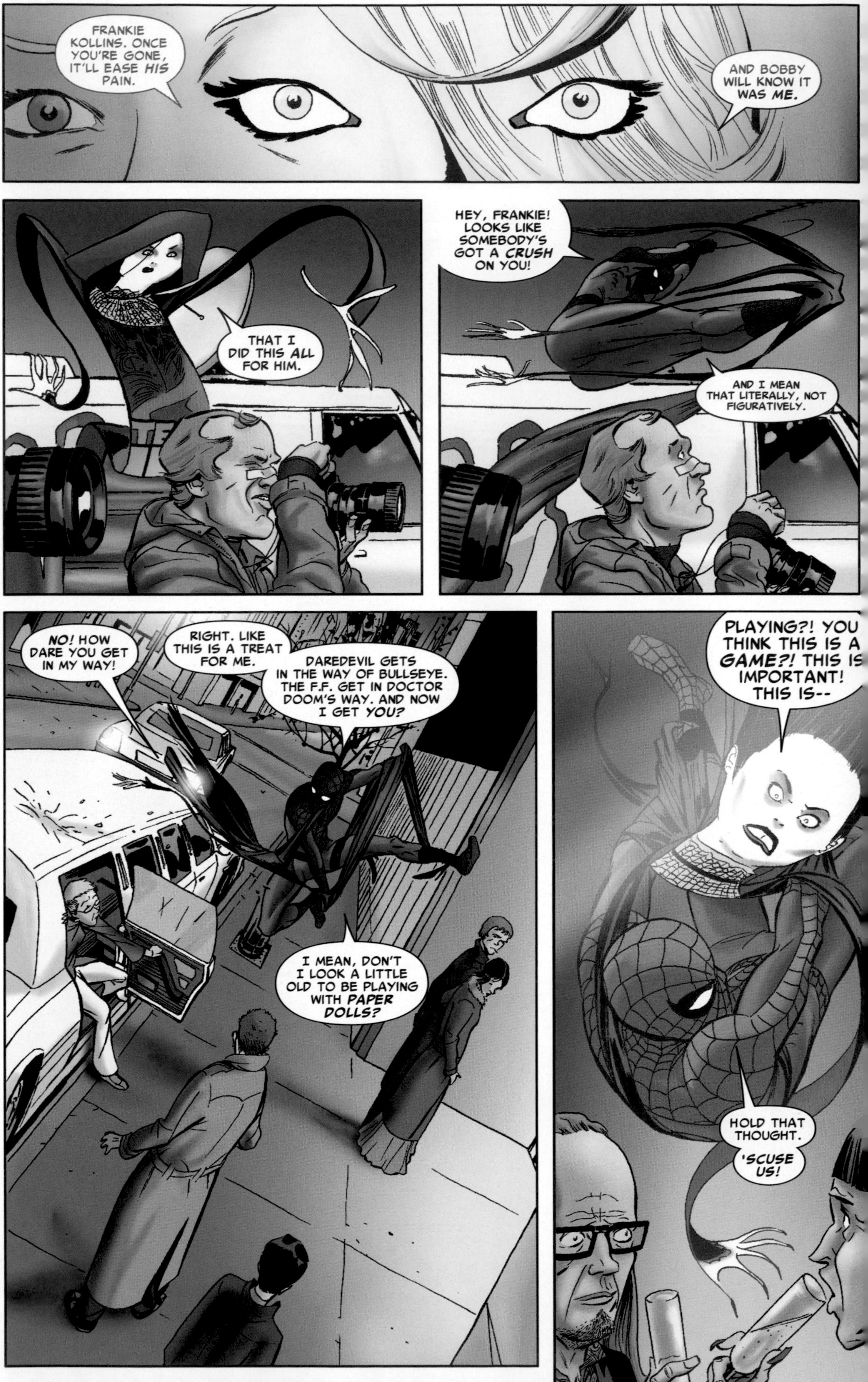
FRANKIE KOLLINS. ONCE YOU'RE GONE, IT'LL EASE HIS PAIN.
AND BOBBY WILL KNOW IT WAS ME.
THAT I DID THIS ALL FOR HIM.
HEY, FRANKIE! LOOKS LIKE SOMEBODY'S GOT A CRUSH ON YOU!
AND I MEAN THAT LITERALLY, NOT FIGURATIVELY.
NO! HOW DARE YOU GET IN MY WAY!
RIGHT. LIKE THIS IS A TREAT FOR ME.
DAREDEVIL GETS IN THE WAY OF BULLSEYE. THE F.F. GET IN DOCTOR DOOM'S WAY. AND NOW I GET YOU?
I MEAN, DON'T I LOOK A LITTLE OLD TO BE PLAYING WITH PAPER DOLLS?
PLAYING?! YOU THINK THIS IS A GAME?! THIS IS IMPORTANT! THIS IS--
HOLD THAT THOUGHT.
'SCUSE US!

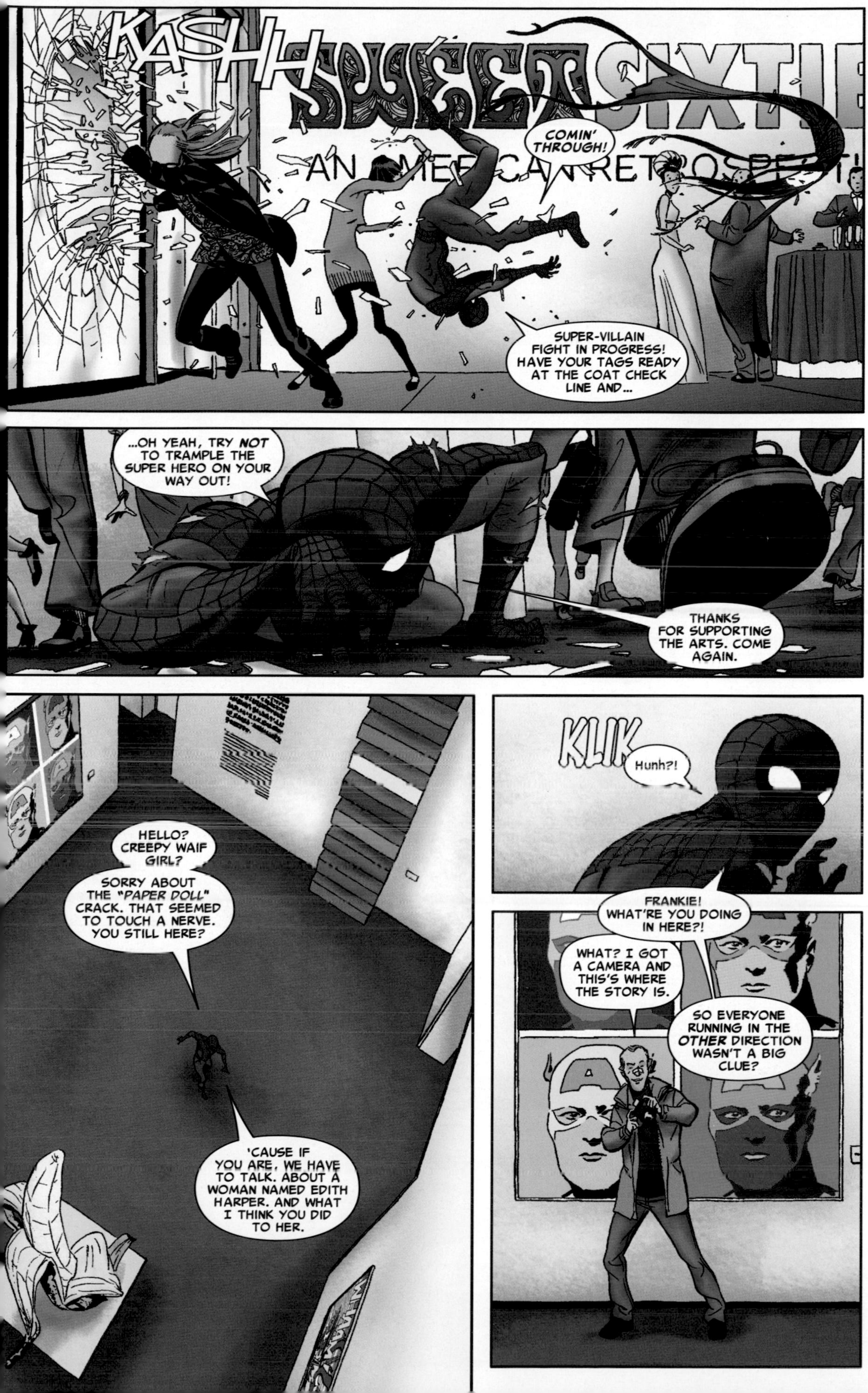
KASHH
SWEET SIXTIE
COMIN' THROUGH!
SUPER-VILLAIN FIGHT IN PROGRESS! HAVE YOUR TAGS READY AT THE COAT CHECK LINE AND...
...OH YEAH, TRY NOT TO TRAMPLE THE SUPER HERO ON YOUR WAY OUT!
THANKS FOR SUPPORTING THE ARTS. COME AGAIN.
HELLO? CREEPY WAIF GIRL?
SORRY ABOUT THE "PAPER DOLL" CRACK. THAT SEEMED TO TOUCH A NERVE. YOU STILL HERE?
'CAUSE IF YOU ARE, WE HAVE TO TALK. ABOUT A WOMAN NAMED EDITH HARPER. AND WHAT I THINK YOU DID TO HER.
KLIK
Hunh?!
FRANKIE! WHAT'RE YOU DOING IN HERE?!
WHAT? I GOT A CAMERA AND THIS'S WHERE THE STORY IS.
SO EVERYONE RUNNING IN THE OTHER DIRECTION WASN'T A BIG CLUE?

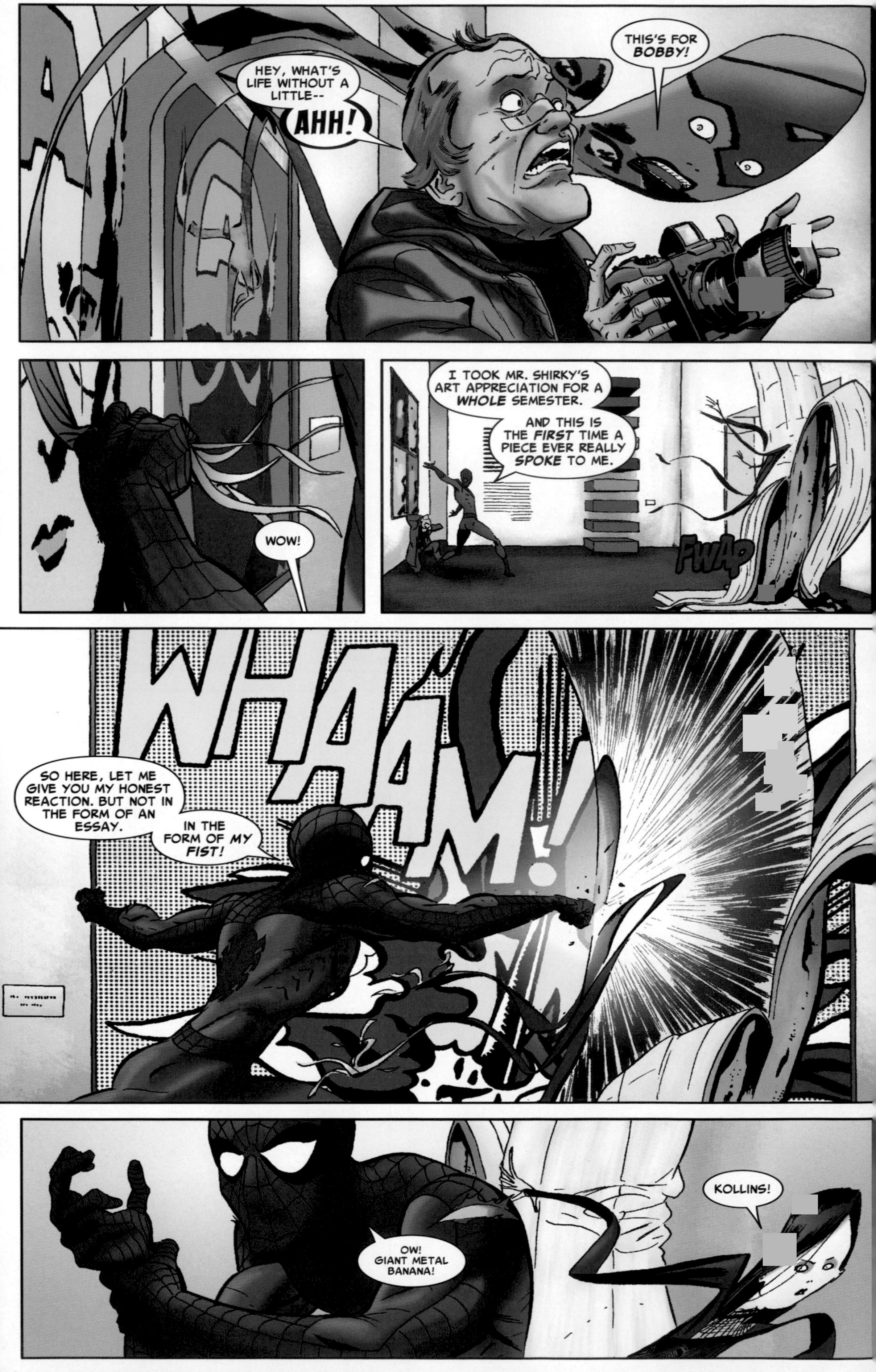
HEY, WHAT'S LIFE WITHOUT A LITTLE--
AHH!
THIS'S FOR BOBBY!
WOW!
I TOOK MR. SHIRKY'S ART APPRECIATION FOR A WHOLE SEMESTER.
AND THIS IS THE FIRST TIME A PIECE EVER REALLY SPOKE TO ME.
FWAP
WHAAM!
SO HERE, LET ME GIVE YOU MY HONEST REACTION. BUT NOT IN THE FORM OF AN ESSAY.
IN THE FORM OF MY FIST!
OW! GIANT METAL BANANA!
KOLLINS!

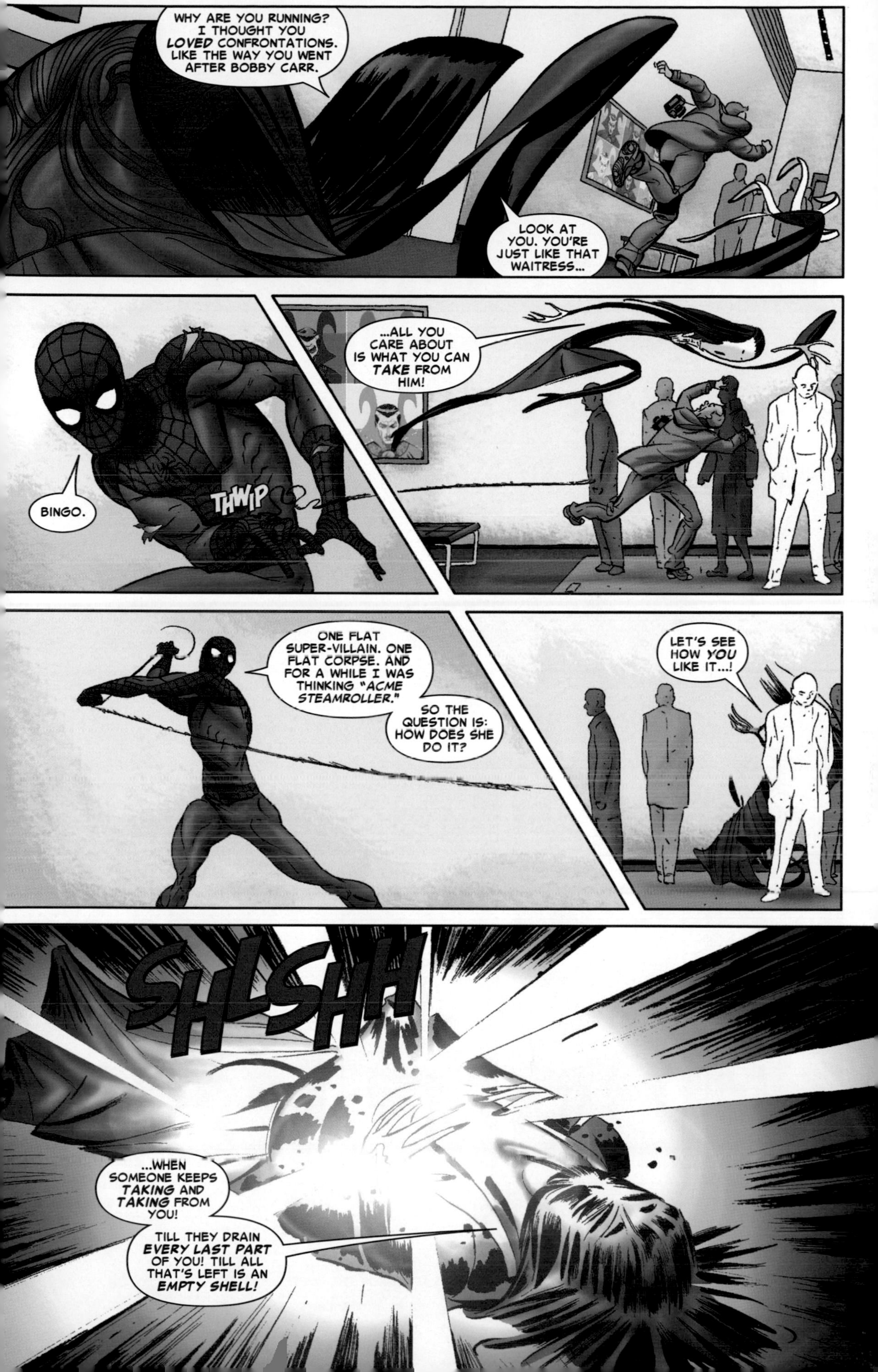
WHY ARE YOU RUNNING? I THOUGHT YOU LOVED CONFRONTATIONS. LIKE THE WAY YOU WENT AFTER BOBBY CARR.
LOOK AT YOU. YOU'RE JUST LIKE THAT WAITRESS...
...ALL YOU CARE ABOUT IS WHAT YOU CAN TAKE FROM HIM!
BINGO.
THWIP
ONE FLAT SUPER-VILLAIN. ONE FLAT CORPSE. AND FOR A WHILE I WAS THINKING "ACME STEAMROLLER."
SO THE QUESTION IS: HOW DOES SHE DO IT?
LET'S SEE HOW YOU LIKE IT...!
SHLSHH
...WHEN SOMEONE KEEPS TAKING AND TAKING FROM YOU!
TILL THEY DRAIN EVERY LAST PART OF YOU! TILL ALL THAT'S LEFT IS AN EMPTY SHELL!

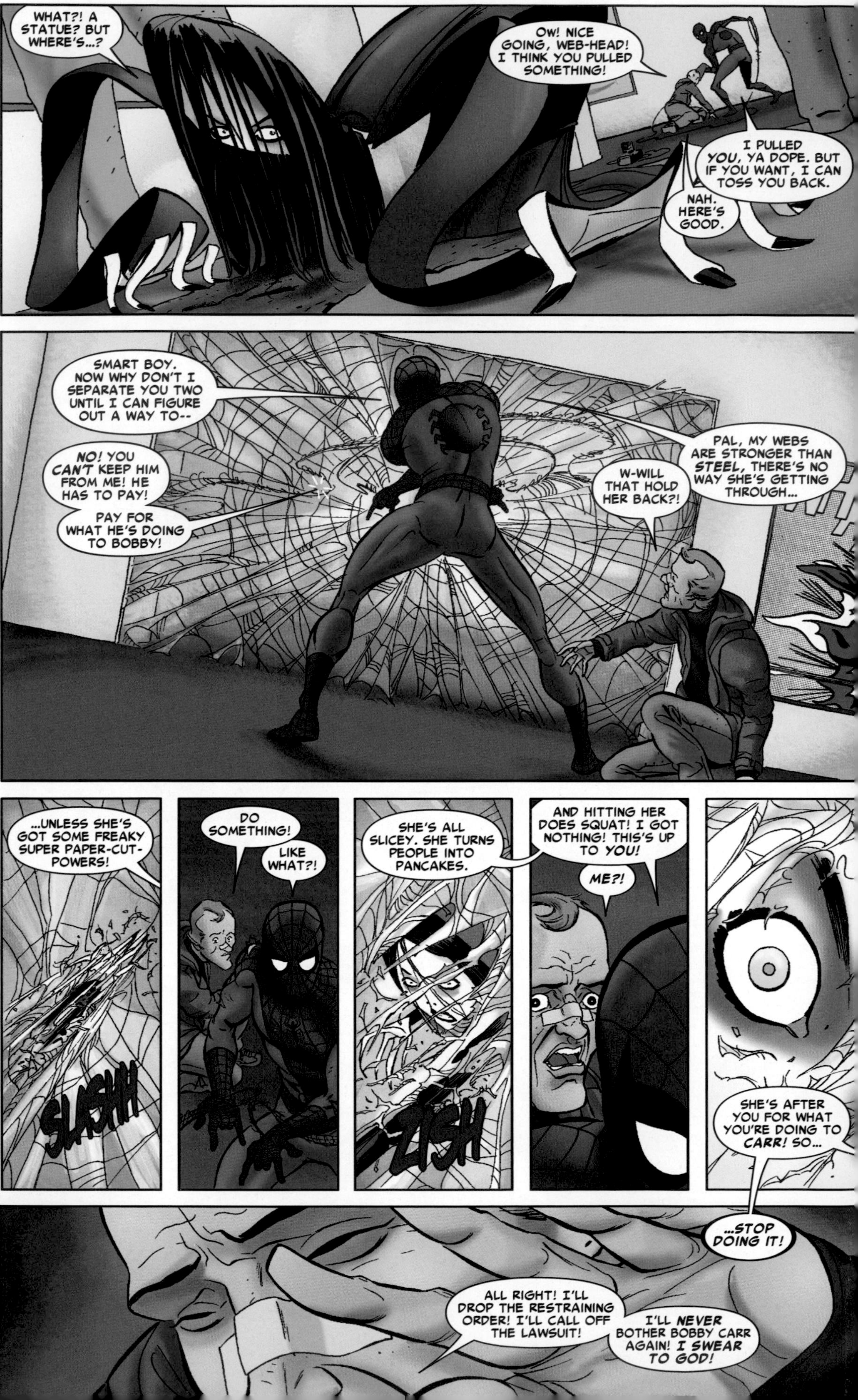
WHAT?! A STATUE? BUT WHERE'S...?
OW! NICE GOING, WEB-HEAD! I THINK YOU PULLED SOMETHING!
I PULLED YOU, YA DOPE. BUT IF YOU WANT, I CAN TOSS YOU BACK.
NAH. HERE'S GOOD.
SMART BOY. NOW WHY DON'T I SEPARATE YOU TWO UNTIL I CAN FIGURE OUT A WAY TO--
NO! YOU CAN'T KEEP HIM FROM ME! HE HAS TO PAY!
PAY FOR WHAT HE'S DOING TO BOBBY!
W-WILL THAT HOLD HER BACK?!
PAL, MY WEBS ARE STRONGER THAN STEEL, THERE'S NO WAY SHE'S GETTING THROUGH...
...UNLESS SHE'S GOT SOME FREAKY SUPER PAPER-CUT-POWERS!
SLSHH
DO SOMETHING!
LIKE WHAT?!
SHE'S ALL SLICEY. SHE TURNS PEOPLE INTO PANCAKES.
ZISH
AND HITTING HER DOES SQUAT! I GOT NOTHING! THIS'S UP TO YOU!
ME?!
SHE'S AFTER YOU FOR WHAT YOU'RE DOING TO CARR! SO...
...STOP DOING IT!
ALL RIGHT! I'LL DROP THE RESTRAINING ORDER! I'LL CALL OFF THE LAWSUIT!
I'LL NEVER BOTHER BOBBY CARR AGAIN! I SWEAR TO GOD!

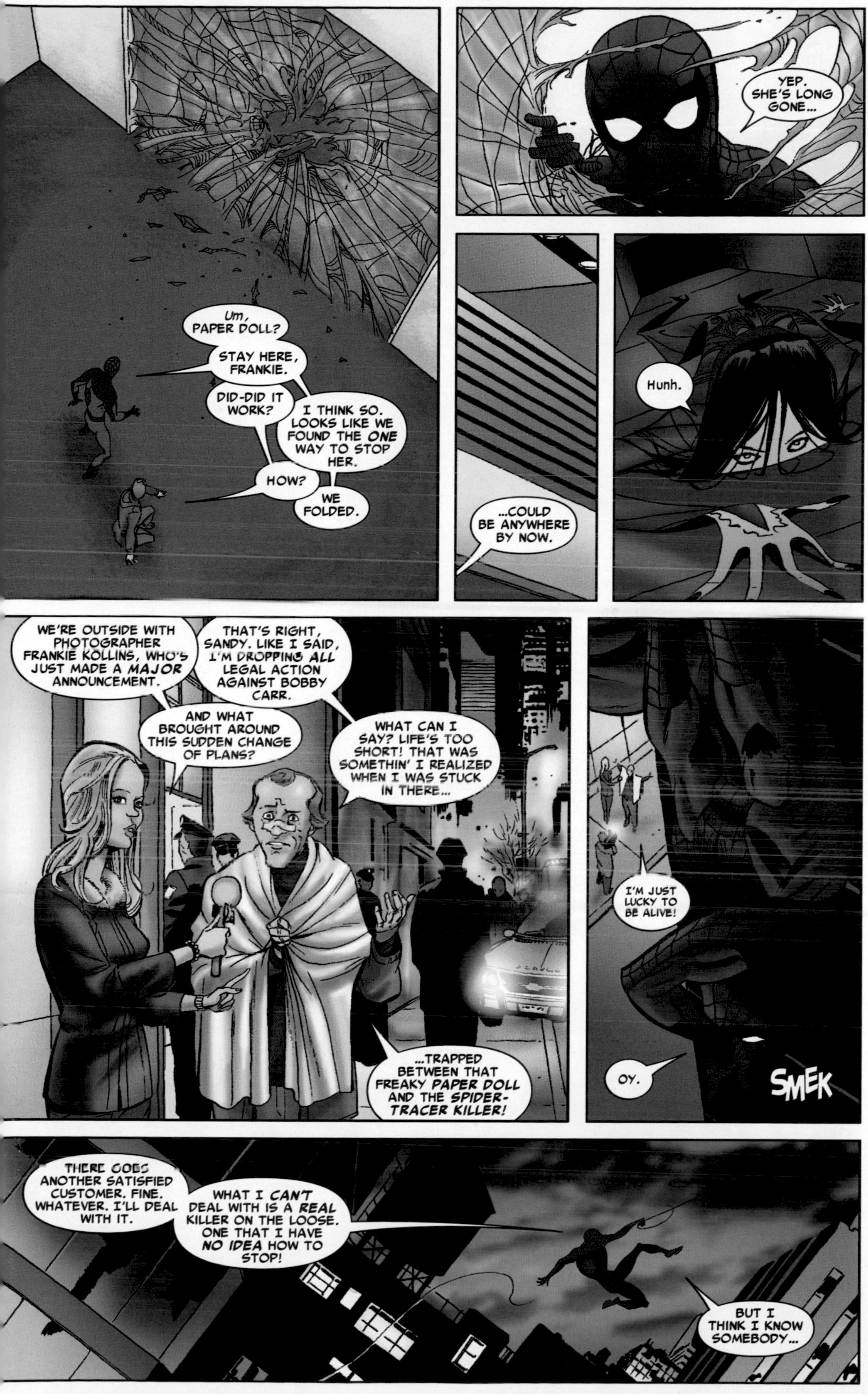
Um, PAPER DOLL?
STAY HERE, FRANKIE.
DID-DID IT WORK?
I THINK SO. LOOKS LIKE WE FOUND THE ONE WAY TO STOP HER.
HOW?
WE FOLDED.
YEP. SHE'S LONG GONE...
...COULD BE ANYWHERE BY NOW.
Hunh.
WE'RE OUTSIDE WITH PHOTOGRAPHER FRANKIE KOLLINS, WHO'S JUST MADE A MAJOR ANNOUNCEMENT.
THAT'S RIGHT, SANDY. LIKE I SAID, I'M DROPPING ALL LEGAL ACTION AGAINST BOBBY CARR.
AND WHAT BROUGHT AROUND THIS SUDDEN CHANGE OF PLANS?
WHAT CAN I SAY? LIFE'S TOO SHORT! THAT WAS SOMETHIN' I REALIZED WHEN I WAS STUCK IN THERE...
...TRAPPED BETWEEN THAT FREAKY PAPER DOLL AND THE SPIDER-TRACER KILLER!
I'M JUST LUCKY TO BE ALIVE!
OY.
SMEK
THERE GOES ANOTHER SATISFIED CUSTOMER. FINE. WHATEVER. I'LL DEAL WITH IT.
WHAT I CAN'T DEAL WITH IS A REAL KILLER ON THE LOOSE. ONE THAT I HAVE NO IDEA HOW TO STOP!
BUT I THINK I KNOW SOMEBODY...

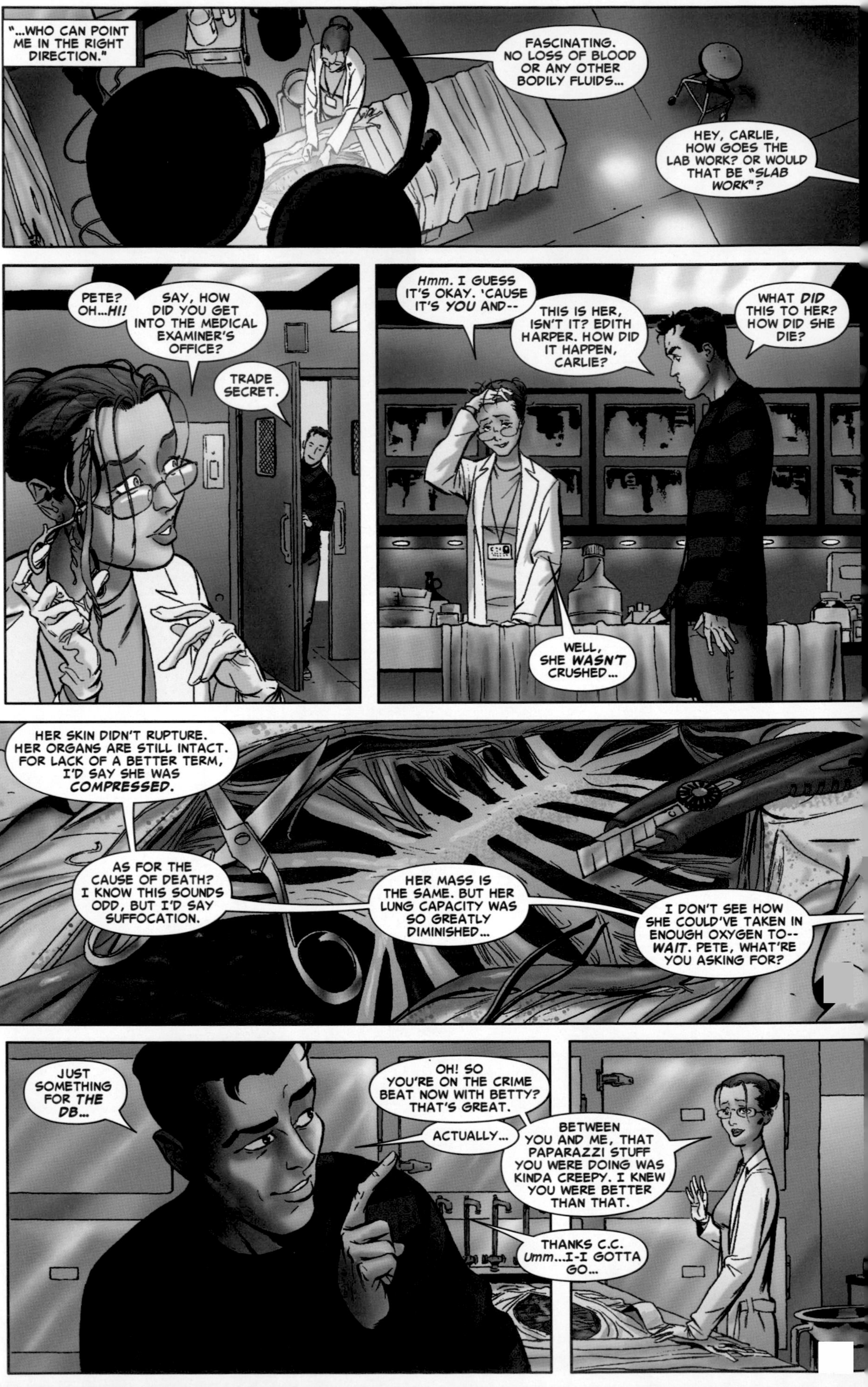
"...WHO CAN POINT ME IN THE RIGHT DIRECTION."
FASCINATING. NO LOSS OF BLOOD OR ANY OTHER BODILY FLUIDS...
HEY, CARLIE, HOW GOES THE LAB WORK? OR WOULD THAT BE "SLAB WORK"?
PETE? OH...HI!
SAY, HOW DID YOU GET INTO THE MEDICAL EXAMINER'S OFFICE?
TRADE SECRET.
Hmm. I GUESS IT'S OKAY. 'CAUSE IT'S YOU AND--
THIS IS HER, ISN'T IT? EDITH HARPER. HOW DID IT HAPPEN, CARLIE?
WHAT DID THIS TO HER? HOW DID SHE DIE?
WELL, SHE WASN'T CRUSHED...
HER SKIN DIDN'T RUPTURE. HER ORGANS ARE STILL INTACT. FOR LACK OF A BETTER TERM, I'D SAY SHE WAS COMPRESSED.
AS FOR THE CAUSE OF DEATH? I KNOW THIS SOUNDS ODD, BUT I'D SAY SUFFOCATION.
HER MASS IS THE SAME. BUT HER LUNG CAPACITY WAS SO GREATLY DIMINISHED...
I DON'T SEE HOW SHE COULD'VE TAKEN IN ENOUGH OXYGEN TO-- WAIT. PETE, WHAT'RE YOU ASKING FOR?
JUST SOMETHING FOR THE DB...
OH! SO YOU'RE ON THE CRIME BEAT NOW WITH BETTY? THAT'S GREAT.
ACTUALLY...
BETWEEN YOU AND ME, THAT PAPARAZZI STUFF YOU WERE DOING WAS KINDA CREEPY. I KNEW YOU WERE BETTER THAN THAT.
THANKS C.C. Umm...I-I GOTTA GO...

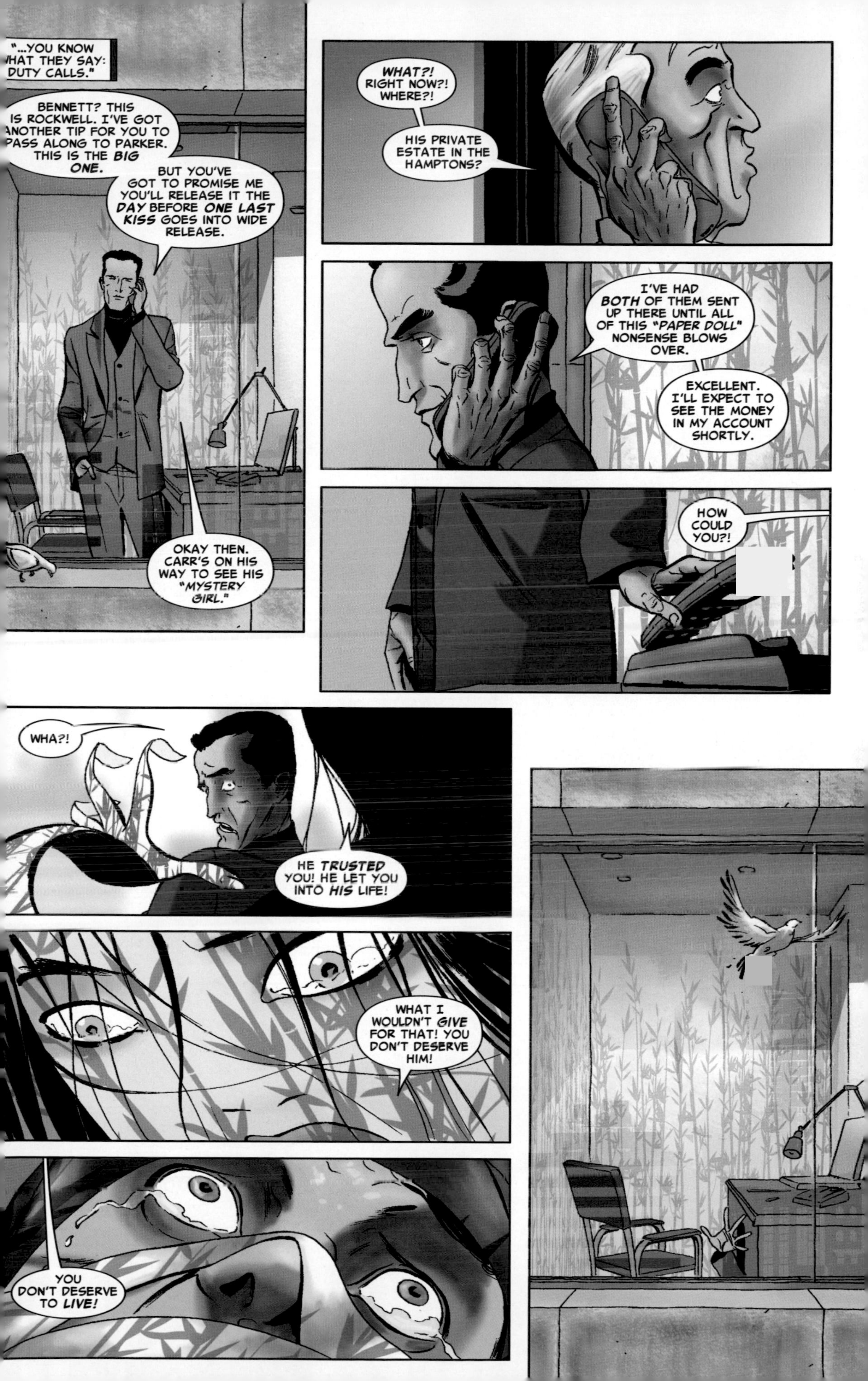
"...YOU KNOW WHAT THEY SAY: DUTY CALLS."
BENNETT? THIS IS ROCKWELL. I'VE GOT ANOTHER TIP FOR YOU TO PASS ALONG TO PARKER. THIS IS THE BIG ONE.
BUT YOU'VE GOT TO PROMISE ME YOU'LL RELEASE IT THE DAY BEFORE ONE LAST KISS GOES INTO WIDE RELEASE.
OKAY THEN. CARR'S ON HIS WAY TO SEE HIS "MYSTERY GIRL."
WHAT?! RIGHT NOW?! WHERE?!
HIS PRIVATE ESTATE IN THE HAMPTONS?
I'VE HAD BOTH OF THEM SENT UP THERE UNTIL ALL OF THIS "PAPER DOLL" NONSENSE BLOWS OVER.
EXCELLENT. I'LL EXPECT TO SEE THE MONEY IN MY ACCOUNT SHORTLY.
HOW COULD YOU?!
WHA?!
HE TRUSTED YOU! HE LET YOU INTO HIS LIFE!
WHAT I WOULDN'T GIVE FOR THAT! YOU DON'T DESERVE HIM!
YOU DON'T DESERVE TO LIVE!

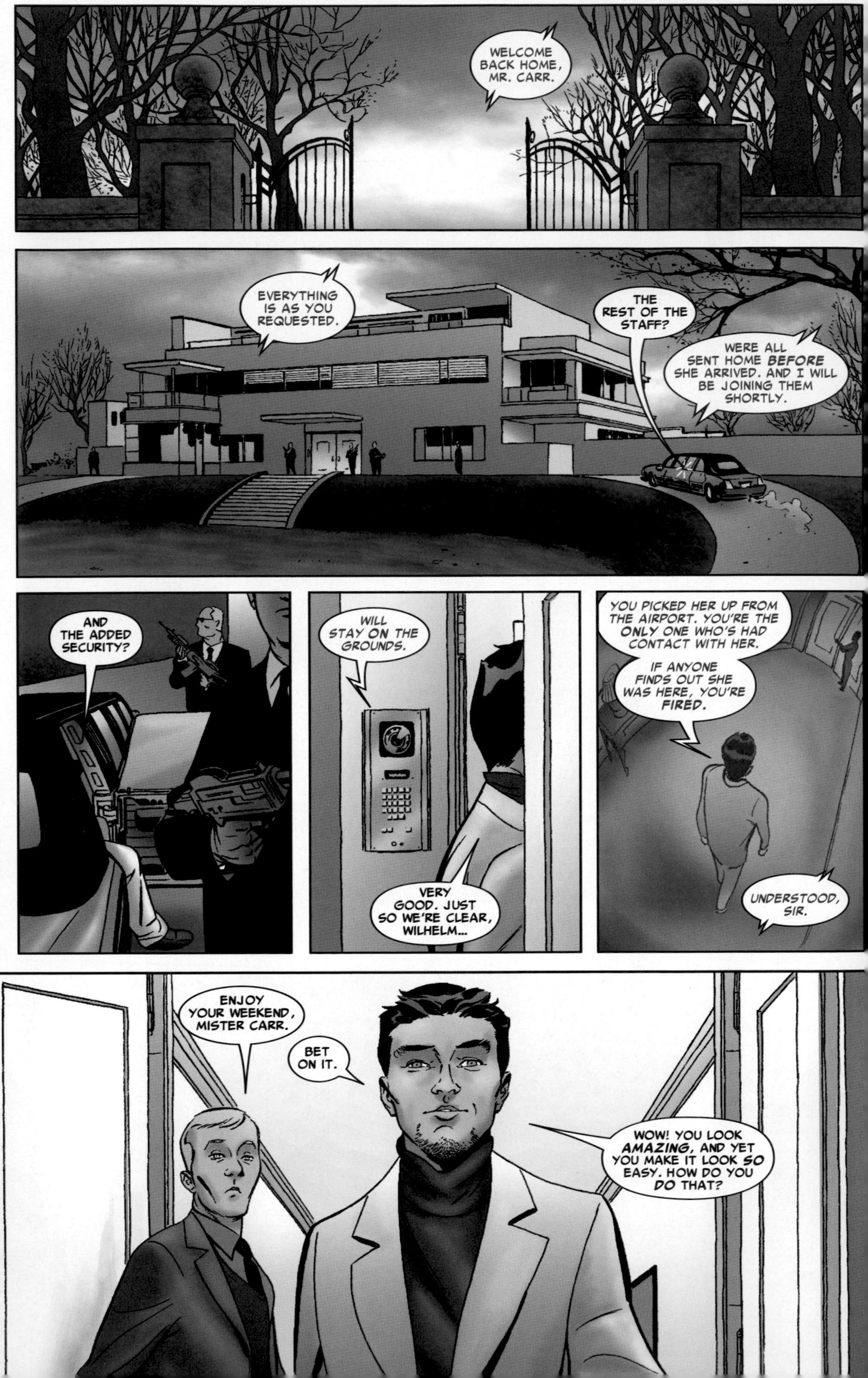
WELCOME BACK HOME, MR. CARR.
EVERYTHING IS AS YOU REQUESTED.
THE REST OF THE STAFF?
WERE ALL SENT HOME BEFORE SHE ARRIVED. AND I WILL BE JOINING THEM SHORTLY.
AND THE ADDED SECURITY?
WILL STAY ON THE GROUNDS.
VERY GOOD. JUST SO WE'RE CLEAR, WILHELM...
YOU PICKED HER UP FROM THE AIRPORT. YOU'RE THE ONLY ONE WHO'S HAD CONTACT WITH HER.
IF ANYONE FINDS OUT SHE WAS HERE, YOU'RE FIRED.
UNDERSTOOD, SIR.
ENJOY YOUR WEEKEND, MISTER CARR.
BET ON IT.
WOW! YOU LOOK AMAZING, AND YET YOU MAKE IT LOOK SO EASY. HOW DO YOU DO THAT?

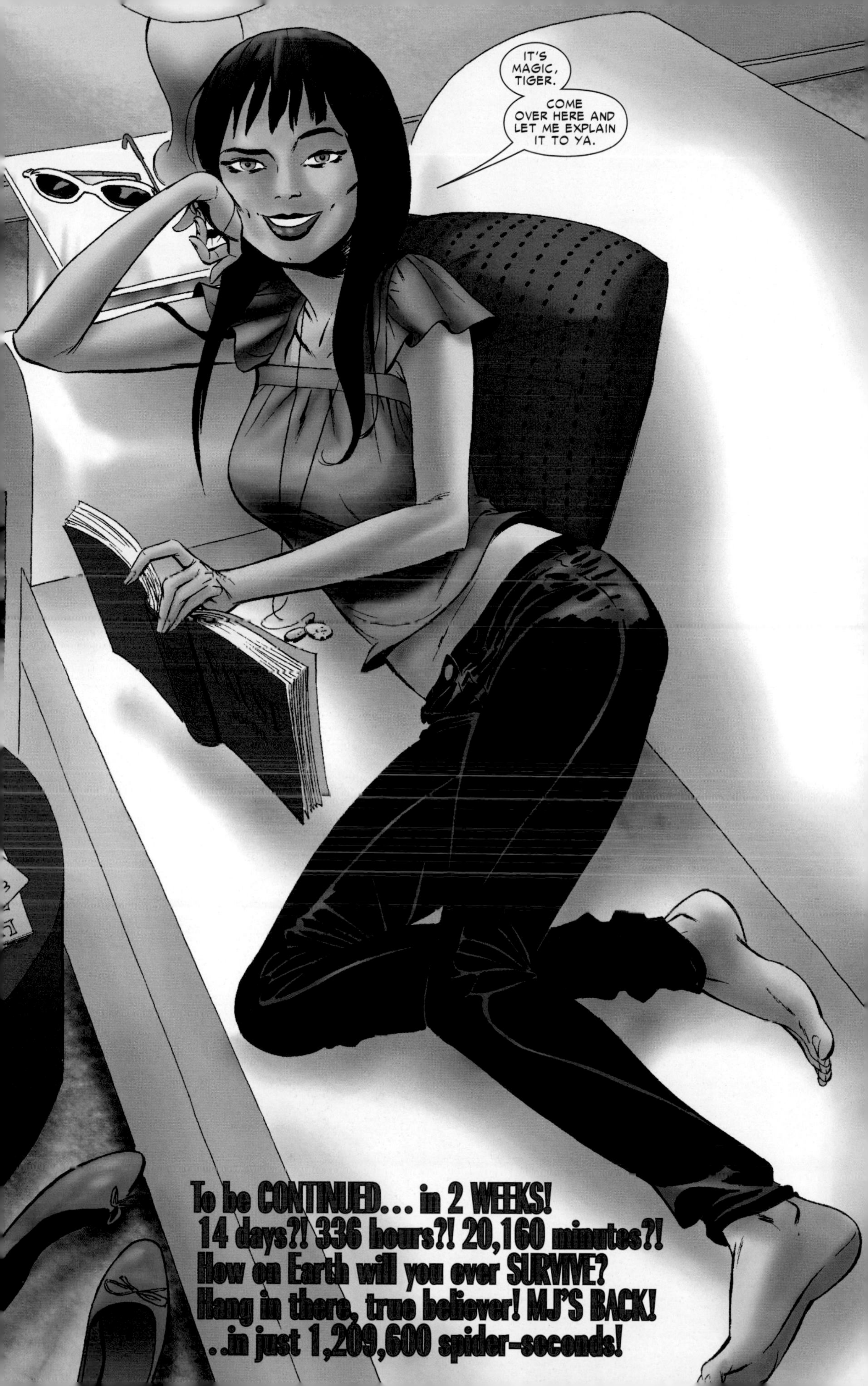
IT'S MAGIC, TIGER.
COME OVER HERE AND LET ME EXPLAIN IT TO YA.
To be CONTINUED... in 2 WEEKS!
14 days?! 336 hours?! 20,160 minutes?!
How on Earth will you ever SURVIVE?
Hang in there, true believer! MJ'S BACK!
..in just 1,209,600 spider-seconds!

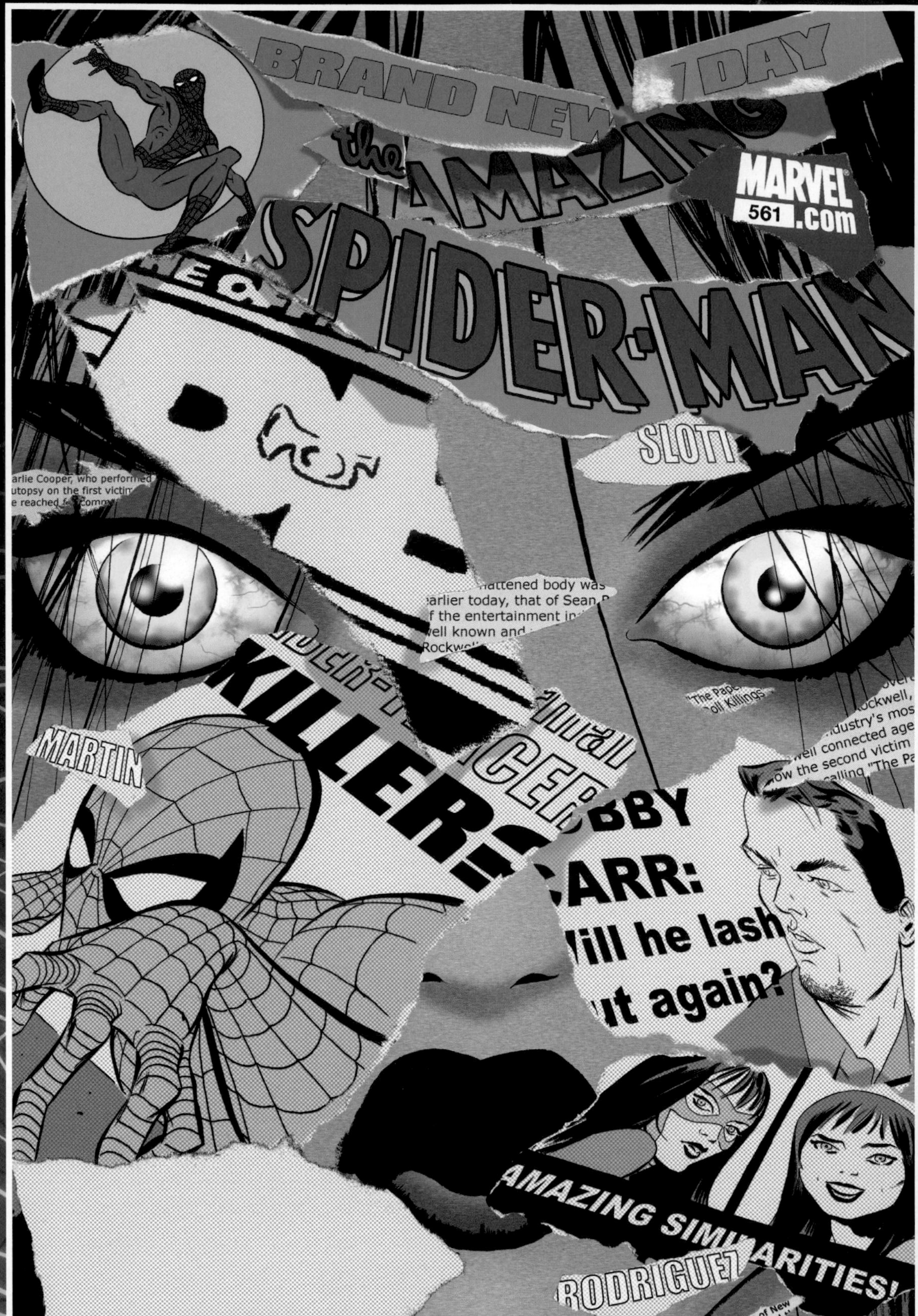
BRAND NEW DAY
the AMAZING SPIDER-MAN
MARVEL
561 .com
SLOTT
arlie Cooper, who performed
utopsy on the first victim
flattened body was
earlier today, that of Sean R
f the entertainment in
well known and
Rockwell
"The Pape
oll Killings
Rockwell,
ndustry's mos
well connected age
ow the second victim
KILLER
MARTIN
BBY
CARR:
Vill he lash
ut again?
AMAZING SIMI ARITIES!
RODRIGUEZ
owever, Jackpot, one of New
ork's licensed heroes, had
o say, "The Paper Doll Kil

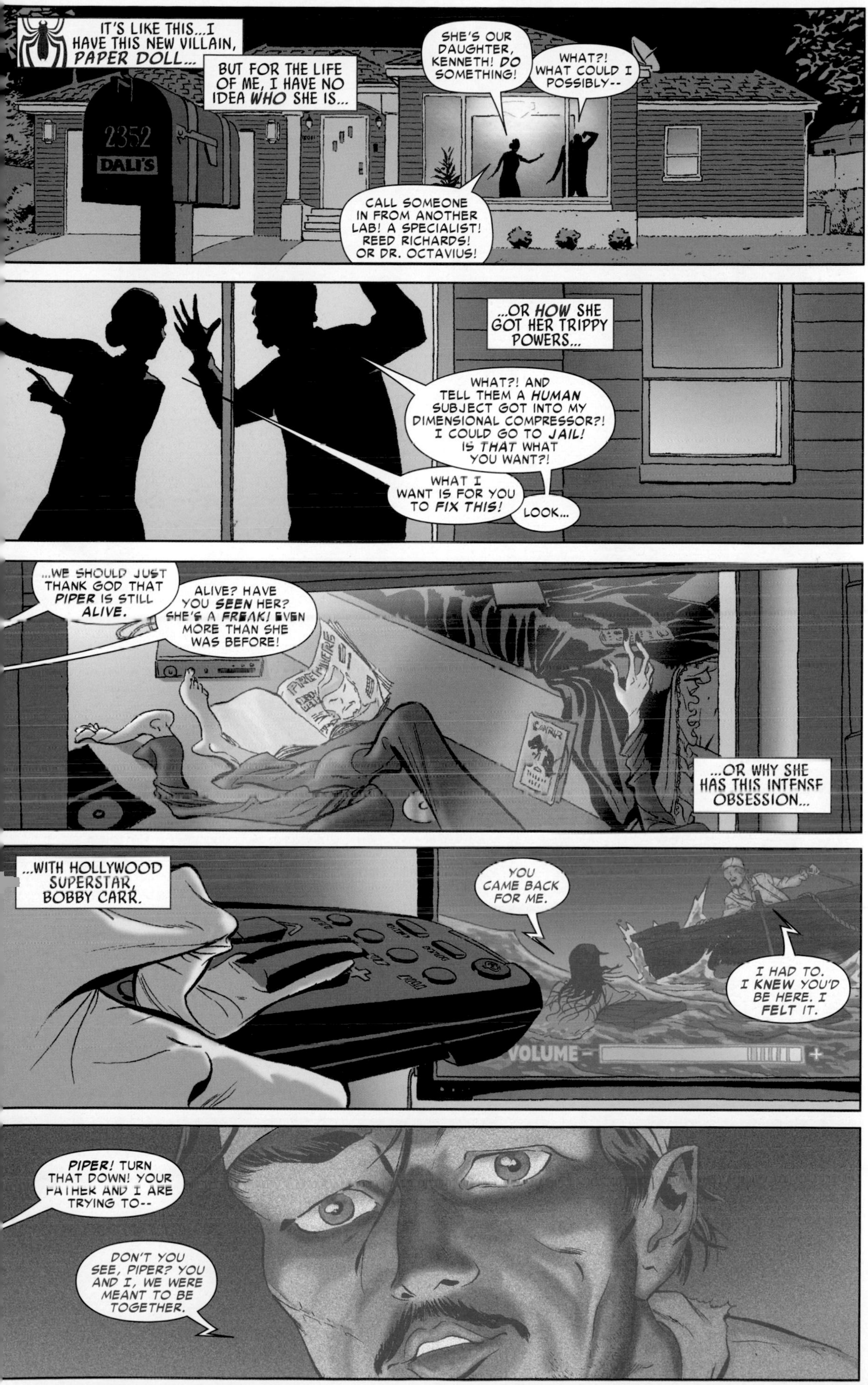
IT'S LIKE THIS...I HAVE THIS NEW VILLAIN, PAPER DOLL...
BUT FOR THE LIFE OF ME, I HAVE NO IDEA WHO SHE IS...
2352
DALI'S
SHE'S OUR DAUGHTER, KENNETH! DO SOMETHING!
WHAT?! WHAT COULD I POSSIBLY--
CALL SOMEONE IN FROM ANOTHER LAB! A SPECIALIST! REED RICHARDS! OR DR. OCTAVIUS!
...OR HOW SHE GOT HER TRIPPY POWERS...
WHAT?! AND TELL THEM A HUMAN SUBJECT GOT INTO MY DIMENSIONAL COMPRESSOR?! I COULD GO TO JAIL! IS THAT WHAT YOU WANT?!
WHAT I WANT IS FOR YOU TO FIX THIS!
LOOK...
...WE SHOULD JUST THANK GOD THAT PIPER IS STILL ALIVE.
ALIVE? HAVE YOU SEEN HER? SHE'S A FREAK! EVEN MORE THAN SHE WAS BEFORE!
...OR WHY SHE HAS THIS INTENSE OBSESSION...
...WITH HOLLYWOOD SUPERSTAR, BOBBY CARR.
YOU CAME BACK FOR ME.
I HAD TO. I KNEW YOU'D BE HERE. I FELT IT.
VOLUME - +
PIPER! TURN THAT DOWN! YOUR FATHER AND I ARE TRYING TO--
DON'T YOU SEE, PIPER? YOU AND I, WE WERE MEANT TO BE TOGETHER.

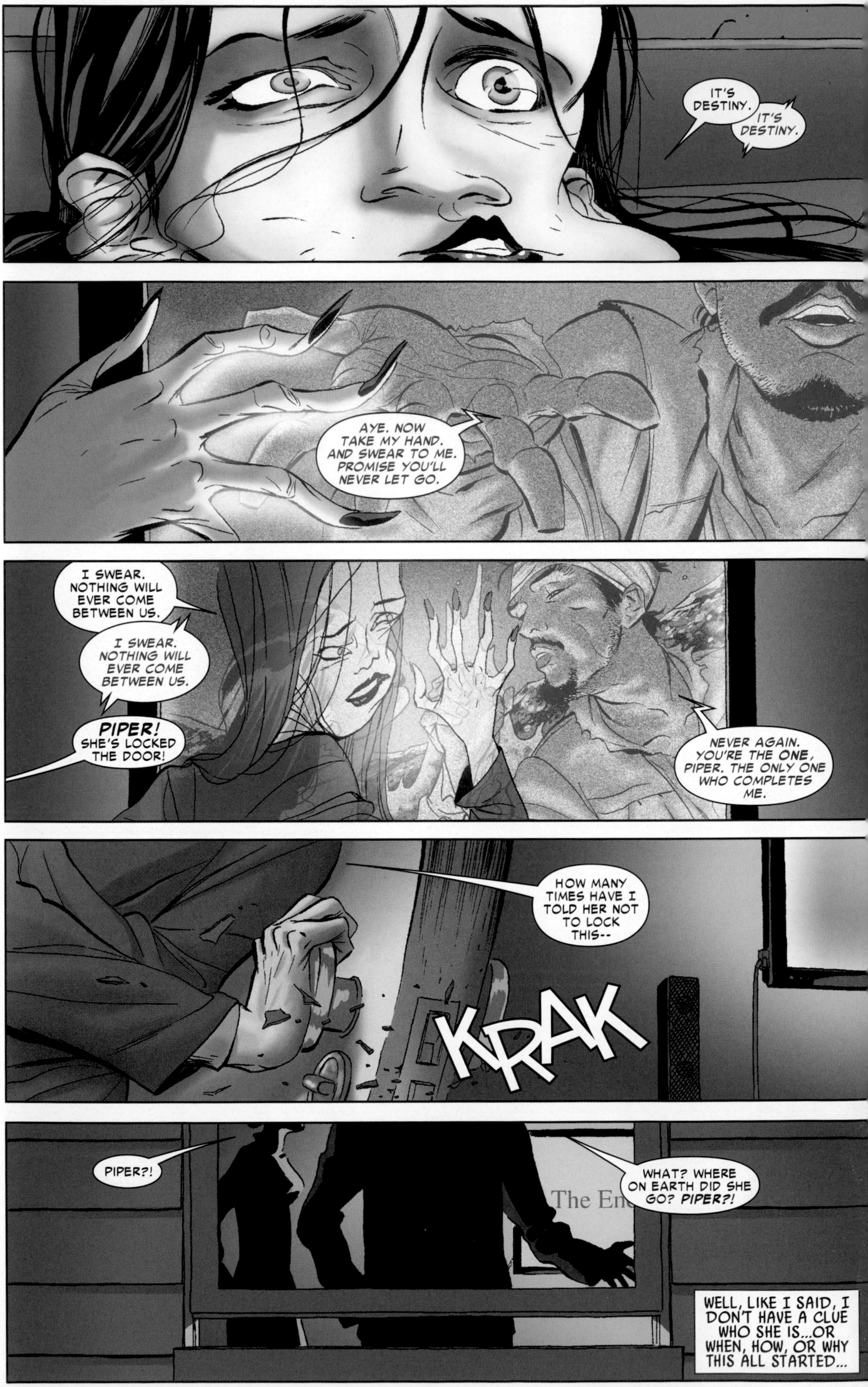
IT'S DESTINY.
IT'S DESTINY.
AYE. NOW TAKE MY HAND. AND SWEAR TO ME. PROMISE YOU'LL NEVER LET GO.
I SWEAR. NOTHING WILL EVER COME BETWEEN US.
I SWEAR. NOTHING WILL EVER COME BETWEEN US.
PIPER! SHE'S LOCKED THE DOOR!
NEVER AGAIN. YOU'RE THE ONE, PIPER. THE ONLY ONE WHO COMPLETES ME.
HOW MANY TIMES HAVE I TOLD HER NOT TO LOCK THIS--
KRAK
PIPER?!
WHAT? WHERE ON EARTH DID SHE GO? PIPER?!
The En
WELL, LIKE I SAID, I DON'T HAVE A CLUE WHO SHE IS...OR WHEN, HOW, OR WHY THIS ALL STARTED...

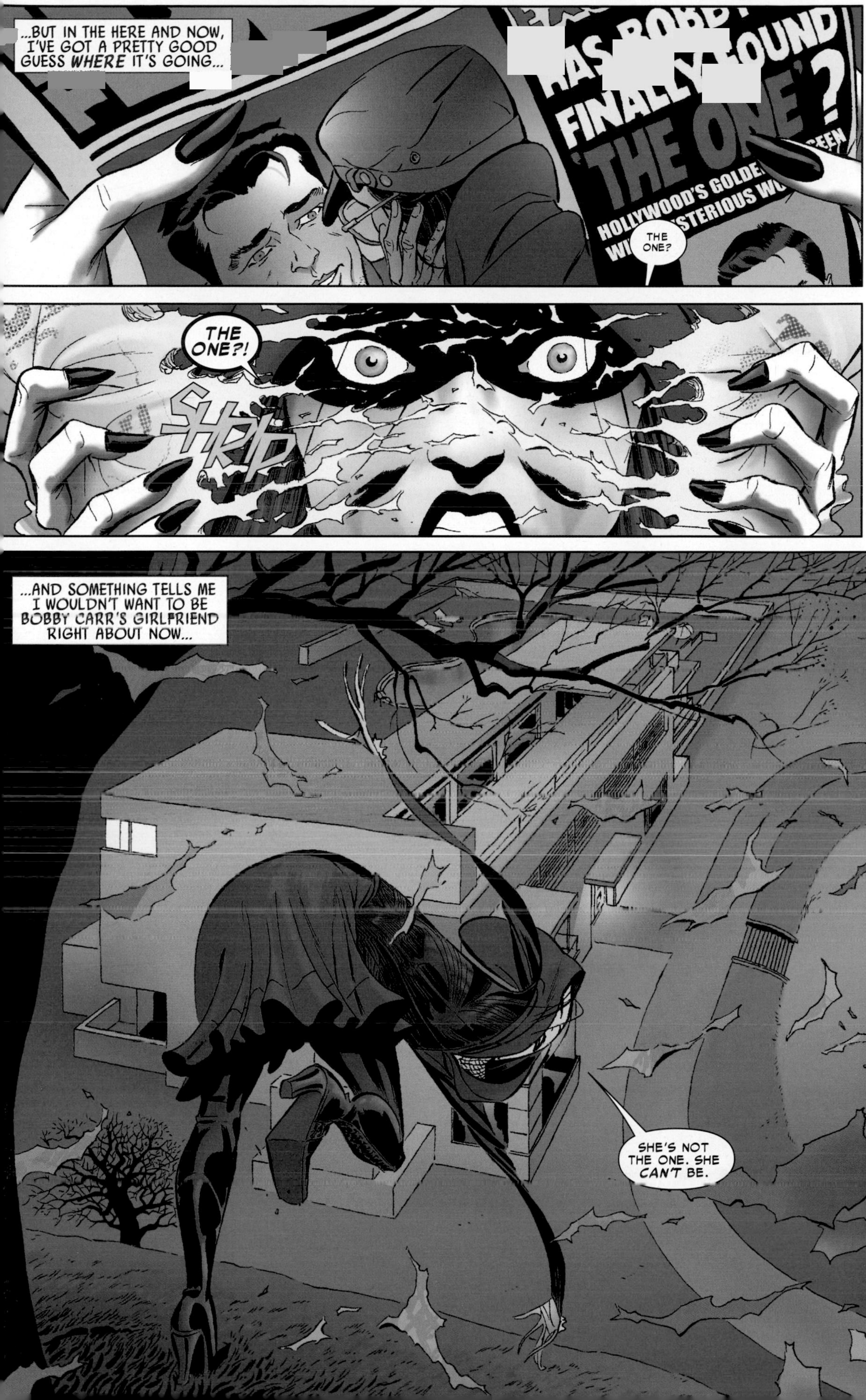
...BUT IN THE HERE AND NOW, I'VE GOT A PRETTY GOOD GUESS WHERE IT'S GOING...
THE ONE?
THE ONE?!
SHRIP
...AND SOMETHING TELLS ME I WOULDN'T WANT TO BE BOBBY CARR'S GIRLFRIEND RIGHT ABOUT NOW...
SHE'S NOT THE ONE. SHE CAN'T BE.

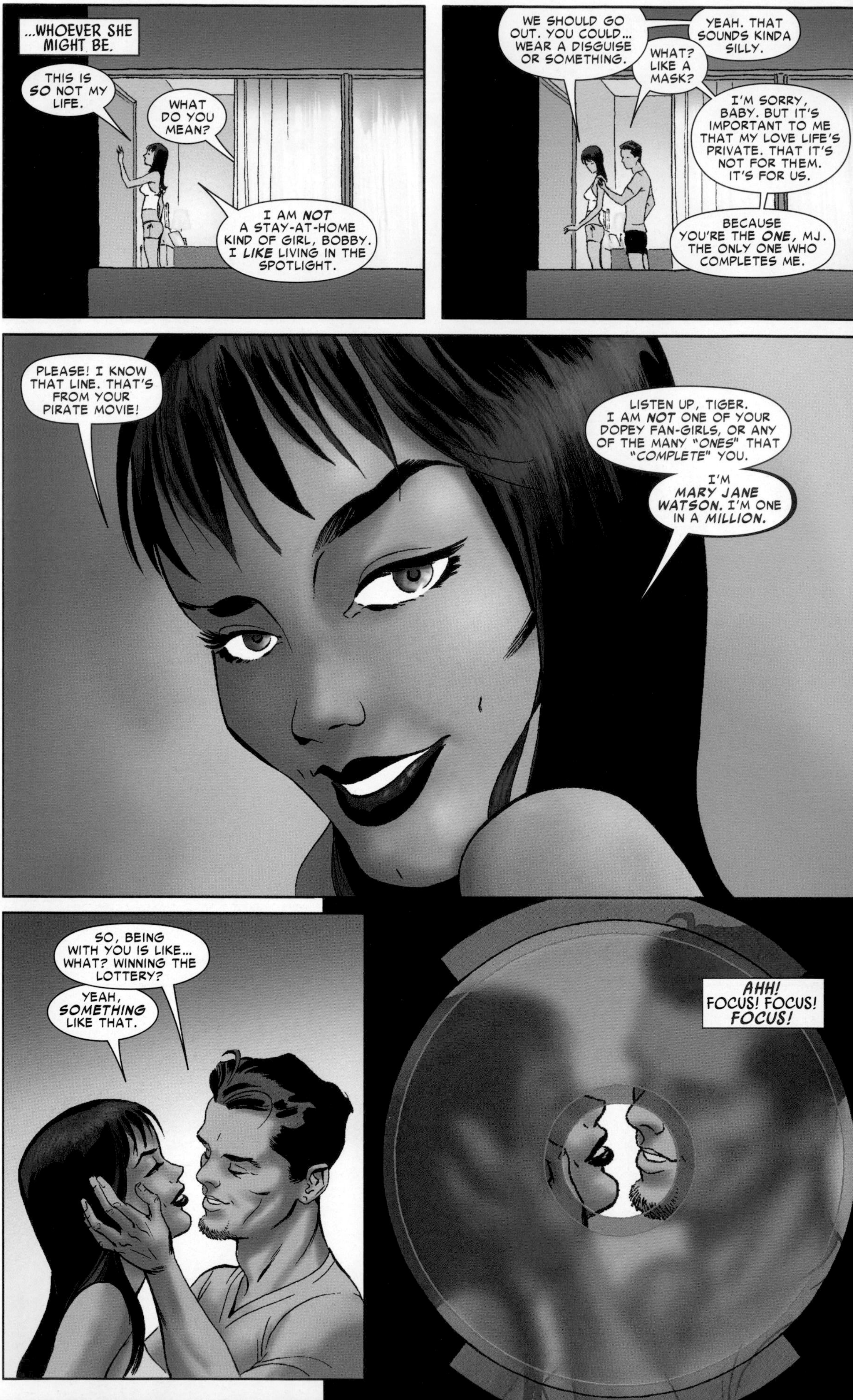
...WHOEVER SHE MIGHT BE.
THIS IS SO NOT MY LIFE.
WHAT DO YOU MEAN?
I AM NOT A STAY-AT-HOME KIND OF GIRL, BOBBY. I LIKE LIVING IN THE SPOTLIGHT.
WE SHOULD GO OUT. YOU COULD... WEAR A DISGUISE OR SOMETHING.
WHAT? LIKE A MASK?
YEAH. THAT SOUNDS KINDA SILLY.
I'M SORRY, BABY. BUT IT'S IMPORTANT TO ME THAT MY LOVE LIFE'S PRIVATE. THAT IT'S NOT FOR THEM. IT'S FOR US.
BECAUSE YOU'RE THE ONE, MJ. THE ONLY ONE WHO COMPLETES ME.
PLEASE! I KNOW THAT LINE. THAT'S FROM YOUR PIRATE MOVIE!
LISTEN UP, TIGER. I AM NOT ONE OF YOUR DOPEY FAN-GIRLS, OR ANY OF THE MANY "ONES" THAT "COMPLETE" YOU.
I'M MARY JANE WATSON. I'M ONE IN A MILLION.
SO, BEING WITH YOU IS LIKE... WHAT? WINNING THE LOTTERY?
YEAH, SOMETHING LIKE THAT.
AHH! FOCUS! FOCUS! FOCUS!

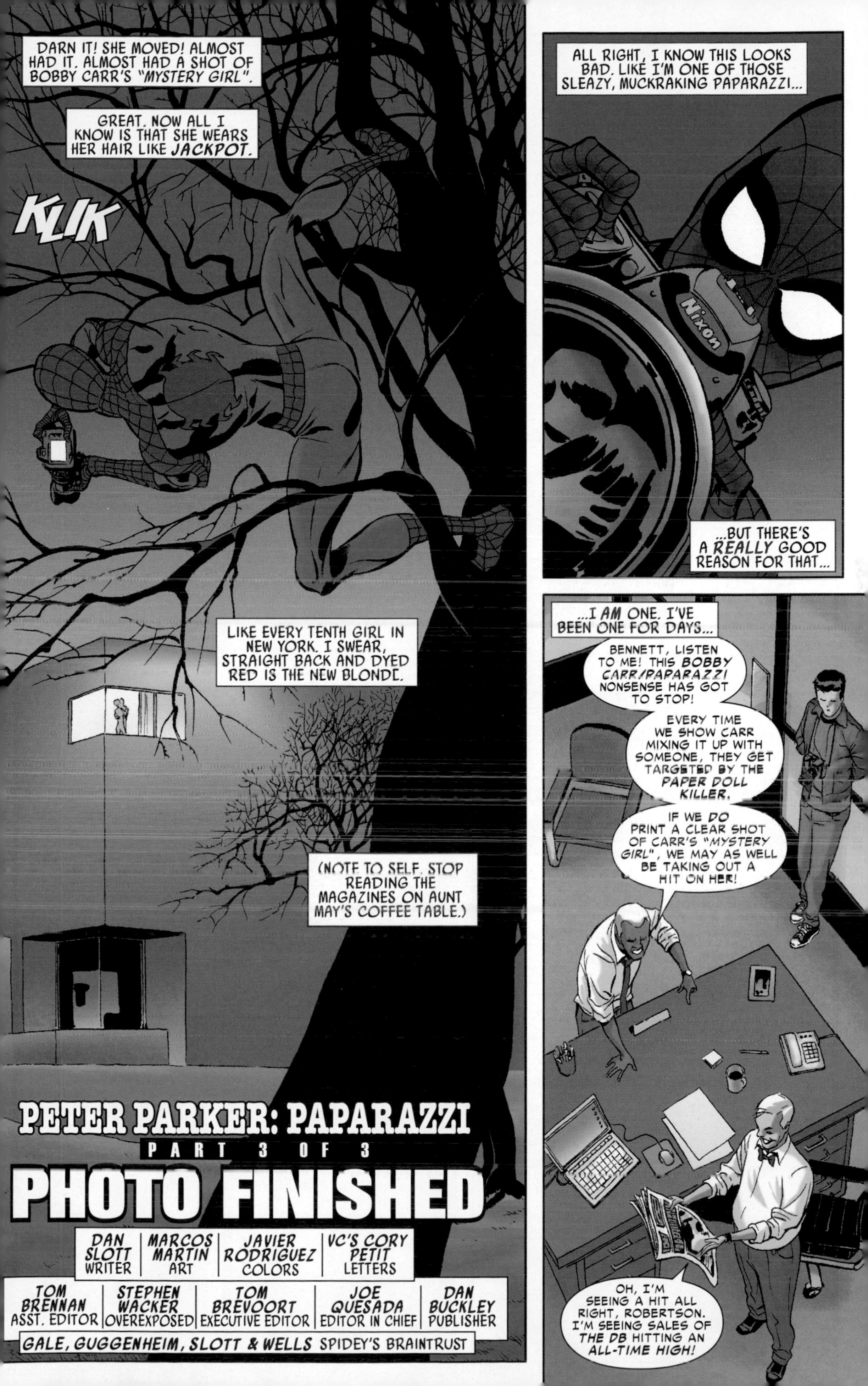
DARN IT! SHE MOVED! ALMOST HAD IT. ALMOST HAD A SHOT OF BOBBY CARR'S "MYSTERY GIRL".
GREAT. NOW ALL I KNOW IS THAT SHE WEARS HER HAIR LIKE JACKPOT.
KLIK
LIKE EVERY TENTH GIRL IN NEW YORK. I SWEAR, STRAIGHT BACK AND DYED RED IS THE NEW BLONDE.
(NOTE TO SELF. STOP READING THE MAGAZINES ON AUNT MAY'S COFFEE TABLE.)
PETER PARKER: PAPARAZZI
PART 3 OF 3
PHOTO FINISHED
DAN SLOTT WRITER
MARCOS MARTIN ART
JAVIER RODRIGUEZ COLORS
VC'S CORY PETIT LETTERS
TOM BRENNAN ASST. EDITOR
STEPHEN WACKER OVEREXPOSED
TOM BREVOORT EXECUTIVE EDITOR
JOE QUESADA EDITOR IN CHIEF
DAN BUCKLEY PUBLISHER
GALE, GUGGENHEIM, SLOTT & WELLS SPIDEY'S BRAINTRUST
ALL RIGHT, I KNOW THIS LOOKS BAD. LIKE I'M ONE OF THOSE SLEAZY, MUCKRAKING PAPARAZZI...
Nixon
...BUT THERE'S A REALLY GOOD REASON FOR THAT...
...I AM ONE. I'VE BEEN ONE FOR DAYS...
BENNETT, LISTEN TO ME! THIS BOBBY CARR/PAPARAZZI NONSENSE HAS GOT TO STOP!
EVERY TIME WE SHOW CARR MIXING IT UP WITH SOMEONE, THEY GET TARGETED BY THE PAPER DOLL KILLER.
IF WE DO PRINT A CLEAR SHOT OF CARR'S "MYSTERY GIRL", WE MAY AS WELL BE TAKING OUT A HIT ON HER!
OH, I'M SEEING A HIT ALL RIGHT, ROBERTSON. I'M SEEING SALES OF THE DB HITTING AN ALL-TIME HIGH!

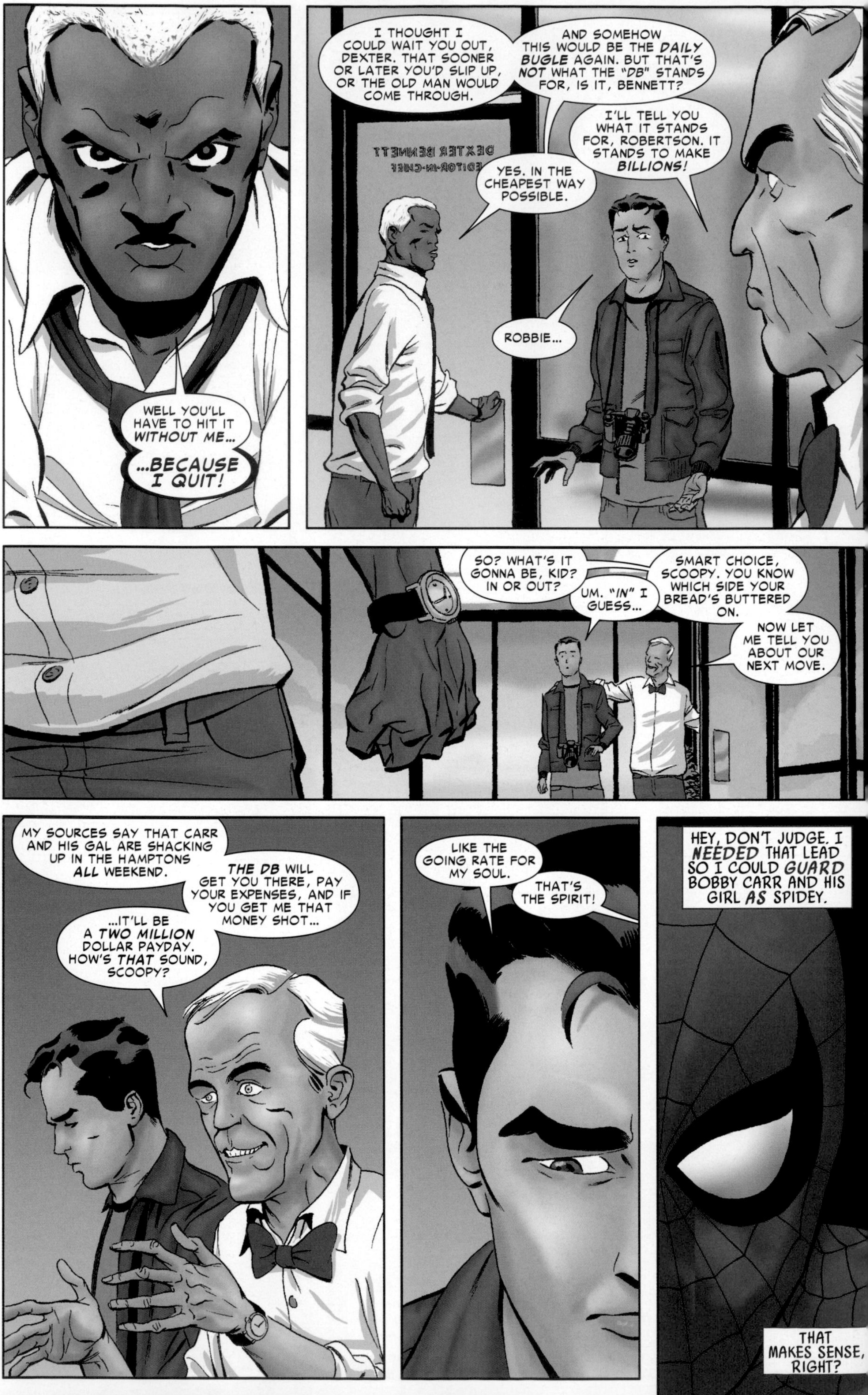
WELL YOU'LL HAVE TO HIT IT WITHOUT ME...
...BECAUSE I QUIT!
I THOUGHT I COULD WAIT YOU OUT, DEXTER. THAT SOONER OR LATER YOU'D SLIP UP, OR THE OLD MAN WOULD COME THROUGH.
AND SOMEHOW THIS WOULD BE THE DAILY BUGLE AGAIN. BUT THAT'S NOT WHAT THE "DB" STANDS FOR, IS IT, BENNETT?
DEXTER BENNETT
EDITOR-IN-CHIEF
I'LL TELL YOU WHAT IT STANDS FOR, ROBERTSON. IT STANDS TO MAKE BILLIONS!
YES. IN THE CHEAPEST WAY POSSIBLE.
ROBBIE...
SO? WHAT'S IT GONNA BE, KID? IN OR OUT?
UM. "IN" I GUESS...
SMART CHOICE, SCOOPY. YOU KNOW WHICH SIDE YOUR BREAD'S BUTTERED ON.
NOW LET ME TELL YOU ABOUT OUR NEXT MOVE.
MY SOURCES SAY THAT CARR AND HIS GAL ARE SHACKING UP IN THE HAMPTONS ALL WEEKEND.
THE DB WILL GET YOU THERE, PAY YOUR EXPENSES, AND IF YOU GET ME THAT MONEY SHOT...
...IT'LL BE A TWO MILLION DOLLAR PAYDAY. HOW'S THAT SOUND, SCOOPY?
LIKE THE GOING RATE FOR MY SOUL.
THAT'S THE SPIRIT!
HEY, DON'T JUDGE. I NEEDED THAT LEAD SO I COULD GUARD BOBBY CARR AND HIS GIRL AS SPIDEY.
THAT MAKES SENSE, RIGHT?

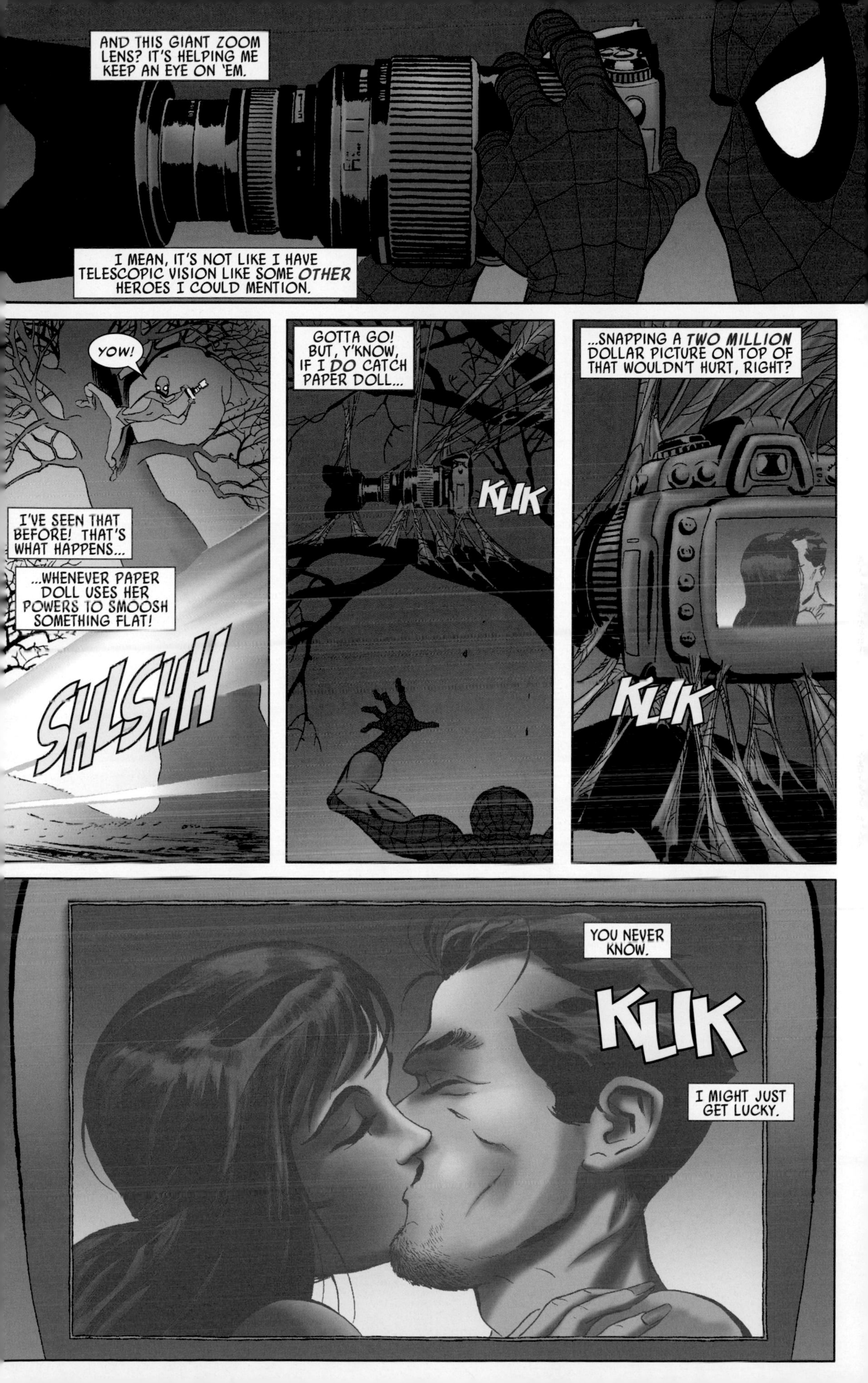
AND THIS GIANT ZOOM LENS? IT'S HELPING ME KEEP AN EYE ON 'EM.
I MEAN, IT'S NOT LIKE I HAVE TELESCOPIC VISION LIKE SOME OTHER HEROES I COULD MENTION.
YOW!
I'VE SEEN THAT BEFORE! THAT'S WHAT HAPPENS...
...WHENEVER PAPER DOLL USES HER POWERS TO SMOOSH SOMETHING FLAT!
SHLSHH
GOTTA GO! BUT, Y'KNOW, IF I DO CATCH PAPER DOLL...
KLIK
...SNAPPING A TWO MILLION DOLLAR PICTURE ON TOP OF THAT WOULDN'T HURT, RIGHT?
KLIK
YOU NEVER KNOW.
KLIK
I MIGHT JUST GET LUCKY.

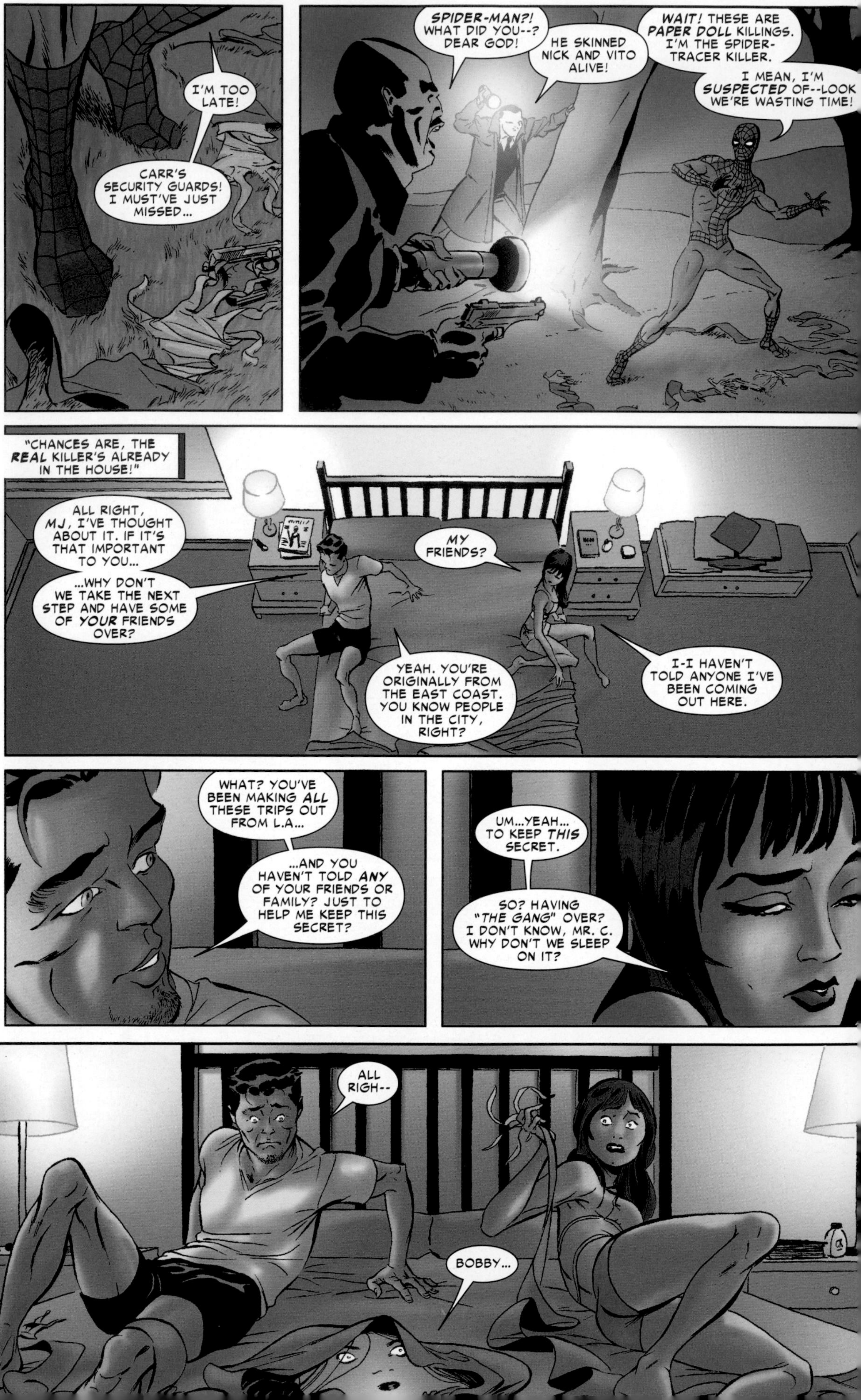

I'M TOO LATE!
CARR'S SECURITY GUARDS! I MUST'VE JUST MISSED...
SPIDER-MAN?! WHAT DID YOU--? DEAR GOD!
HE SKINNED NICK AND VITO ALIVE!
WAIT! THESE ARE PAPER DOLL KILLINGS. I'M THE SPIDER-TRACER KILLER.
I MEAN, I'M SUSPECTED OF--LOOK WE'RE WASTING TIME!
"CHANCES ARE, THE REAL KILLER'S ALREADY IN THE HOUSE!"
ALL RIGHT, MJ, I'VE THOUGHT ABOUT IT. IF IT'S THAT IMPORTANT TO YOU...
...WHY DON'T WE TAKE THE NEXT STEP AND HAVE SOME OF YOUR FRIENDS OVER?
MY FRIENDS?
YEAH. YOU'RE ORIGINALLY FROM THE EAST COAST. YOU KNOW PEOPLE IN THE CITY, RIGHT?
I-I HAVEN'T TOLD ANYONE I'VE BEEN COMING OUT HERE.
WHAT? YOU'VE BEEN MAKING ALL THESE TRIPS OUT FROM L.A...
...AND YOU HAVEN'T TOLD ANY OF YOUR FRIENDS OR FAMILY? JUST TO HELP ME KEEP THIS SECRET?
UM...YEAH... TO KEEP THIS SECRET.
SO? HAVING "THE GANG" OVER? I DON'T KNOW, MR. C. WHY DON'T WE SLEEP ON IT?
ALL RIGH--
BOBBY...

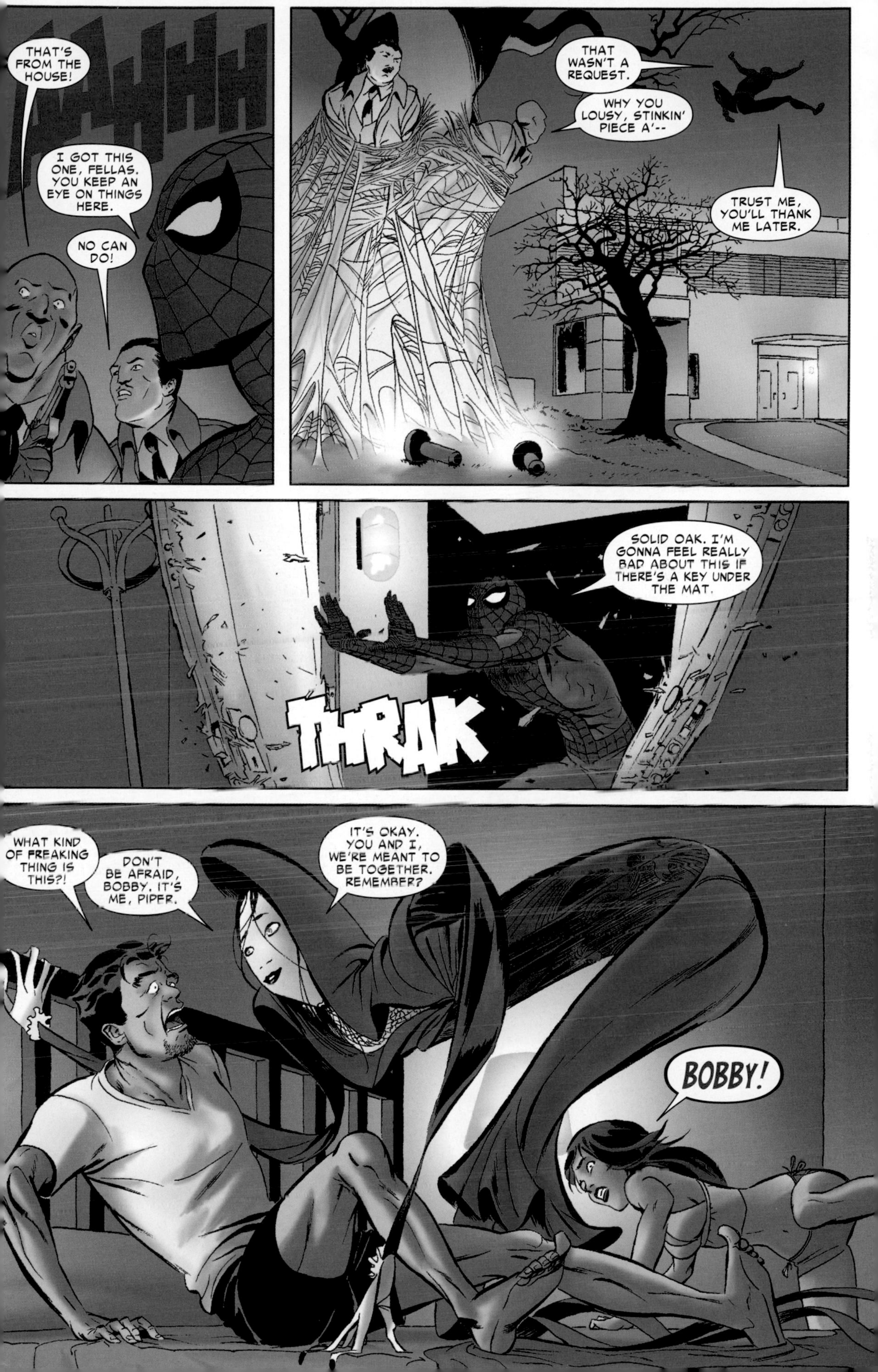
AAAHHH
THAT'S FROM THE HOUSE!
I GOT THIS ONE, FELLAS. YOU KEEP AN EYE ON THINGS HERE.
NO CAN DO!
THAT WASN'T A REQUEST.
WHY YOU LOUSY, STINKIN' PIECE A'--
TRUST ME, YOU'LL THANK ME LATER.
SOLID OAK. I'M GONNA FEEL REALLY BAD ABOUT THIS IF THERE'S A KEY UNDER THE MAT.
THRAK
WHAT KIND OF FREAKING THING IS THIS?!
DON'T BE AFRAID, BOBBY. IT'S ME, PIPER.
IT'S OKAY. YOU AND I, WE'RE MEANT TO BE TOGETHER. REMEMBER?
BOBBY!

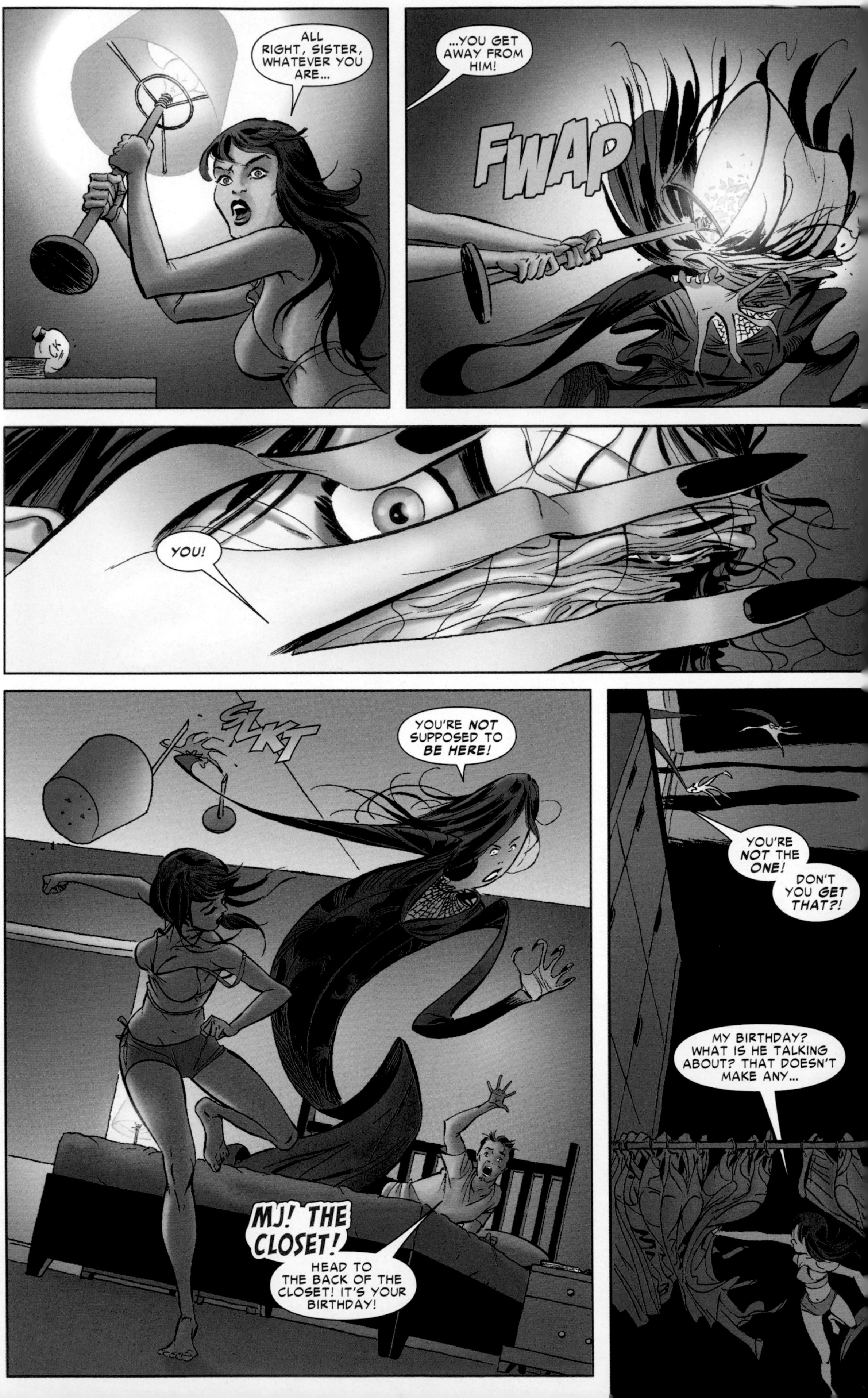
ALL RIGHT, SISTER, WHATEVER YOU ARE...
...YOU GET AWAY FROM HIM!
FWAP
YOU!
SLKT
YOU'RE NOT SUPPOSED TO BE HERE!
MJ! THE CLOSET!
HEAD TO THE BACK OF THE CLOSET! IT'S YOUR BIRTHDAY!
YOU'RE NOT THE ONE!
DON'T YOU GET THAT?!
MY BIRTHDAY? WHAT IS HE TALKING ABOUT? THAT DOESN'T MAKE ANY...

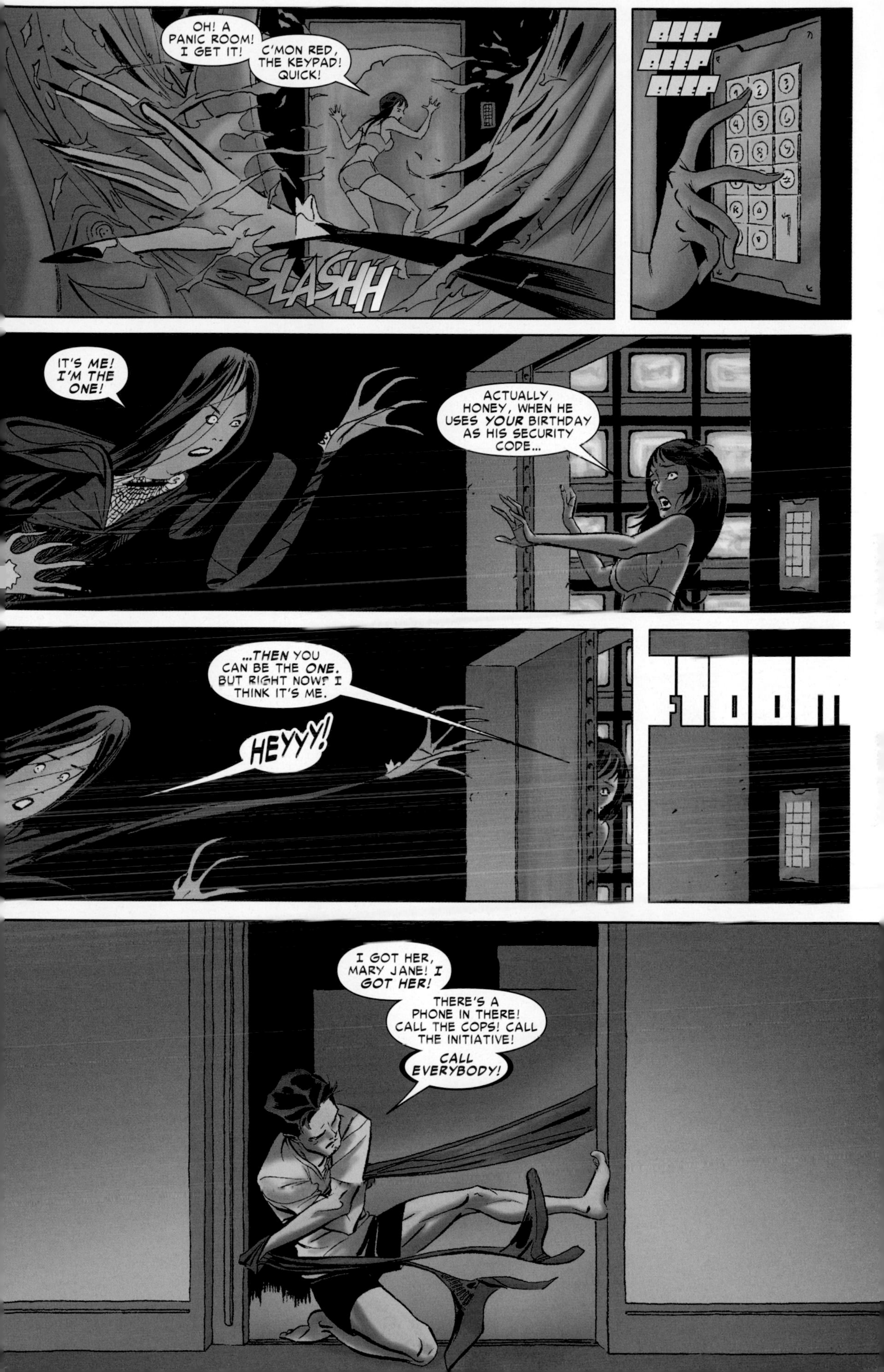

OH! A PANIC ROOM! I GET IT!
C'MON RED, THE KEYPAD! QUICK!
SLASHH
BEEP BEEP BEEP
IT'S ME! I'M THE ONE!
ACTUALLY, HONEY, WHEN HE USES YOUR BIRTHDAY AS HIS SECURITY CODE...
...THEN YOU CAN BE THE ONE. BUT RIGHT NOW? I THINK IT'S ME.
HEYYY!
FTOOM
I GOT HER, MARY JANE! I GOT HER!
THERE'S A PHONE IN THERE! CALL THE COPS! CALL THE INITIATIVE!
CALL EVERYBODY!

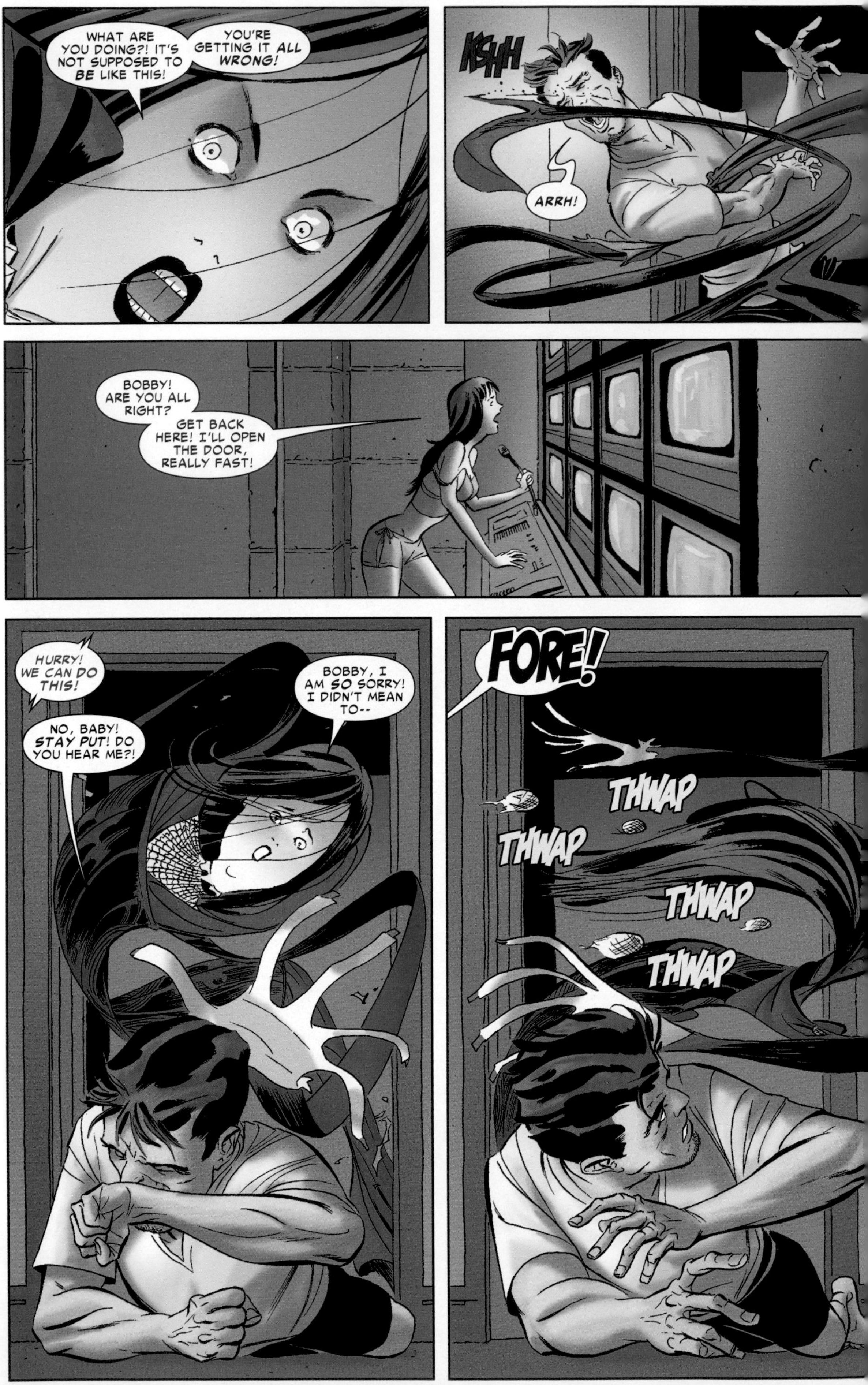
WHAT ARE YOU DOING?! IT'S NOT SUPPOSED TO BE LIKE THIS!
YOU'RE GETTING IT ALL WRONG!
KSHH
ARRH!
BOBBY! ARE YOU ALL RIGHT?
GET BACK HERE! I'LL OPEN THE DOOR, REALLY FAST!
HURRY! WE CAN DO THIS!
NO, BABY! STAY PUT! DO YOU HEAR ME?!
BOBBY, I AM SO SORRY! I DIDN'T MEAN TO--
FORE!
THWAP
THWAP
THWAP
THWAP

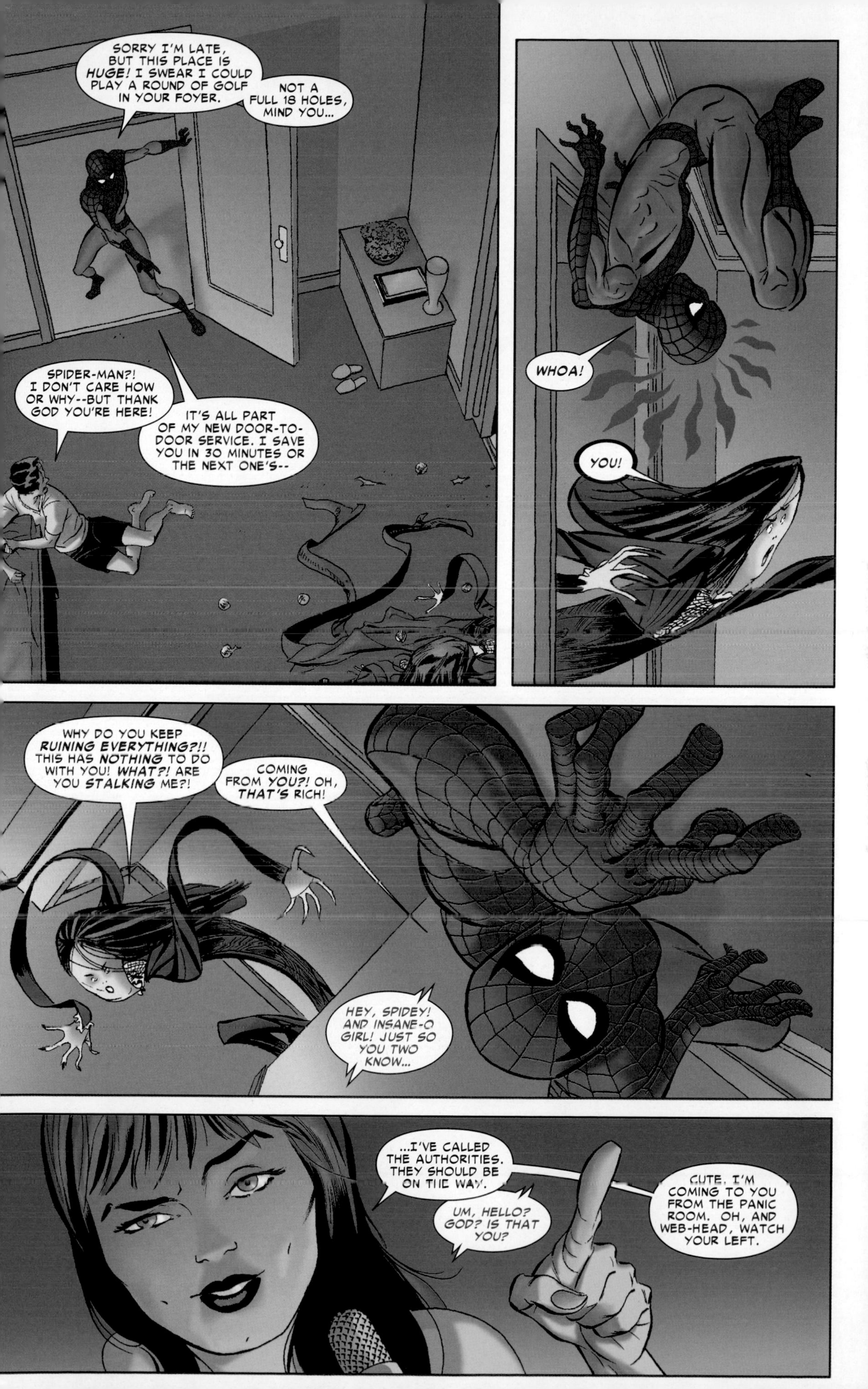
SORRY I'M LATE, BUT THIS PLACE IS HUGE! I SWEAR I COULD PLAY A ROUND OF GOLF IN YOUR FOYER.
NOT A FULL 18 HOLES, MIND YOU...
SPIDER-MAN?! I DON'T CARE HOW OR WHY--BUT THANK GOD YOU'RE HERE!
IT'S ALL PART OF MY NEW DOOR-TO-DOOR SERVICE. I SAVE YOU IN 30 MINUTES OR THE NEXT ONE'S--
WHOA!
YOU!
WHY DO YOU KEEP RUINING EVERYTHING?!! THIS HAS NOTHING TO DO WITH YOU! WHAT?! ARE YOU STALKING ME?!
COMING FROM YOU?! OH, THAT'S RICH!
HEY, SPIDEY! AND INSANE-O GIRL! JUST SO YOU TWO KNOW...
...I'VE CALLED THE AUTHORITIES. THEY SHOULD BE ON THE WAY.
UM, HELLO? GOD? IS THAT YOU?
CUTE. I'M COMING TO YOU FROM THE PANIC ROOM. OH, AND WEB-HEAD, WATCH YOUR LEFT.

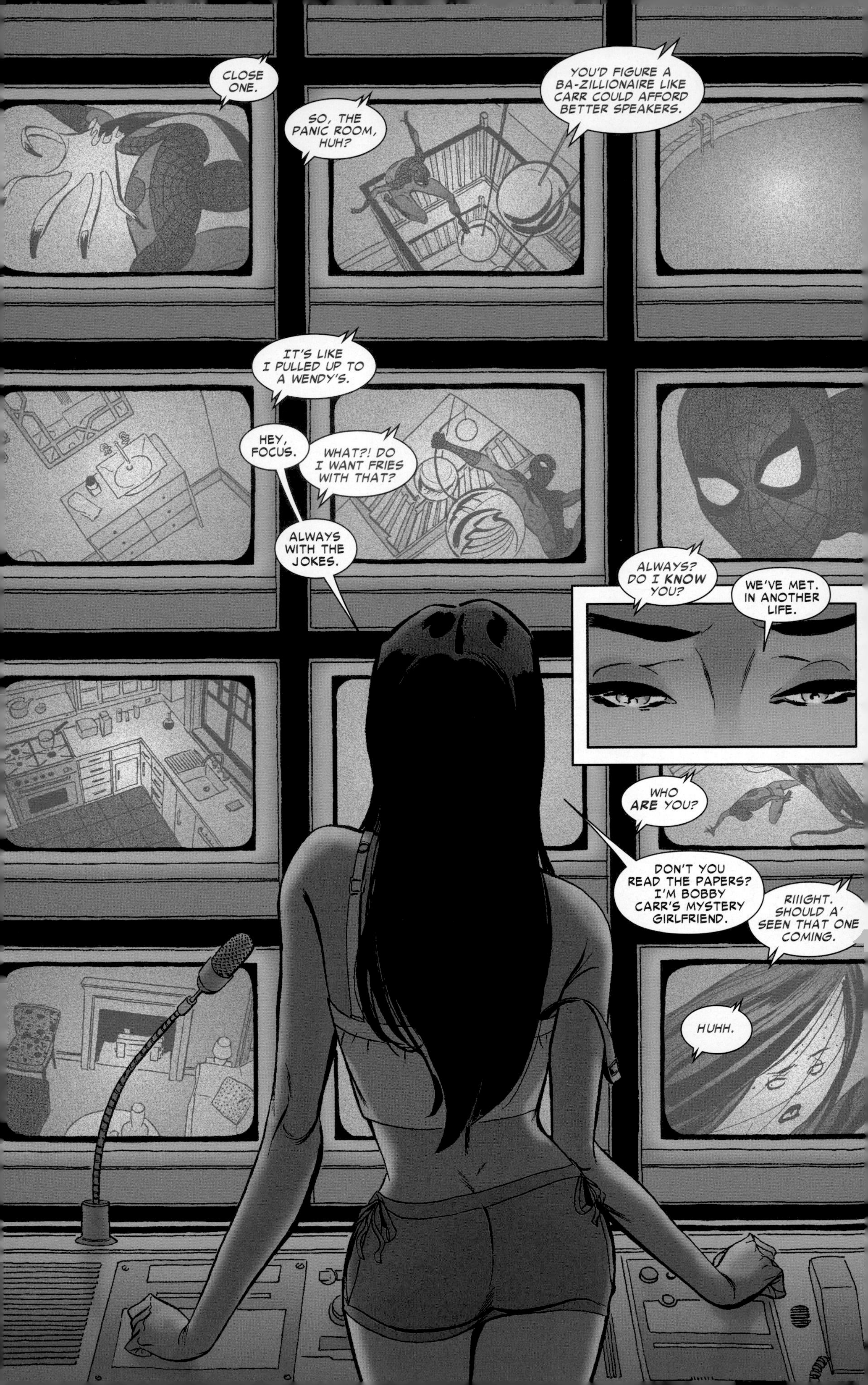
CLOSE ONE.
SO, THE PANIC ROOM, HUH?
YOU'D FIGURE A BA-ZILLIONAIRE LIKE CARR COULD AFFORD BETTER SPEAKERS.
IT'S LIKE I PULLED UP TO A WENDY'S.
HEY, FOCUS.
WHAT?! DO I WANT FRIES WITH THAT?
ALWAYS WITH THE JOKES.
ALWAYS? DO I KNOW YOU?
WE'VE MET. IN ANOTHER LIFE.
WHO ARE YOU?
DON'T YOU READ THE PAPERS? I'M BOBBY CARR'S MYSTERY GIRLFRIEND.
RIIIGHT. SHOULD A' SEEN THAT ONE COMING.
HUHH.

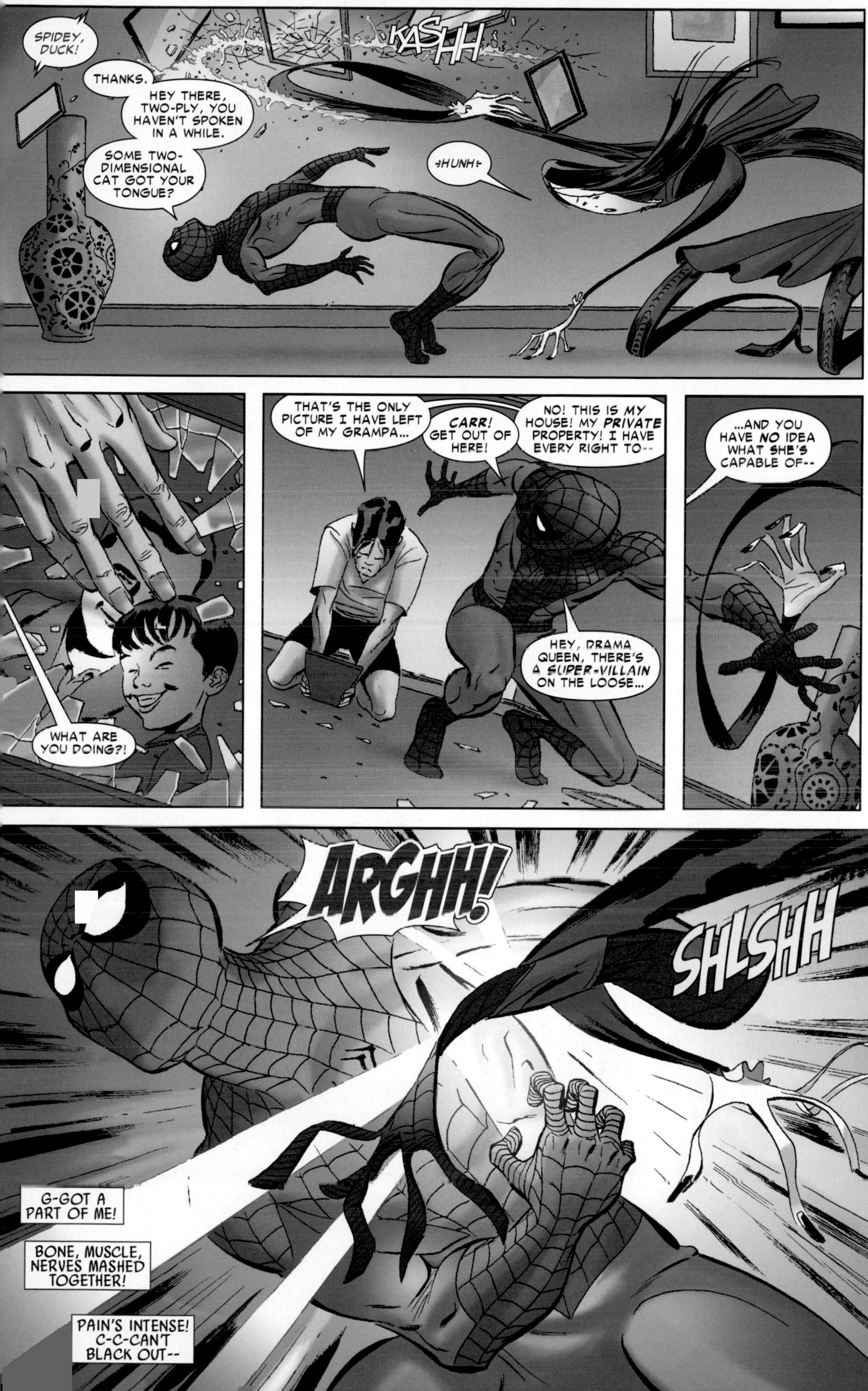
SPIDEY, DUCK!
KASHH
THANKS.
HEY THERE, TWO-PLY, YOU HAVEN'T SPOKEN IN A WHILE.
SOME TWO-DIMENSIONAL CAT GOT YOUR TONGUE?
HUNH
WHAT ARE YOU DOING?!
THAT'S THE ONLY PICTURE I HAVE LEFT OF MY GRAMPA...
CARR! GET OUT OF HERE!
NO! THIS IS MY HOUSE! MY PRIVATE PROPERTY! I HAVE EVERY RIGHT TO--
HEY, DRAMA QUEEN, THERE'S A SUPER-VILLAIN ON THE LOOSE...
...AND YOU HAVE NO IDEA WHAT SHE'S CAPABLE OF--
ARGHH!
SHLSHH
G-GOT A PART OF ME!
BONE, MUSCLE, NERVES MASHED TOGETHER!
PAIN'S INTENSE! C-C-CAN'T BLACK OUT--

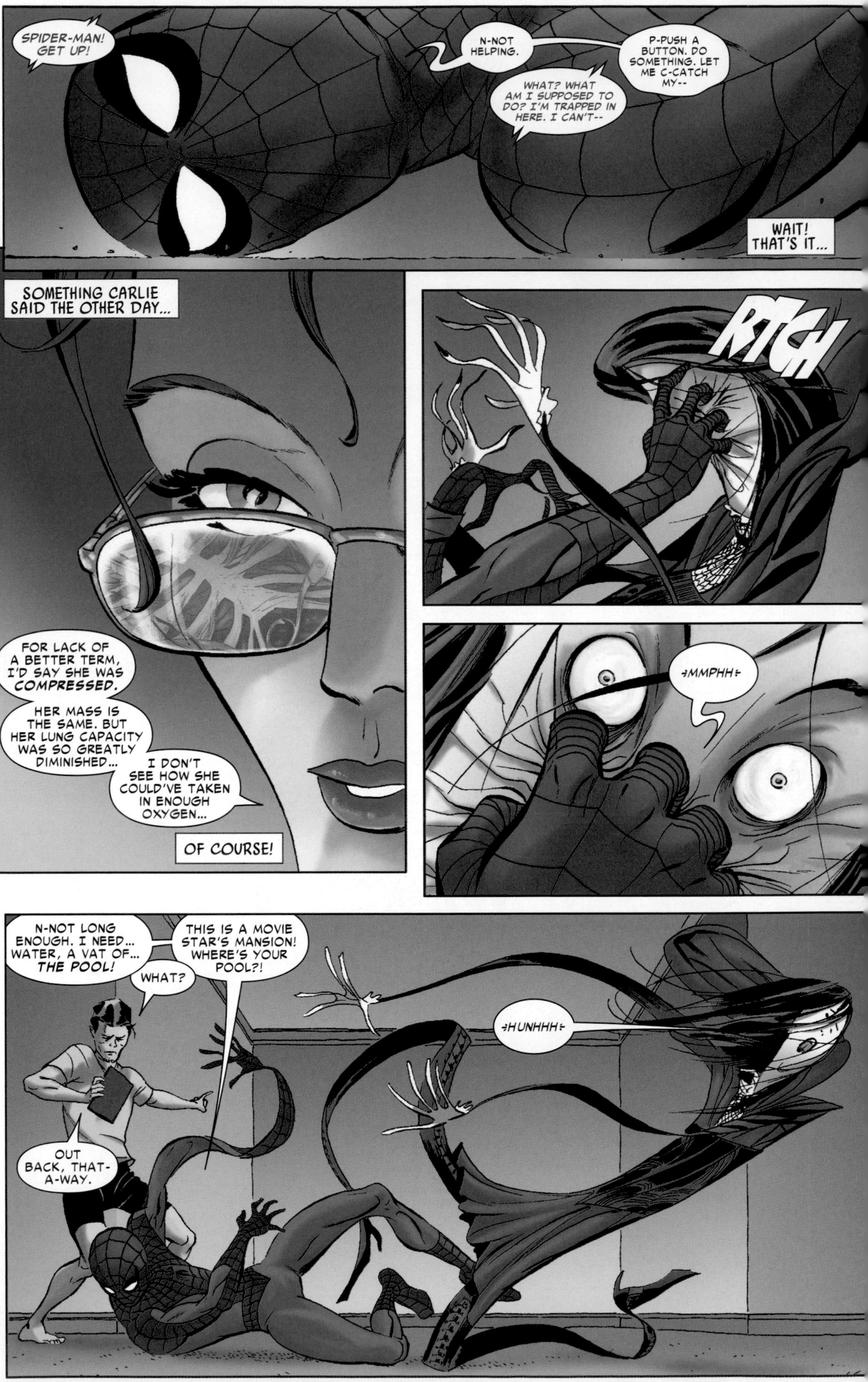
SPIDER-MAN! GET UP!
N-NOT HELPING.
WHAT? WHAT AM I SUPPOSED TO DO? I'M TRAPPED IN HERE. I CAN'T--
P-PUSH A BUTTON. DO SOMETHING. LET ME C-CATCH MY--
WAIT! THAT'S IT...
SOMETHING CARLIE SAID THE OTHER DAY...
FOR LACK OF A BETTER TERM, I'D SAY SHE WAS COMPRESSED.
HER MASS IS THE SAME. BUT HER LUNG CAPACITY WAS SO GREATLY DIMINISHED...
I DON'T SEE HOW SHE COULD'VE TAKEN IN ENOUGH OXYGEN...
OF COURSE!
RTCH
MMPHH
N-NOT LONG ENOUGH. I NEED... WATER, A VAT OF... THE POOL!
WHAT?
THIS IS A MOVIE STAR'S MANSION! WHERE'S YOUR POOL?!
OUT BACK, THAT-A-WAY.
HUNHHH

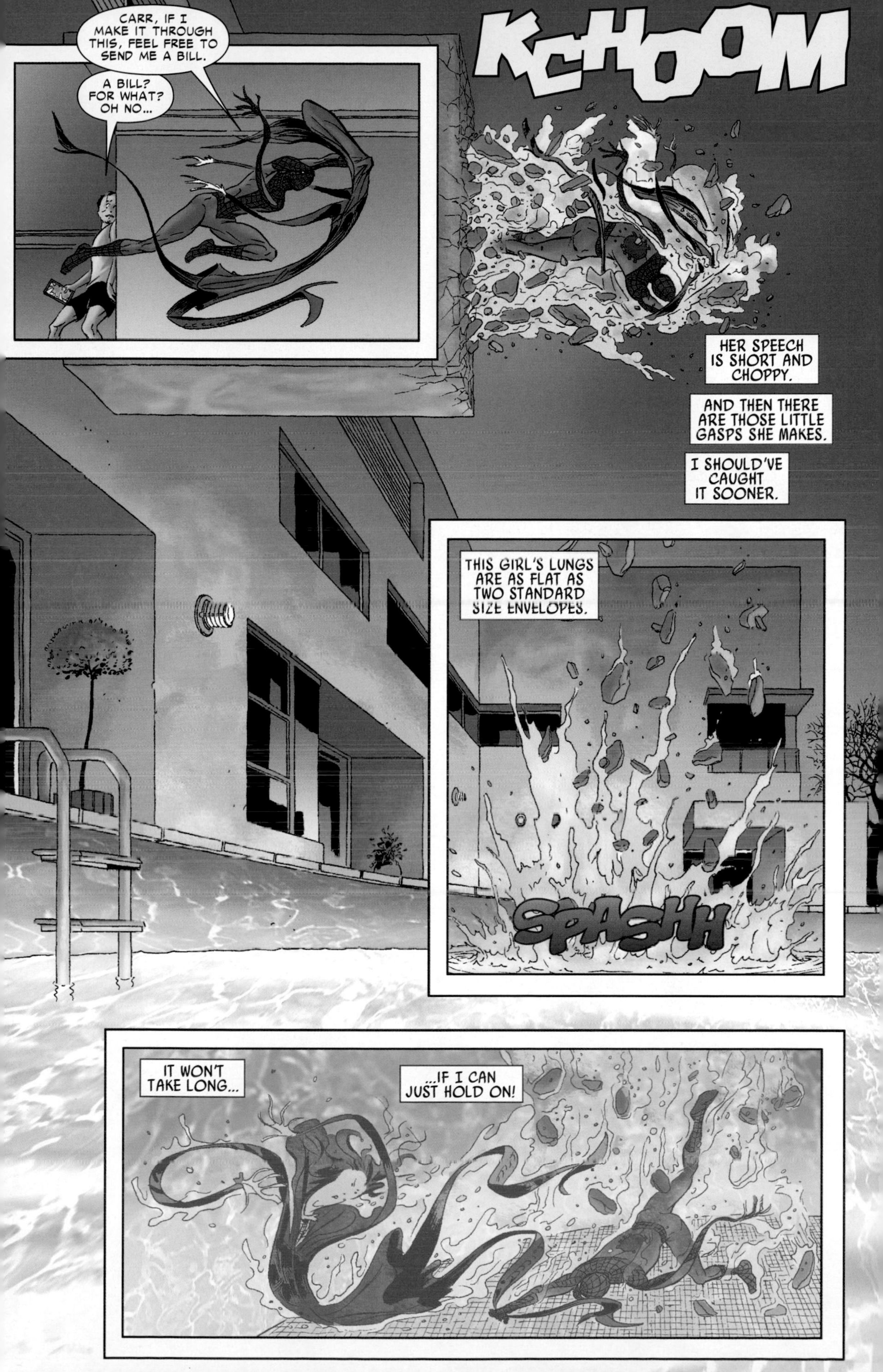
CARR, IF I MAKE IT THROUGH THIS, FEEL FREE TO SEND ME A BILL.
A BILL? FOR WHAT? OH NO...
KCHOOM
HER SPEECH IS SHORT AND CHOPPY.
AND THEN THERE ARE THOSE LITTLE GASPS SHE MAKES.
I SHOULD'VE CAUGHT IT SOONER.
THIS GIRL'S LUNGS ARE AS FLAT AS TWO STANDARD SIZE ENVELOPES.
SPASHH
IT WON'T TAKE LONG...
...IF I CAN JUST HOLD ON!

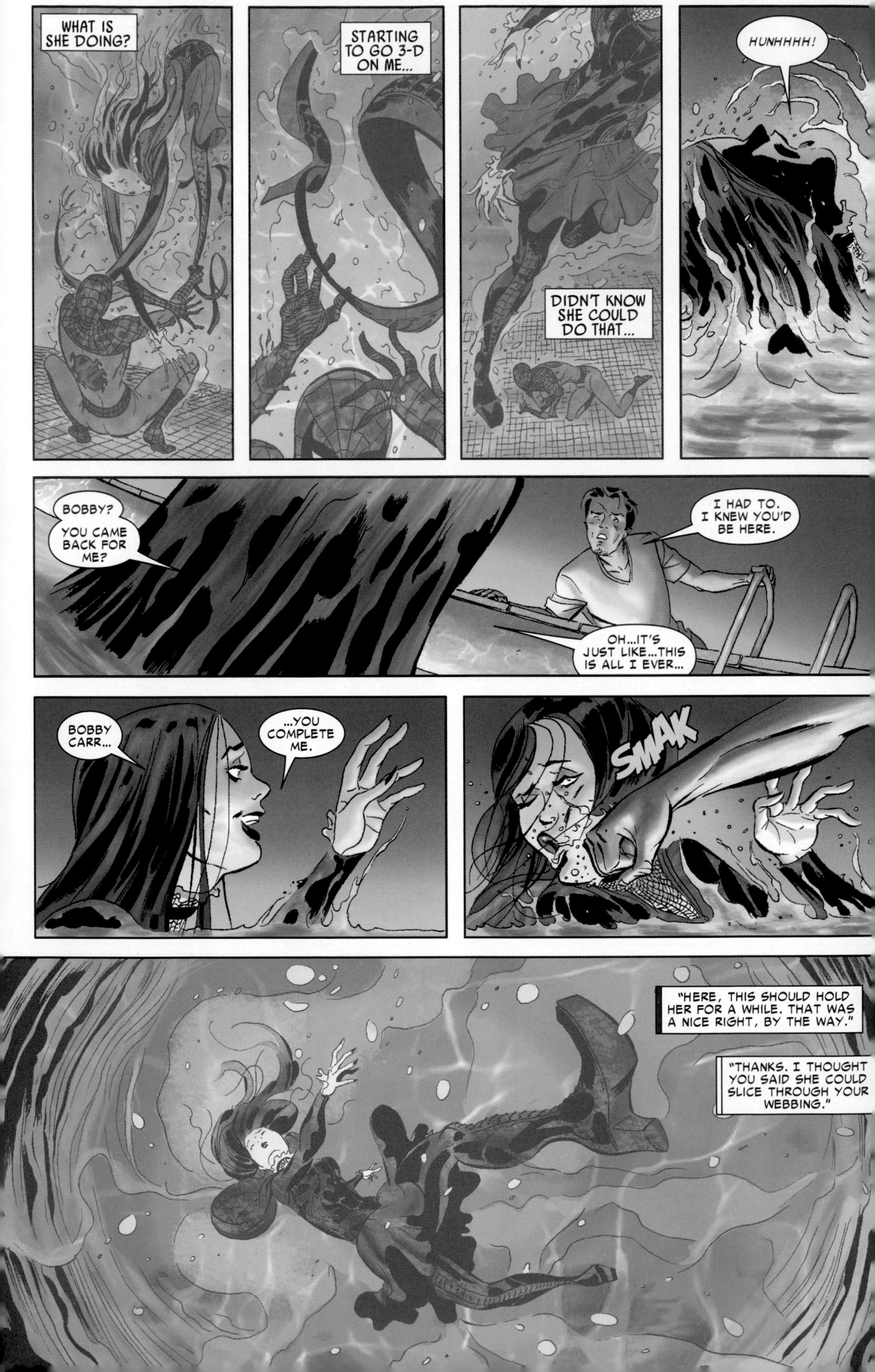
WHAT IS SHE DOING?
STARTING TO GO 3-D ON ME...
DIDN'T KNOW SHE COULD DO THAT...
HUNHHHH!
BOBBY?
YOU CAME BACK FOR ME?
I HAD TO. I KNEW YOU'D BE HERE.
OH...IT'S JUST LIKE...THIS IS ALL I EVER...
BOBBY CARR...
...YOU COMPLETE ME.
SMAK
"HERE, THIS SHOULD HOLD HER FOR A WHILE. THAT WAS A NICE RIGHT, BY THE WAY."
"THANKS. I THOUGHT YOU SAID SHE COULD SLICE THROUGH YOUR WEBBING."

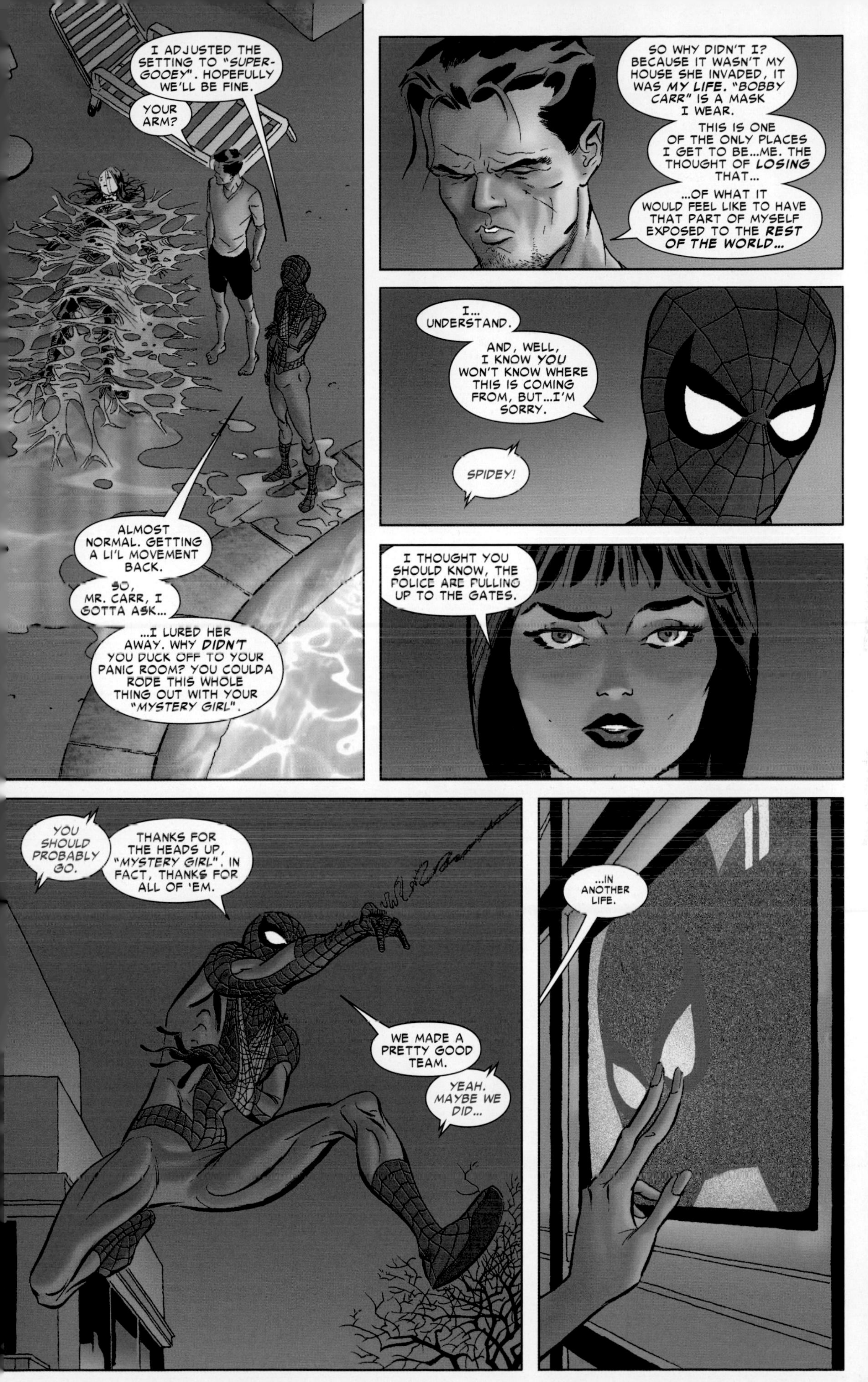
I ADJUSTED THE SETTING TO "SUPER-GOOEY". HOPEFULLY WE'LL BE FINE.
YOUR ARM?
ALMOST NORMAL. GETTING A LI'L MOVEMENT BACK.
SO, MR. CARR, I GOTTA ASK...
...I LURED HER AWAY. WHY DIDN'T YOU DUCK OFF TO YOUR PANIC ROOM? YOU COULDA RODE THIS WHOLE THING OUT WITH YOUR "MYSTERY GIRL".
SO WHY DIDN'T I? BECAUSE IT WASN'T MY HOUSE SHE INVADED, IT WAS MY LIFE. "BOBBY CARR" IS A MASK I WEAR.
THIS IS ONE OF THE ONLY PLACES I GET TO BE...ME. THE THOUGHT OF LOSING THAT...
...OF WHAT IT WOULD FEEL LIKE TO HAVE THAT PART OF MYSELF EXPOSED TO THE REST OF THE WORLD...
I... UNDERSTAND.
AND, WELL, I KNOW YOU WON'T KNOW WHERE THIS IS COMING FROM, BUT...I'M SORRY.
SPIDEY!
I THOUGHT YOU SHOULD KNOW, THE POLICE ARE PULLING UP TO THE GATES.
YOU SHOULD PROBABLY GO.
THANKS FOR THE HEADS UP, "MYSTERY GIRL". IN FACT, THANKS FOR ALL OF 'EM.
WE MADE A PRETTY GOOD TEAM.
YEAH. MAYBE WE DID...
...IN ANOTHER LIFE.

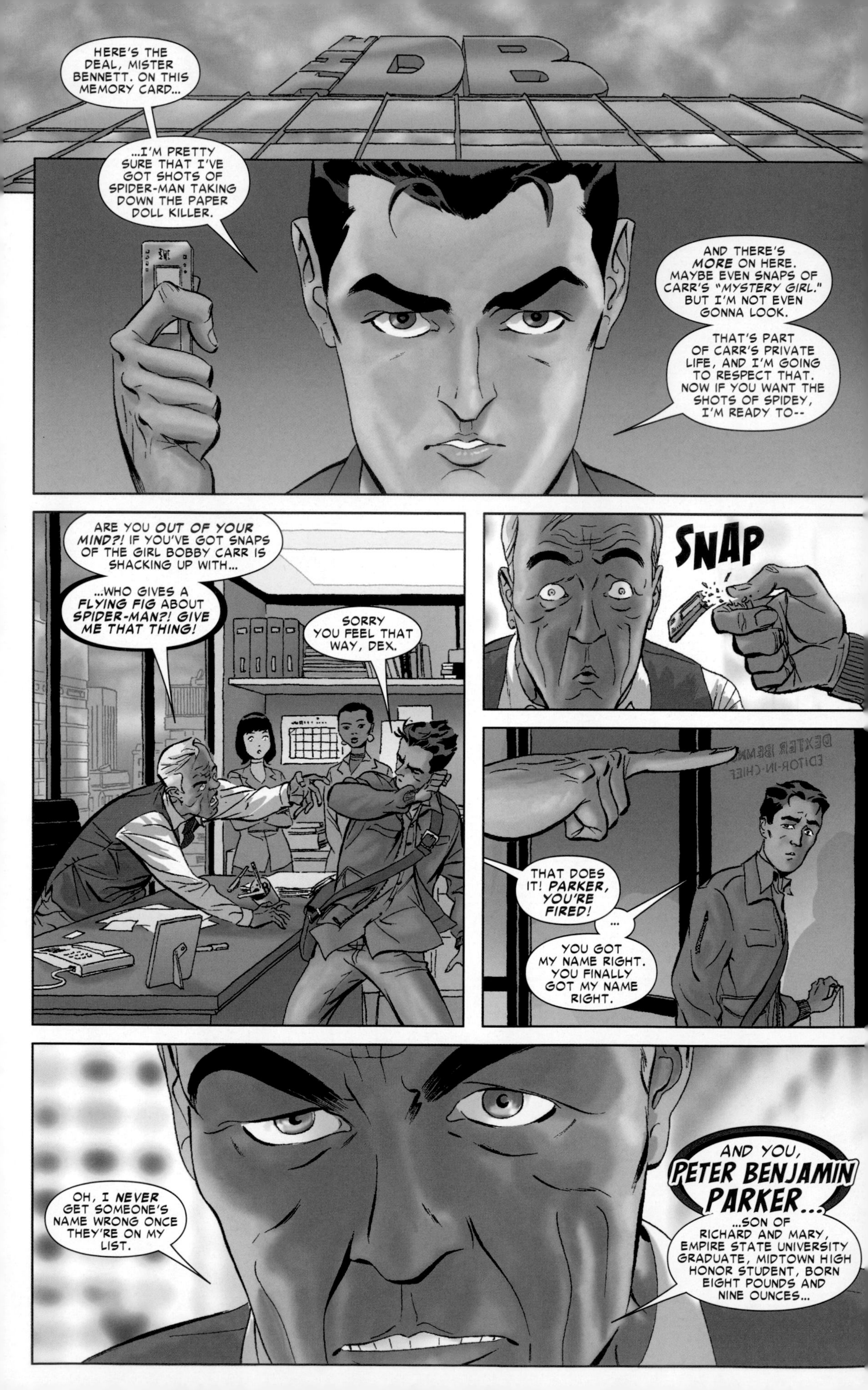

THE DB
HERE'S THE DEAL, MISTER BENNETT. ON THIS MEMORY CARD...
...I'M PRETTY SURE THAT I'VE GOT SHOTS OF SPIDER-MAN TAKING DOWN THE PAPER DOLL KILLER.
AND THERE'S MORE ON HERE. MAYBE EVEN SNAPS OF CARR'S "MYSTERY GIRL." BUT I'M NOT EVEN GONNA LOOK.
THAT'S PART OF CARR'S PRIVATE LIFE, AND I'M GOING TO RESPECT THAT. NOW IF YOU WANT THE SHOTS OF SPIDEY, I'M READY TO--
ARE YOU OUT OF YOUR MIND?! IF YOU'VE GOT SNAPS OF THE GIRL BOBBY CARR IS SHACKING UP WITH...
...WHO GIVES A FLYING FIG ABOUT SPIDER-MAN?! GIVE ME THAT THING!
SORRY YOU FEEL THAT WAY, DEX.
SNAP
DEXTER BENNETT EDITOR-IN-CHIEF
THAT DOES IT! PARKER, YOU'RE FIRED!
...
YOU GOT MY NAME RIGHT. YOU FINALLY GOT MY NAME RIGHT.
OH, I NEVER GET SOMEONE'S NAME WRONG ONCE THEY'RE ON MY LIST.
AND YOU, PETER BENJAMIN PARKER...
...SON OF RICHARD AND MARY, EMPIRE STATE UNIVERSITY GRADUATE, MIDTOWN HIGH HONOR STUDENT, BORN EIGHT POUNDS AND NINE OUNCES...

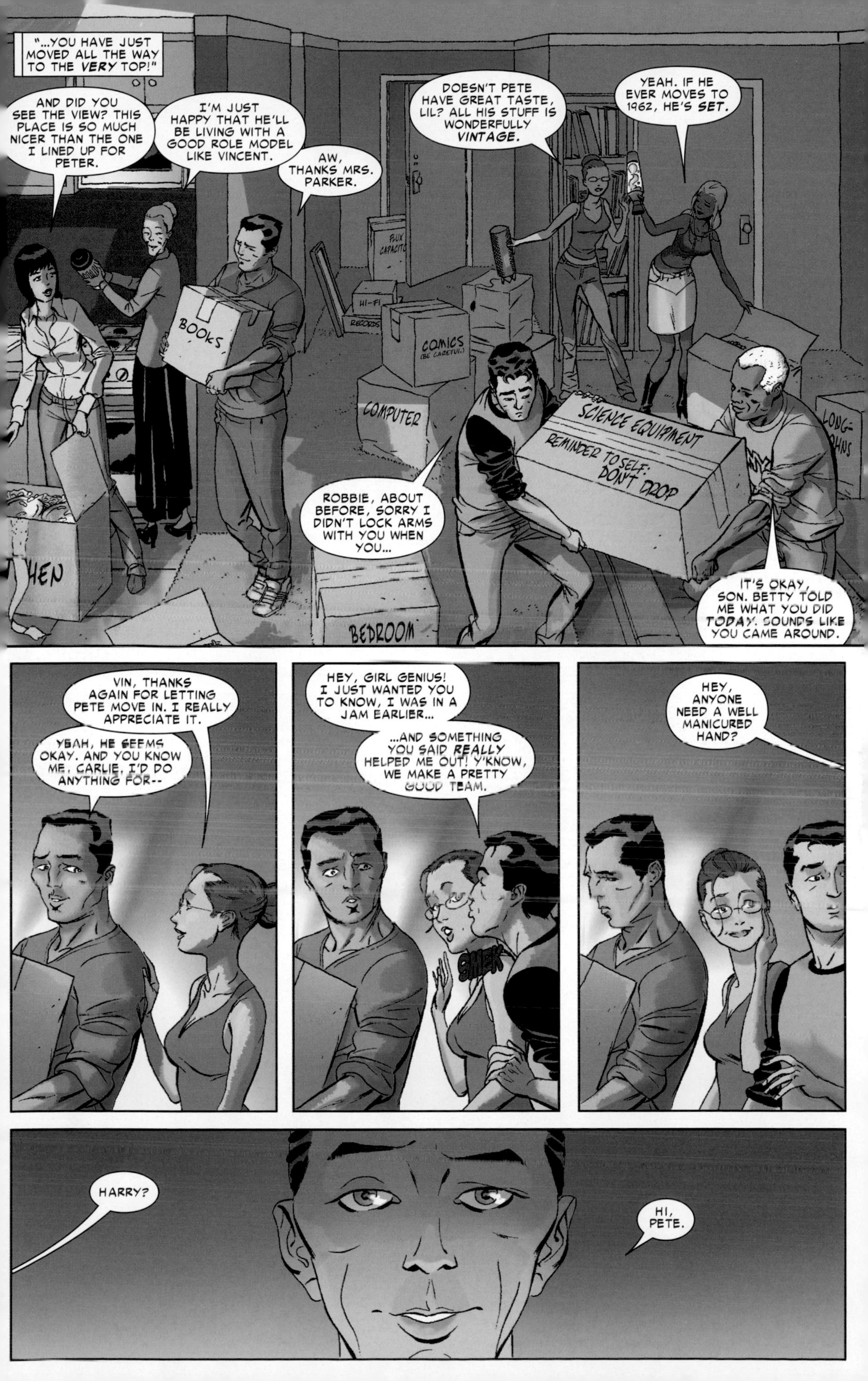
"...YOU HAVE JUST MOVED ALL THE WAY TO THE *VERY* TOP!"
AND DID YOU SEE THE VIEW? THIS PLACE IS SO MUCH NICER THAN THE ONE I LINED UP FOR PETER.
I'M JUST HAPPY THAT HE'LL BE LIVING WITH A GOOD ROLE MODEL LIKE VINCENT.
AW, THANKS MRS. PARKER.
DOESN'T PETE HAVE GREAT TASTE, LIL? ALL HIS STUFF IS WONDERFULLY *VINTAGE.*
YEAH. IF HE EVER MOVES TO 1962, HE'S *SET.*
BOOKS
COMICS (BE CAREFUL!)
COMPUTER
RECORDS
HI-FI
SCIENCE EQUIPMENT
REMINDER TO SELF: DON'T DROP
BEDROOM
ROBBIE, ABOUT BEFORE, SORRY I DIDN'T LOCK ARMS WITH YOU WHEN YOU...
IT'S OKAY, SON. BETTY TOLD ME WHAT YOU DID *TODAY*. SOUNDS LIKE YOU CAME AROUND.
VIN, THANKS AGAIN FOR LETTING PETE MOVE IN. I REALLY APPRECIATE IT.
YEAH, HE SEEMS OKAY. AND YOU KNOW ME, CARLIE, I'D DO ANYTHING FOR--
HEY, GIRL GENIUS! I JUST WANTED YOU TO KNOW, I WAS IN A JAM EARLIER...
...AND SOMETHING YOU SAID *REALLY* HELPED ME OUT! Y'KNOW, WE MAKE A PRETTY GOOD TEAM.
SMEK
HEY, ANYONE NEED A WELL MANICURED HAND?
HARRY?
HI, PETE.

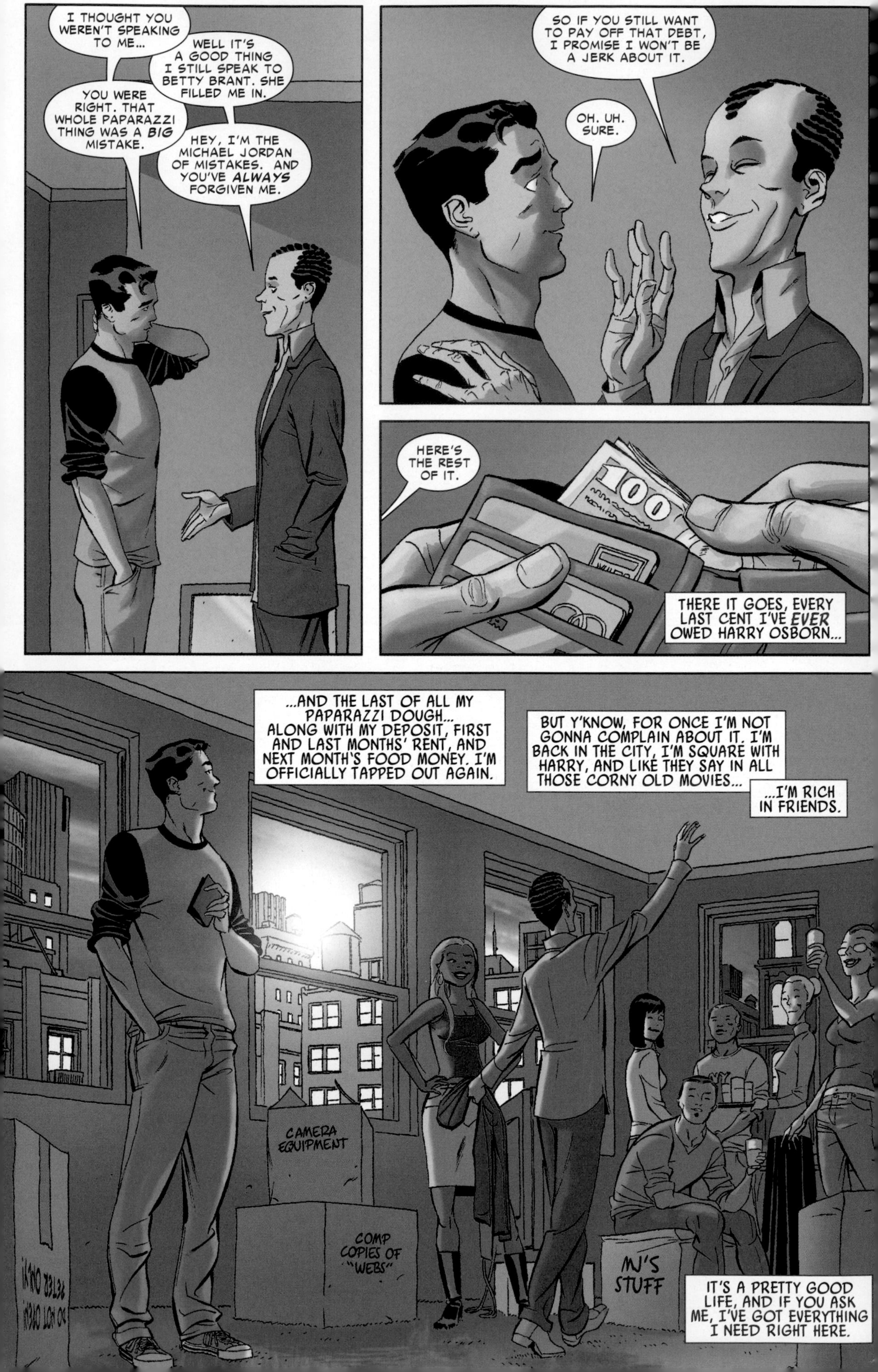
I THOUGHT YOU WEREN'T SPEAKING TO ME...
WELL IT'S A GOOD THING I STILL SPEAK TO BETTY BRANT. SHE FILLED ME IN.
YOU WERE RIGHT. THAT WHOLE PAPARAZZI THING WAS A BIG MISTAKE.
HEY, I'M THE MICHAEL JORDAN OF MISTAKES. AND YOU'VE ALWAYS FORGIVEN ME.
SO IF YOU STILL WANT TO PAY OFF THAT DEBT, I PROMISE I WON'T BE A JERK ABOUT IT.
OH. UH. SURE.
HERE'S THE REST OF IT.
THERE IT GOES, EVERY LAST CENT I'VE EVER OWED HARRY OSBORN...
...AND THE LAST OF ALL MY PAPARAZZI DOUGH... ALONG WITH MY DEPOSIT, FIRST AND LAST MONTHS' RENT, AND NEXT MONTH'S FOOD MONEY. I'M OFFICIALLY TAPPED OUT AGAIN.
BUT Y'KNOW, FOR ONCE I'M NOT GONNA COMPLAIN ABOUT IT. I'M BACK IN THE CITY, I'M SQUARE WITH HARRY, AND LIKE THEY SAY IN ALL THOSE CORNY OLD MOVIES...
...I'M RICH IN FRIENDS.
CAMERA EQUIPMENT
COMP COPIES OF "WEBS"
MJ'S STUFF
IT'S A PRETTY GOOD LIFE, AND IF YOU ASK ME, I'VE GOT EVERYTHING I NEED RIGHT HERE.

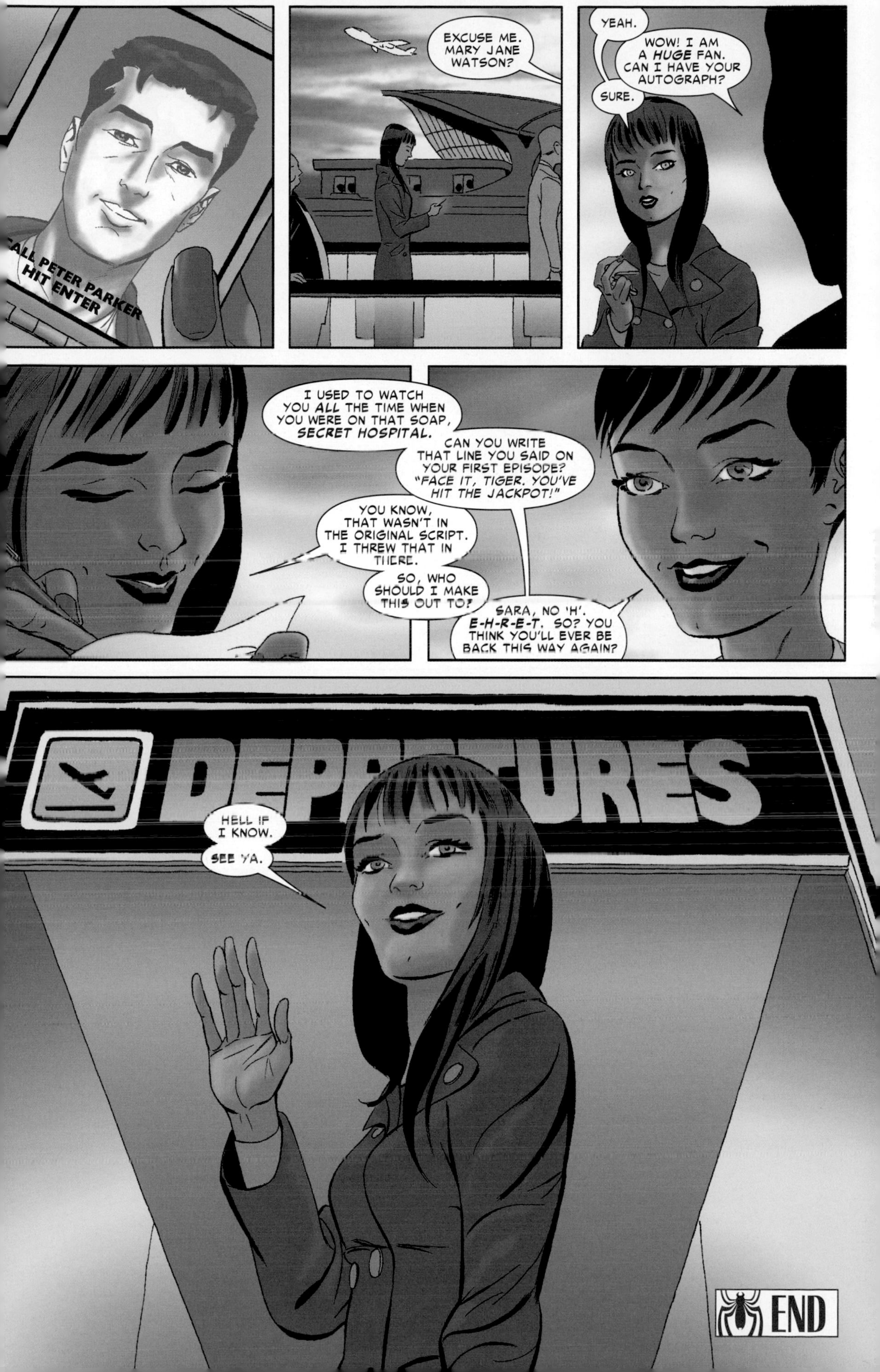
CALL PETER PARKER
HIT ENTER
EXCUSE ME. MARY JANE WATSON?
YEAH.
WOW! I AM A HUGE FAN. CAN I HAVE YOUR AUTOGRAPH?
SURE.
I USED TO WATCH YOU ALL THE TIME WHEN YOU WERE ON THAT SOAP, SECRET HOSPITAL.
CAN YOU WRITE THAT LINE YOU SAID ON YOUR FIRST EPISODE? "FACE IT, TIGER. YOU'VE HIT THE JACKPOT!"
YOU KNOW, THAT WASN'T IN THE ORIGINAL SCRIPT. I THREW THAT IN THERE.
SO, WHO SHOULD I MAKE THIS OUT TO?
SARA, NO 'H'. E-H-R-E-T. SO? YOU THINK YOU'LL EVER BE BACK THIS WAY AGAIN?
DEPARTURES
HELL IF I KNOW.
SEE YA.
END

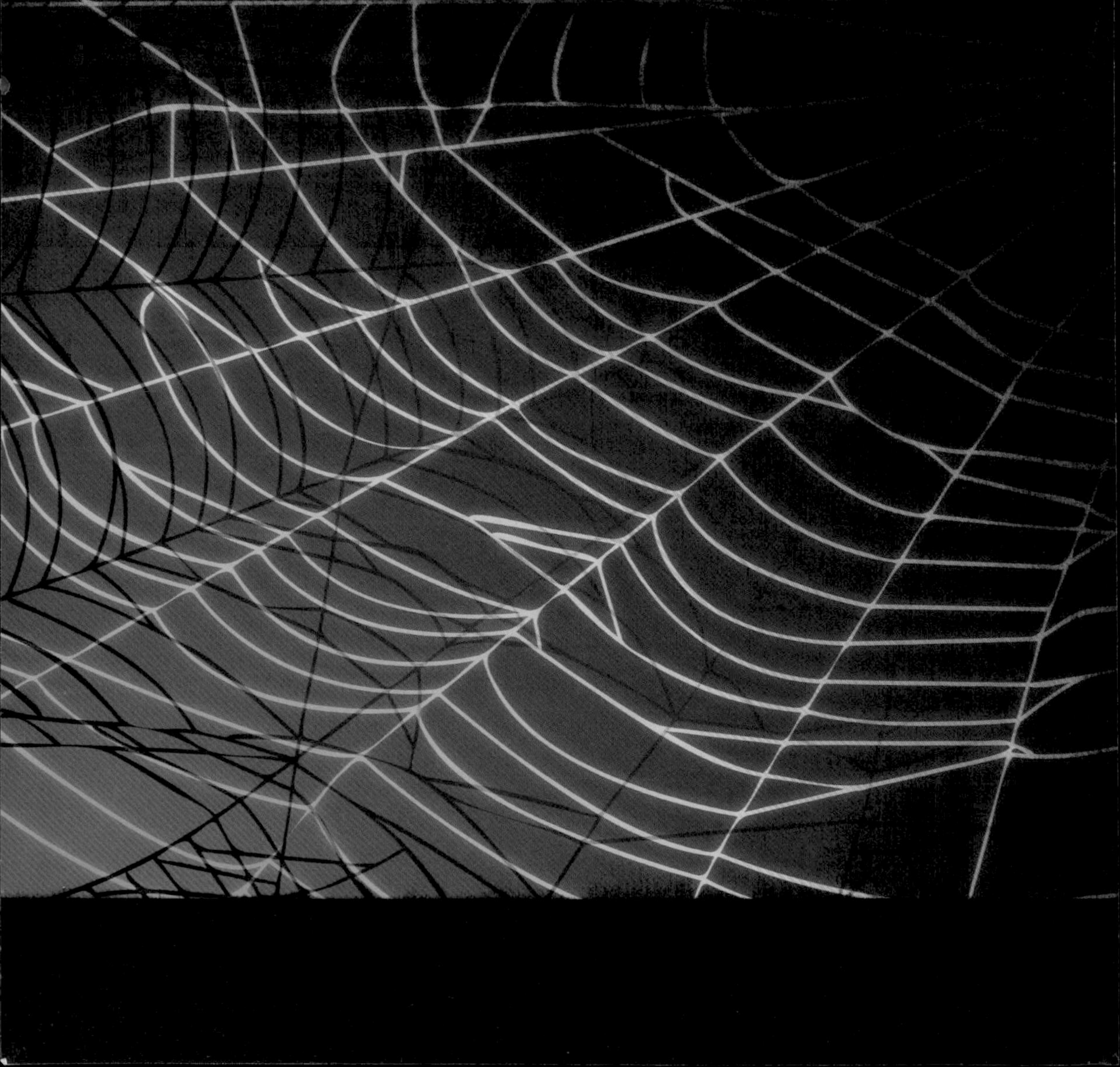

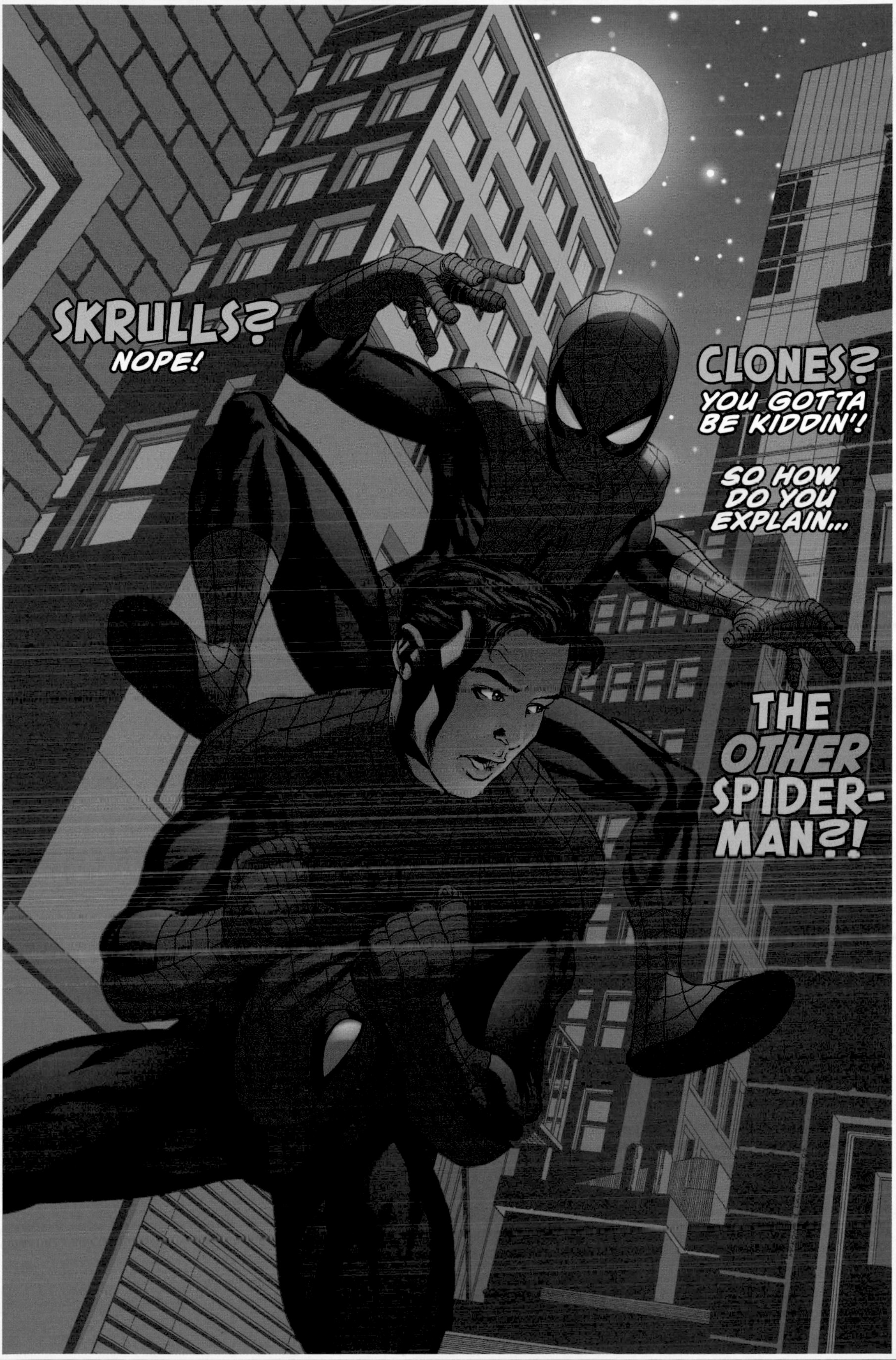
SKRULLS?
NOPE!
CLONES?
YOU GOTTA BE KIDDIN'!
SO HOW DO YOU EXPLAIN...
THE OTHER SPIDER-MAN?!

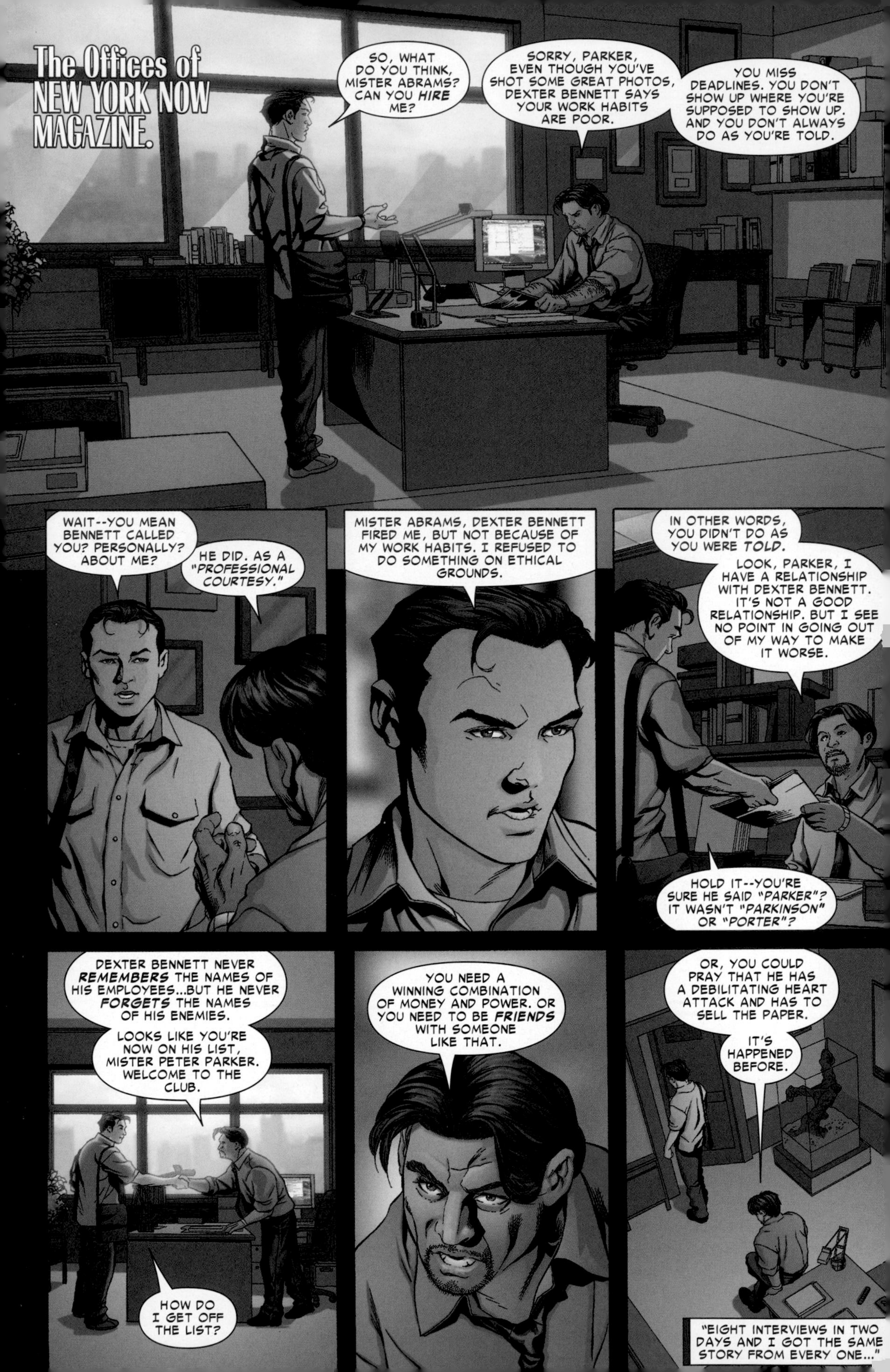
The Offices of NEW YORK NOW MAGAZINE.
SO, WHAT DO YOU THINK, MISTER ABRAMS? CAN YOU HIRE ME?
SORRY, PARKER, EVEN THOUGH YOU'VE SHOT SOME GREAT PHOTOS, DEXTER BENNETT SAYS YOUR WORK HABITS ARE POOR.
YOU MISS DEADLINES. YOU DON'T SHOW UP WHERE YOU'RE SUPPOSED TO SHOW UP. AND YOU DON'T ALWAYS DO AS YOU'RE TOLD.
WAIT--YOU MEAN BENNETT CALLED YOU? PERSONALLY? ABOUT ME?
HE DID. AS A "PROFESSIONAL COURTESY."
MISTER ABRAMS, DEXTER BENNETT FIRED ME, BUT NOT BECAUSE OF MY WORK HABITS. I REFUSED TO DO SOMETHING ON ETHICAL GROUNDS.
IN OTHER WORDS, YOU DIDN'T DO AS YOU WERE TOLD.
LOOK, PARKER, I HAVE A RELATIONSHIP WITH DEXTER BENNETT. IT'S NOT A GOOD RELATIONSHIP. BUT I SEE NO POINT IN GOING OUT OF MY WAY TO MAKE IT WORSE.
HOLD IT--YOU'RE SURE HE SAID "PARKER"? IT WASN'T "PARKINSON" OR "PORTER"?
DEXTER BENNETT NEVER REMEMBERS THE NAMES OF HIS EMPLOYEES...BUT HE NEVER FORGETS THE NAMES OF HIS ENEMIES.
LOOKS LIKE YOU'RE NOW ON HIS LIST, MISTER PETER PARKER. WELCOME TO THE CLUB.
HOW DO I GET OFF THE LIST?
YOU NEED A WINNING COMBINATION OF MONEY AND POWER. OR YOU NEED TO BE FRIENDS WITH SOMEONE LIKE THAT.
OR, YOU COULD PRAY THAT HE HAS A DEBILITATING HEART ATTACK AND HAS TO SELL THE PAPER.
IT'S HAPPENED BEFORE.
"EIGHT INTERVIEWS IN TWO DAYS AND I GOT THE SAME STORY FROM EVERY ONE..."

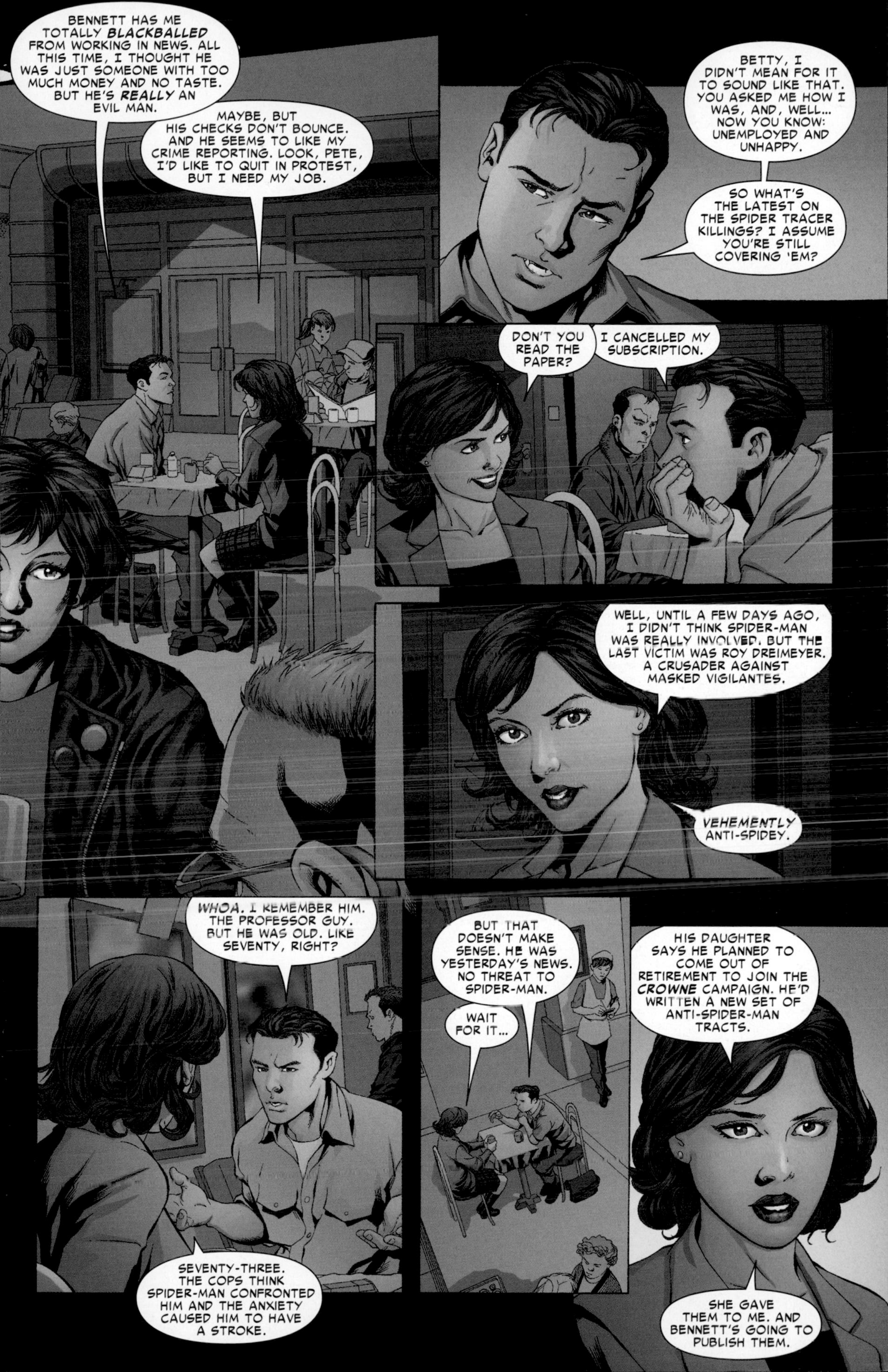
BENNETT HAS ME TOTALLY BLACKBALLED FROM WORKING IN NEWS. ALL THIS TIME, I THOUGHT HE WAS JUST SOMEONE WITH TOO MUCH MONEY AND NO TASTE. BUT HE'S REALLY AN EVIL MAN.
MAYBE, BUT HIS CHECKS DON'T BOUNCE. AND HE SEEMS TO LIKE MY CRIME REPORTING. LOOK, PETE, I'D LIKE TO QUIT IN PROTEST, BUT I NEED MY JOB.
BETTY, I DIDN'T MEAN FOR IT TO SOUND LIKE THAT. YOU ASKED ME HOW I WAS, AND, WELL... NOW YOU KNOW: UNEMPLOYED AND UNHAPPY.
SO WHAT'S THE LATEST ON THE SPIDER TRACER KILLINGS? I ASSUME YOU'RE STILL COVERING 'EM?
DON'T YOU READ THE PAPER?
I CANCELLED MY SUBSCRIPTION.
WELL, UNTIL A FEW DAYS AGO, I DIDN'T THINK SPIDER-MAN WAS REALLY INVOLVED. BUT THE LAST VICTIM WAS ROY DREIMEYER. A CRUSADER AGAINST MASKED VIGILANTES.
VEHEMENTLY ANTI-SPIDEY.
WHOA. I REMEMBER HIM. THE PROFESSOR GUY. BUT HE WAS OLD. LIKE SEVENTY, RIGHT?
SEVENTY-THREE. THE COPS THINK SPIDER-MAN CONFRONTED HIM AND THE ANXIETY CAUSED HIM TO HAVE A STROKE.
BUT THAT DOESN'T MAKE SENSE. HE WAS YESTERDAY'S NEWS. NO THREAT TO SPIDER-MAN.
WAIT FOR IT...
HIS DAUGHTER SAYS HE PLANNED TO COME OUT OF RETIREMENT TO JOIN THE CROWNE CAMPAIGN. HE'D WRITTEN A NEW SET OF ANTI-SPIDER-MAN TRACTS.
SHE GAVE THEM TO ME. AND BENNETT'S GOING TO PUBLISH THEM.

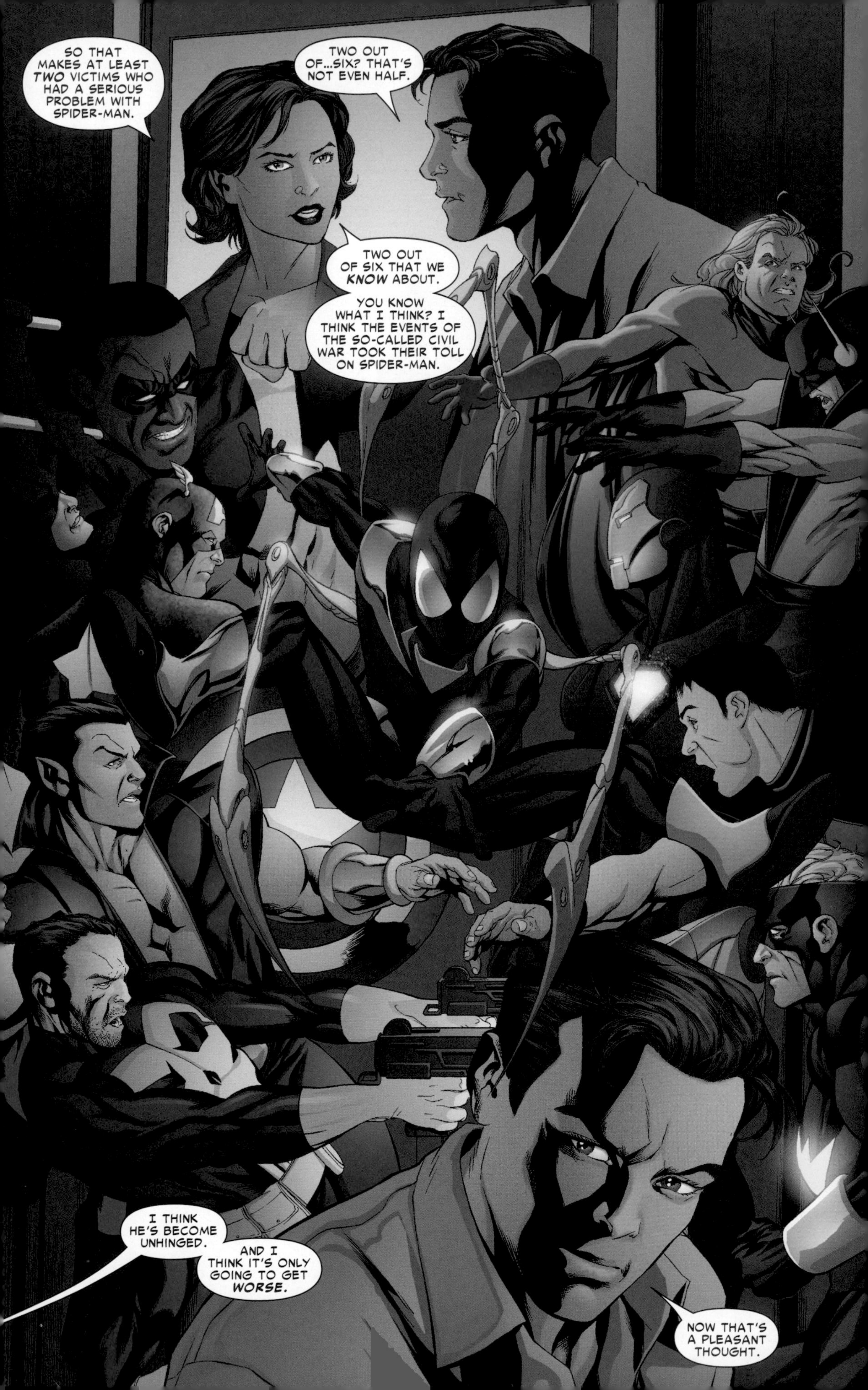
SO THAT MAKES AT LEAST TWO VICTIMS WHO HAD A SERIOUS PROBLEM WITH SPIDER-MAN.
TWO OUT OF...SIX? THAT'S NOT EVEN HALF.
TWO OUT OF SIX THAT WE KNOW ABOUT.
YOU KNOW WHAT I THINK? I THINK THE EVENTS OF THE SO-CALLED CIVIL WAR TOOK THEIR TOLL ON SPIDER-MAN.
I THINK HE'S BECOME UNHINGED.
AND I THINK IT'S ONLY GOING TO GET WORSE.
NOW THAT'S A PLEASANT THOUGHT.

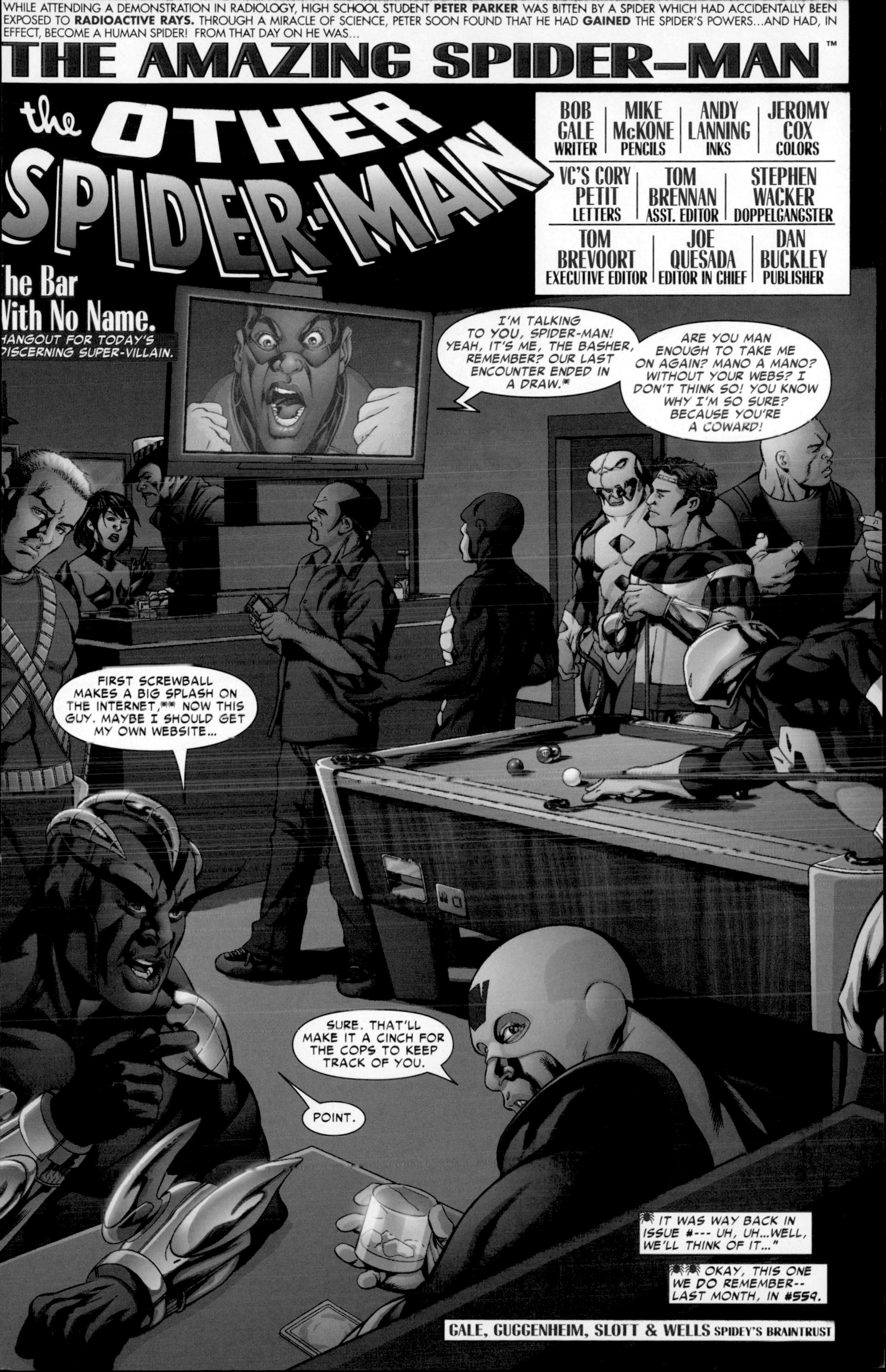

WHILE ATTENDING A DEMONSTRATION IN RADIOLOGY, HIGH SCHOOL STUDENT PETER PARKER WAS BITTEN BY A SPIDER WHICH HAD ACCIDENTALLY BEEN EXPOSED TO RADIOACTIVE RAYS. THROUGH A MIRACLE OF SCIENCE, PETER SOON FOUND THAT HE HAD GAINED THE SPIDER'S POWERS...AND HAD, IN EFFECT, BECOME A HUMAN SPIDER! FROM THAT DAY ON HE WAS...
THE AMAZING SPIDER-MAN™
the OTHER SPIDER-MAN
BOB GALE WRITER | MIKE McKONE PENCILS | ANDY LANNING INKS | JEROMY COX COLORS
VC'S CORY PETIT LETTERS | TOM BRENNAN ASST. EDITOR | STEPHEN WACKER DOPPELGANGSTER
TOM BREVOORT EXECUTIVE EDITOR | JOE QUESADA EDITOR IN CHIEF | DAN BUCKLEY PUBLISHER
The Bar With No Name.
HANGOUT FOR TODAY'S DISCERNING SUPER-VILLAIN.
I'M TALKING TO YOU, SPIDER-MAN! YEAH, IT'S ME, THE BASHER, REMEMBER? OUR LAST ENCOUNTER ENDED IN A DRAW.*
ARE YOU MAN ENOUGH TO TAKE ME ON AGAIN? MANO A MANO? WITHOUT YOUR WEBS? I DON'T THINK SO! YOU KNOW WHY I'M SO SURE? BECAUSE YOU'RE A COWARD!
FIRST SCREWBALL MAKES A BIG SPLASH ON THE INTERNET,** NOW THIS GUY. MAYBE I SHOULD GET MY OWN WEBSITE...
SURE. THAT'LL MAKE IT A CINCH FOR THE COPS TO KEEP TRACK OF YOU.
POINT.
*IT WAS WAY BACK IN ISSUE #--- UH, UH...WELL, WE'LL THINK OF IT..."
**OKAY, THIS ONE WE DO REMEMBER-- LAST MONTH, IN #559.
GALE, GUGGENHEIM, SLOTT & WELLS SPIDEY'S BRAINTRUST

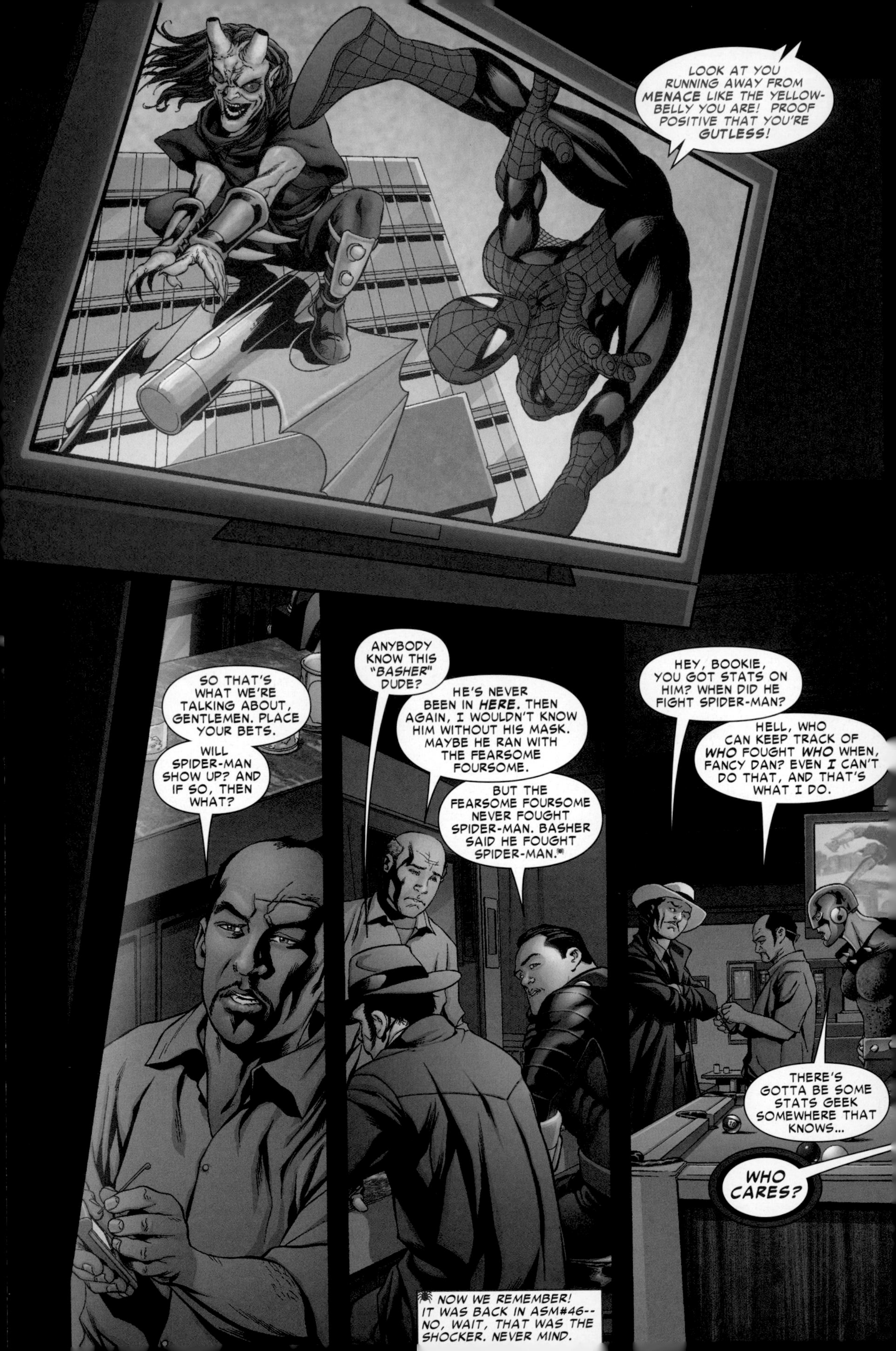
LOOK AT YOU RUNNING AWAY FROM MENACE LIKE THE YELLOW-BELLY YOU ARE! PROOF POSITIVE THAT YOU'RE GUTLESS!
SO THAT'S WHAT WE'RE TALKING ABOUT, GENTLEMEN. PLACE YOUR BETS.
WILL SPIDER-MAN SHOW UP? AND IF SO, THEN WHAT?
ANYBODY KNOW THIS "BASHER" DUDE?
HE'S NEVER BEEN IN HERE. THEN AGAIN, I WOULDN'T KNOW HIM WITHOUT HIS MASK. MAYBE HE RAN WITH THE FEARSOME FOURSOME.
BUT THE FEARSOME FOURSOME NEVER FOUGHT SPIDER-MAN. BASHER SAID HE FOUGHT SPIDER-MAN.*
HEY, BOOKIE, YOU GOT STATS ON HIM? WHEN DID HE FIGHT SPIDER-MAN?
HELL, WHO CAN KEEP TRACK OF WHO FOUGHT WHO WHEN, FANCY DAN? EVEN I CAN'T DO THAT, AND THAT'S WHAT I DO.
THERE'S GOTTA BE SOME STATS GEEK SOMEWHERE THAT KNOWS...
WHO CARES?
NOW WE REMEMBER! IT WAS BACK IN ASM#46-- NO, WAIT, THAT WAS THE SHOCKER. NEVER MIND.

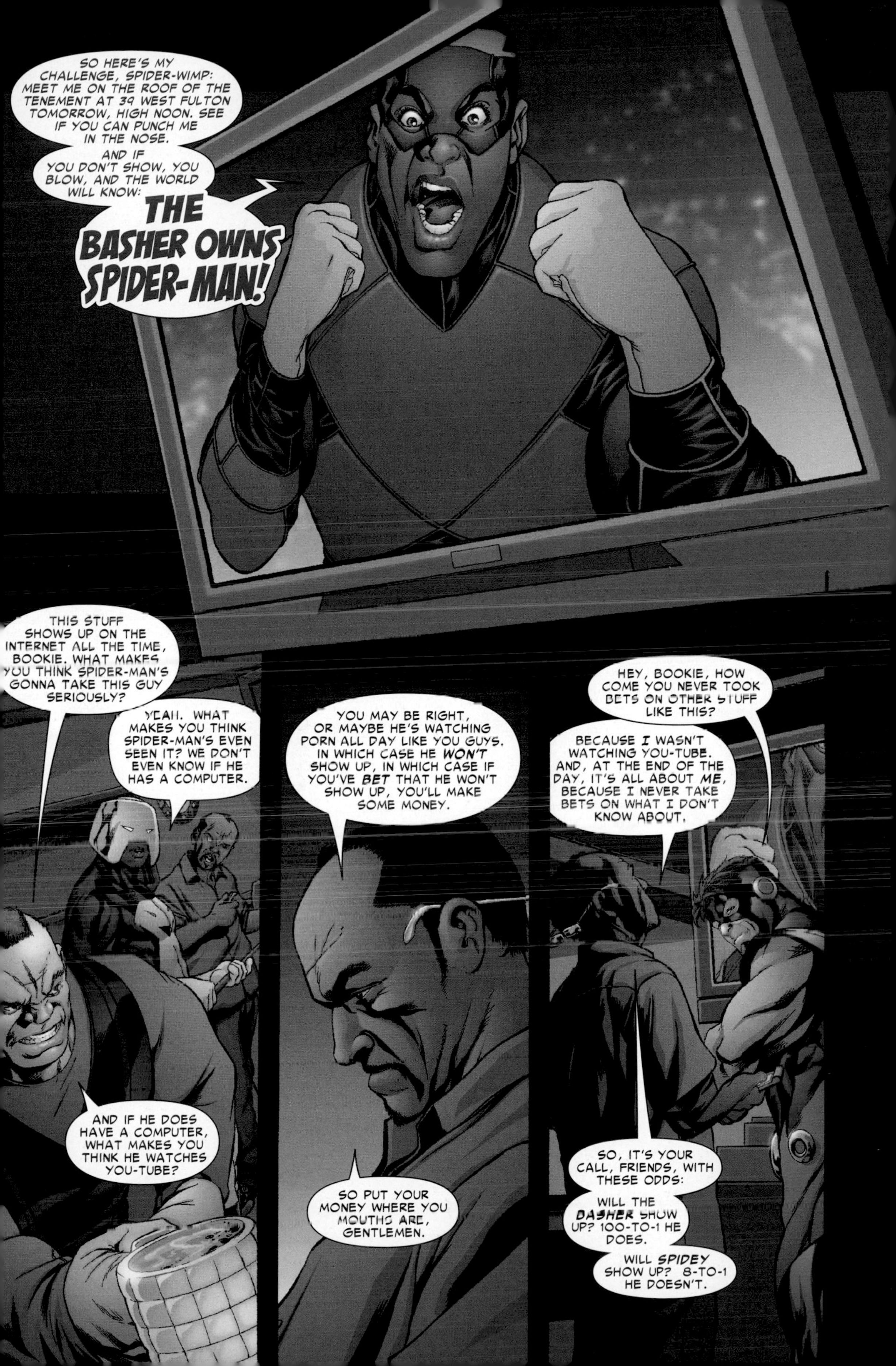
SO HERE'S MY CHALLENGE, SPIDER-WIMP: MEET ME ON THE ROOF OF THE TENEMENT AT 39 WEST FULTON TOMORROW, HIGH NOON. SEE IF YOU CAN PUNCH ME IN THE NOSE.
AND IF YOU DON'T SHOW, YOU BLOW, AND THE WORLD WILL KNOW:
THE BASHER OWNS SPIDER-MAN!
THIS STUFF SHOWS UP ON THE INTERNET ALL THE TIME, BOOKIE. WHAT MAKES YOU THINK SPIDER-MAN'S GONNA TAKE THIS GUY SERIOUSLY?
YEAH. WHAT MAKES YOU THINK SPIDER-MAN'S EVEN SEEN IT? WE DON'T EVEN KNOW IF HE HAS A COMPUTER.
AND IF HE DOES HAVE A COMPUTER, WHAT MAKES YOU THINK HE WATCHES YOU-TUBE?
YOU MAY BE RIGHT, OR MAYBE HE'S WATCHING PORN ALL DAY LIKE YOU GUYS. IN WHICH CASE HE WON'T SHOW UP, IN WHICH CASE IF YOU'VE BET THAT HE WON'T SHOW UP, YOU'LL MAKE SOME MONEY.
SO PUT YOUR MONEY WHERE YOU MOUTHS ARE, GENTLEMEN.
HEY, BOOKIE, HOW COME YOU NEVER TOOK BETS ON OTHER STUFF LIKE THIS?
BECAUSE I WASN'T WATCHING YOU-TUBE. AND, AT THE END OF THE DAY, IT'S ALL ABOUT ME, BECAUSE I NEVER TAKE BETS ON WHAT I DON'T KNOW ABOUT.
SO, IT'S YOUR CALL, FRIENDS, WITH THESE ODDS:
WILL THE BASHER SHOW UP? 100-TO-1 HE DOES.
WILL SPIDEY SHOW UP? 8-TO-1 HE DOESN'T.

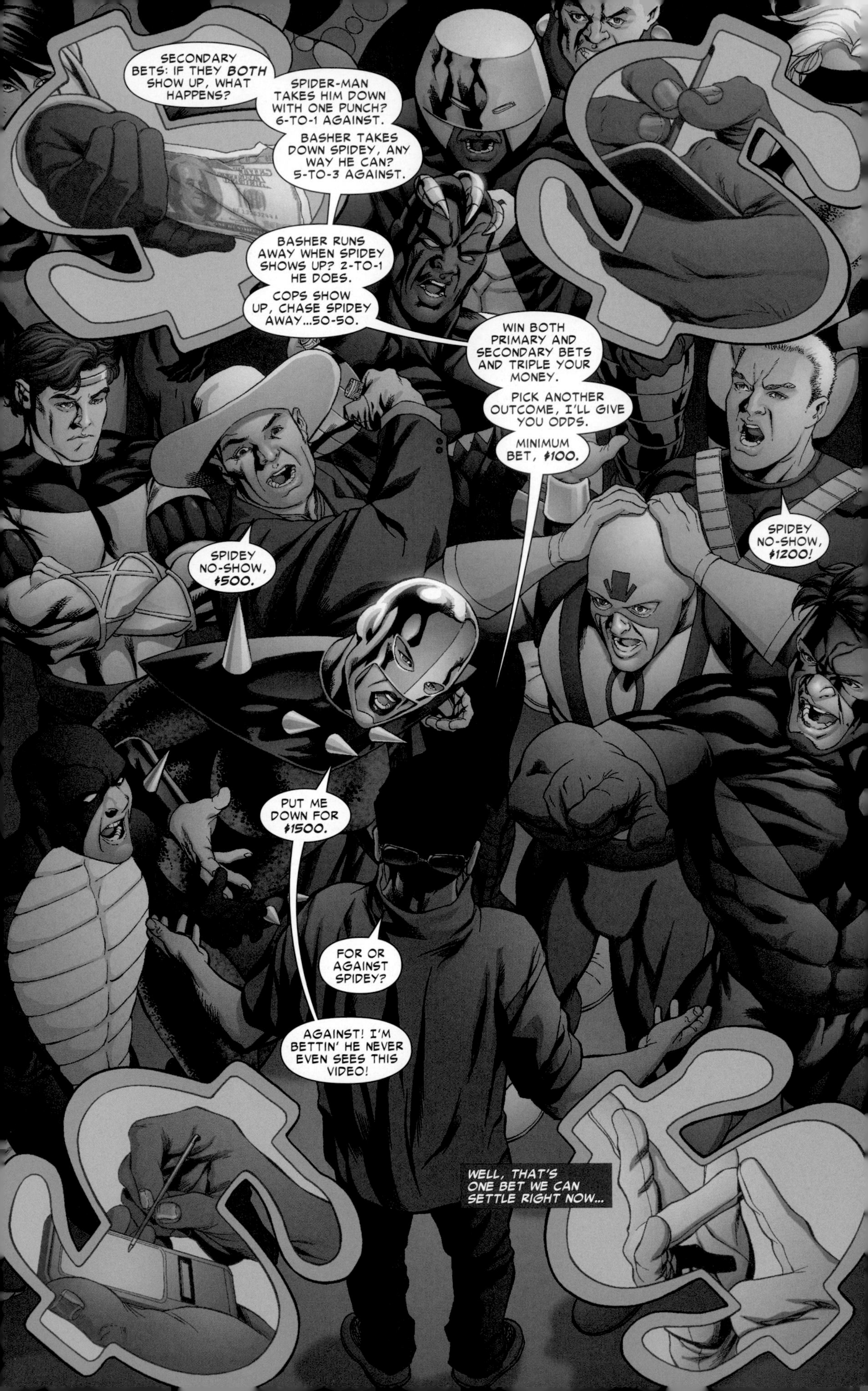
SECONDARY BETS: IF THEY *BOTH* SHOW UP, WHAT HAPPENS?
SPIDER-MAN TAKES HIM DOWN WITH ONE PUNCH? 6-TO-1 AGAINST.
BASHER TAKES DOWN SPIDEY, ANY WAY HE CAN? 5-TO-3 AGAINST.
BASHER RUNS AWAY WHEN SPIDEY SHOWS UP? 2-TO-1 HE DOES.
COPS SHOW UP, CHASE SPIDEY AWAY...50-50.
WIN BOTH PRIMARY AND SECONDARY BETS AND TRIPLE YOUR MONEY.
PICK ANOTHER OUTCOME, I'LL GIVE YOU ODDS.
MINIMUM BET, **$100.**
SPIDEY NO-SHOW, **$500.**
SPIDEY NO-SHOW, **$1200!**
PUT ME DOWN FOR **$1500.**
FOR OR AGAINST SPIDEY?
AGAINST! I'M BETTIN' HE NEVER EVEN SEES THIS VIDEO!
WELL, THAT'S ONE BET WE CAN SETTLE RIGHT NOW...

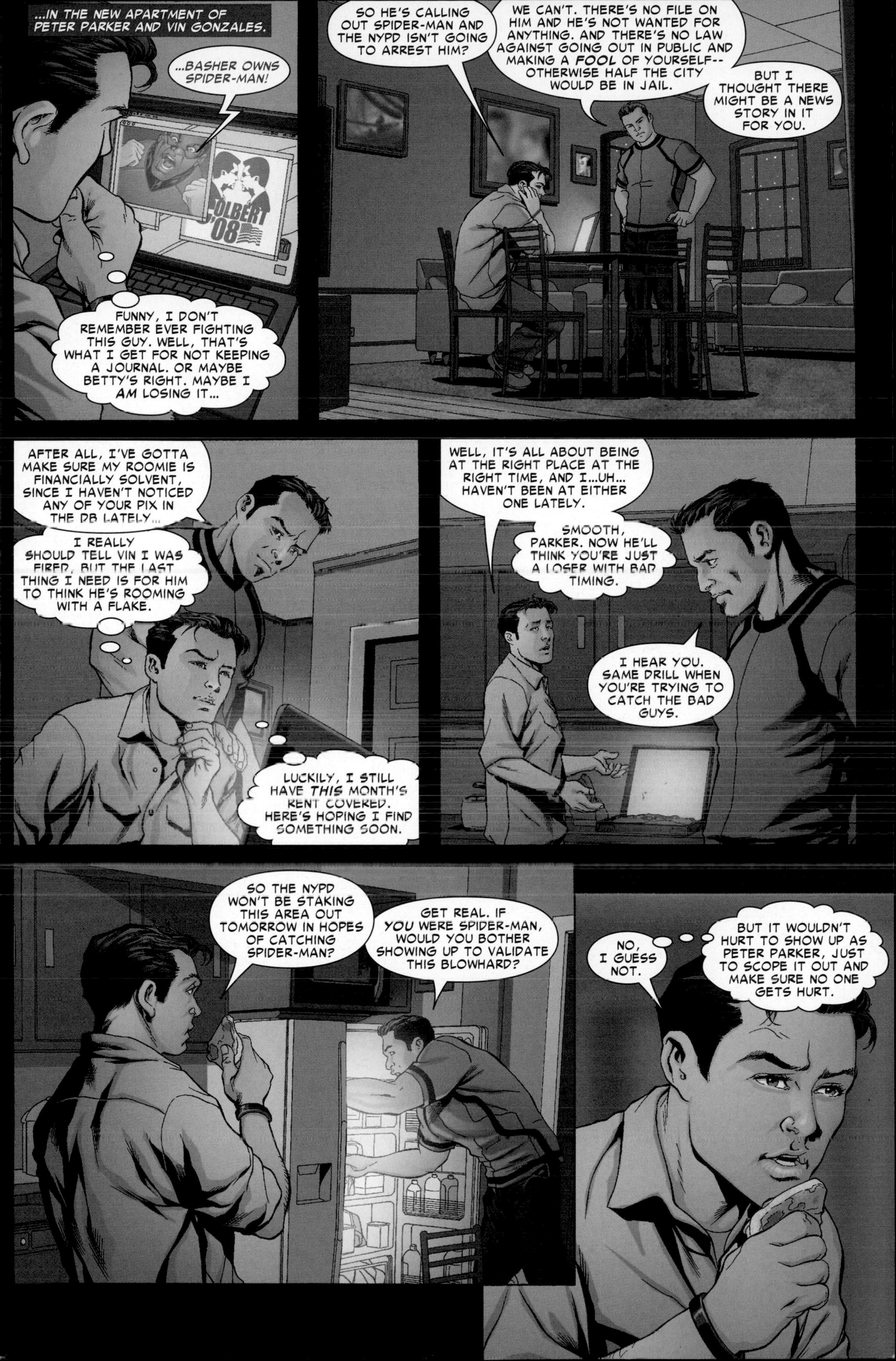
...IN THE NEW APARTMENT OF PETER PARKER AND VIN GONZALES.
...BASHER OWNS SPIDER-MAN!
COLBERT '08
FUNNY, I DON'T REMEMBER EVER FIGHTING THIS GUY. WELL, THAT'S WHAT I GET FOR NOT KEEPING A JOURNAL. OR MAYBE BETTY'S RIGHT. MAYBE I AM LOSING IT...
SO HE'S CALLING OUT SPIDER-MAN AND THE NYPD ISN'T GOING TO ARREST HIM?
WE CAN'T. THERE'S NO FILE ON HIM AND HE'S NOT WANTED FOR ANYTHING. AND THERE'S NO LAW AGAINST GOING OUT IN PUBLIC AND MAKING A FOOL OF YOURSELF-- OTHERWISE HALF THE CITY WOULD BE IN JAIL.
BUT I THOUGHT THERE MIGHT BE A NEWS STORY IN IT FOR YOU.
AFTER ALL, I'VE GOTTA MAKE SURE MY ROOMIE IS FINANCIALLY SOLVENT, SINCE I HAVEN'T NOTICED ANY OF YOUR PIX IN THE DB LATELY...
I REALLY SHOULD TELL VIN I WAS FIRED, BUT THE LAST THING I NEED IS FOR HIM TO THINK HE'S ROOMING WITH A FLAKE.
LUCKILY, I STILL HAVE THIS MONTH'S RENT COVERED. HERE'S HOPING I FIND SOMETHING SOON.
WELL, IT'S ALL ABOUT BEING AT THE RIGHT PLACE AT THE RIGHT TIME, AND I...UH... HAVEN'T BEEN AT EITHER ONE LATELY.
SMOOTH, PARKER. NOW HE'LL THINK YOU'RE JUST A LOSER WITH BAD TIMING.
I HEAR YOU. SAME DRILL WHEN YOU'RE TRYING TO CATCH THE BAD GUYS.
SO THE NYPD WON'T BE STAKING THIS AREA OUT TOMORROW IN HOPES OF CATCHING SPIDER-MAN?
GET REAL. IF YOU WERE SPIDER-MAN, WOULD YOU BOTHER SHOWING UP TO VALIDATE THIS BLOWHARD?
NO, I GUESS NOT.
BUT IT WOULDN'T HURT TO SHOW UP AS PETER PARKER, JUST TO SCOPE IT OUT AND MAKE SURE NO ONE GETS HURT.

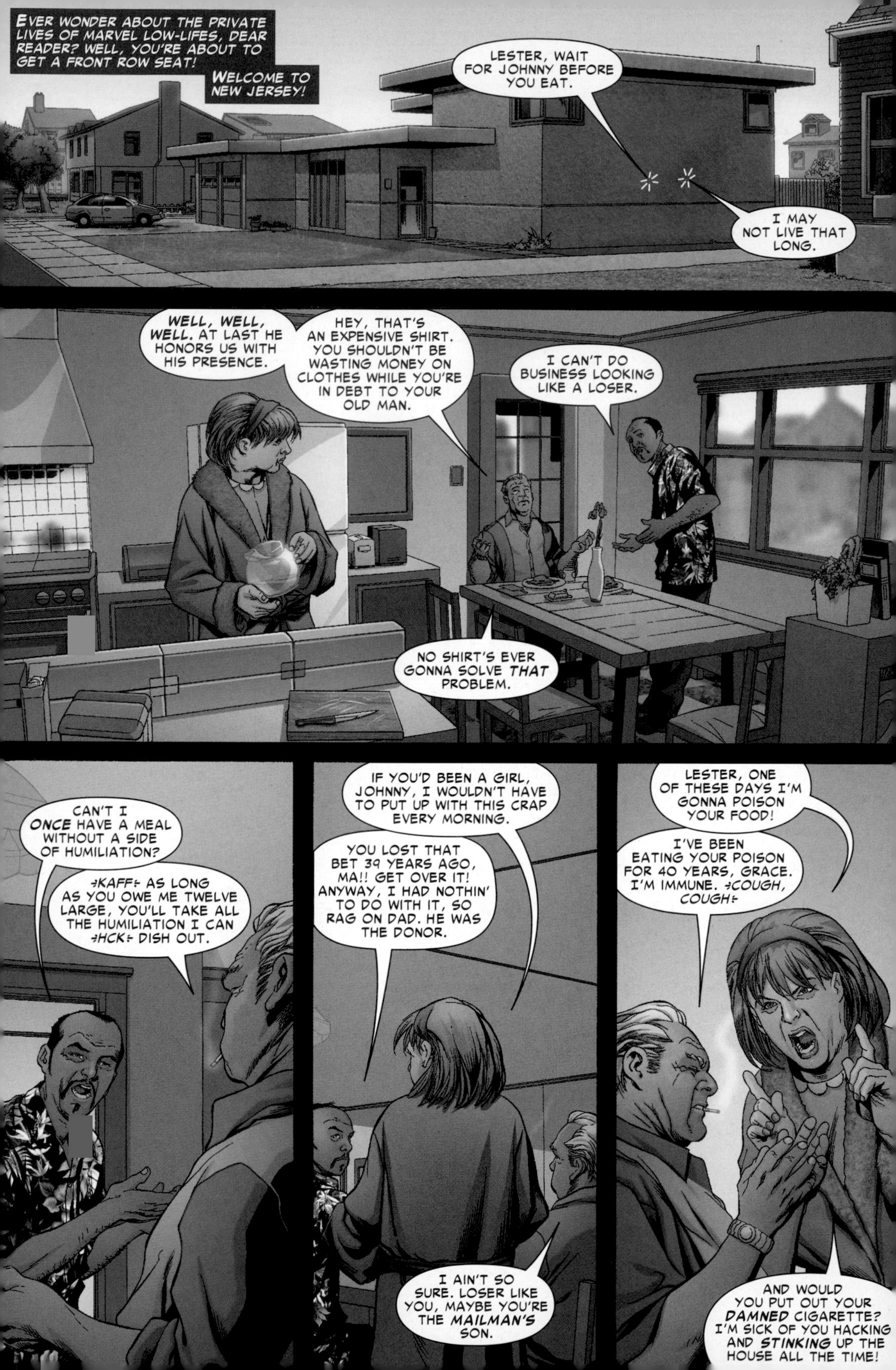
EVER WONDER ABOUT THE PRIVATE LIVES OF MARVEL LOW-LIFES, DEAR READER? WELL, YOU'RE ABOUT TO GET A FRONT ROW SEAT!
WELCOME TO NEW JERSEY!
LESTER, WAIT FOR JOHNNY BEFORE YOU EAT.
I MAY NOT LIVE THAT LONG.
WELL, WELL, WELL. AT LAST HE HONORS US WITH HIS PRESENCE.
HEY, THAT'S AN EXPENSIVE SHIRT. YOU SHOULDN'T BE WASTING MONEY ON CLOTHES WHILE YOU'RE IN DEBT TO YOUR OLD MAN.
I CAN'T DO BUSINESS LOOKING LIKE A LOSER.
NO SHIRT'S EVER GONNA SOLVE THAT PROBLEM.
CAN'T I ONCE HAVE A MEAL WITHOUT A SIDE OF HUMILIATION?
⊰KAFF⊱ AS LONG AS YOU OWE ME TWELVE LARGE, YOU'LL TAKE ALL THE HUMILIATION I CAN ⊰HCK⊱ DISH OUT.
IF YOU'D BEEN A GIRL, JOHNNY, I WOULDN'T HAVE TO PUT UP WITH THIS CRAP EVERY MORNING.
YOU LOST THAT BET 39 YEARS AGO, MA!! GET OVER IT! ANYWAY, I HAD NOTHIN' TO DO WITH IT, SO RAG ON DAD. HE WAS THE DONOR.
I AIN'T SO SURE. LOSER LIKE YOU, MAYBE YOU'RE THE MAILMAN'S SON.
LESTER, ONE OF THESE DAYS I'M GONNA POISON YOUR FOOD!
I'VE BEEN EATING YOUR POISON FOR 40 YEARS, GRACE. I'M IMMUNE. ⊰COUGH, COUGH⊱
AND WOULD YOU PUT OUT YOUR DAMNED CIGARETTE? I'M SICK OF YOU HACKING AND STINKING UP THE HOUSE ALL THE TIME!

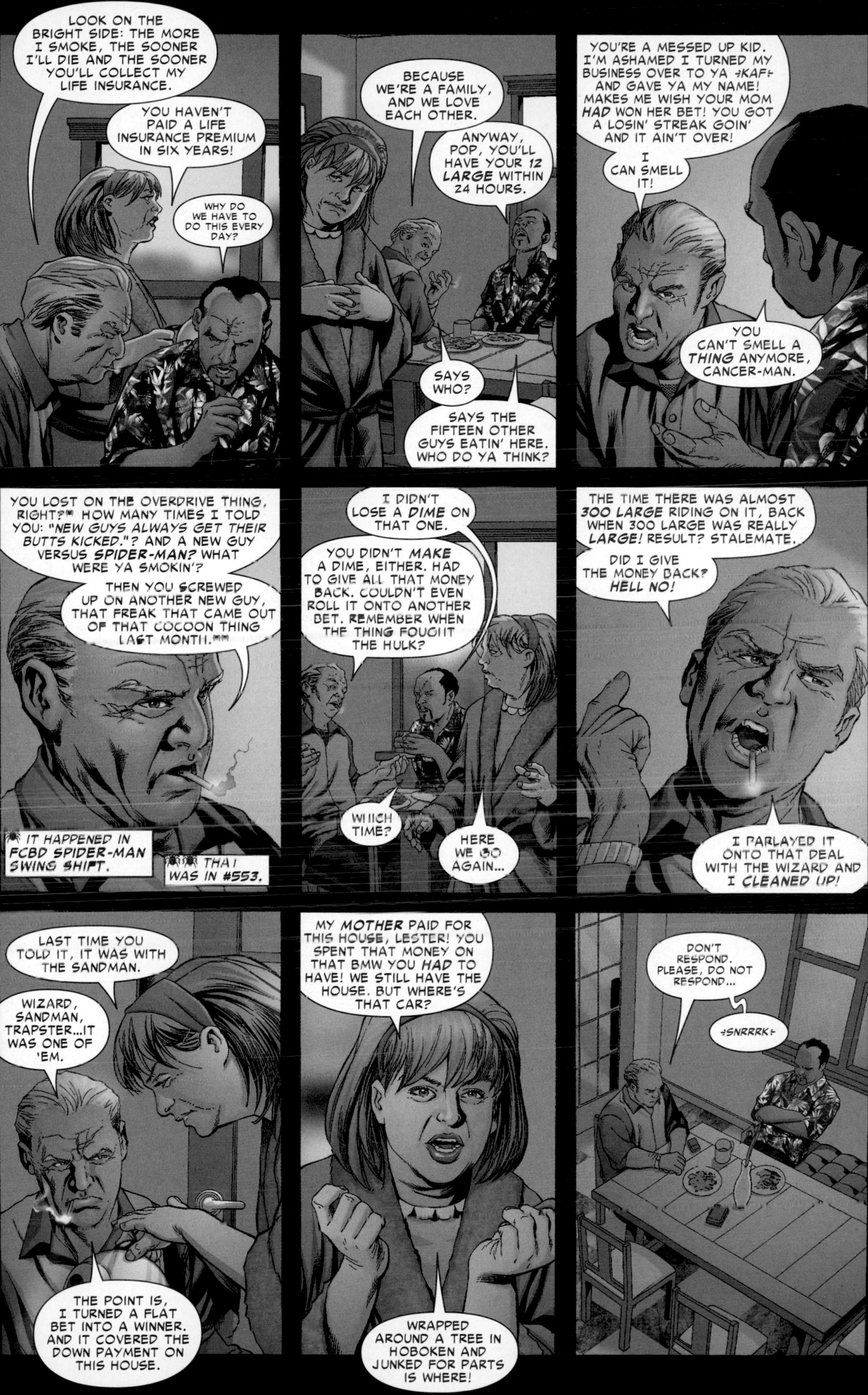

LOOK ON THE BRIGHT SIDE: THE MORE I SMOKE, THE SOONER I'LL DIE AND THE SOONER YOU'LL COLLECT MY LIFE INSURANCE.
YOU HAVEN'T PAID A LIFE INSURANCE PREMIUM IN SIX YEARS!
WHY DO WE HAVE TO DO THIS EVERY DAY?
BECAUSE WE'RE A FAMILY, AND WE LOVE EACH OTHER.
ANYWAY, POP, YOU'LL HAVE YOUR 12 LARGE WITHIN 24 HOURS.
SAYS WHO?
SAYS THE FIFTEEN OTHER GUYS EATIN' HERE. WHO DO YA THINK?
YOU'RE A MESSED UP KID. I'M ASHAMED I TURNED MY BUSINESS OVER TO YA -KAF- AND GAVE YA MY NAME! MAKES ME WISH YOUR MOM HAD WON HER BET! YOU GOT A LOSIN' STREAK GOIN' AND IT AIN'T OVER!
I CAN SMELL IT!
YOU CAN'T SMELL A THING ANYMORE, CANCER-MAN.
YOU LOST ON THE OVERDRIVE THING, RIGHT?* HOW MANY TIMES I TOLD YOU: "NEW GUYS ALWAYS GET THEIR BUTTS KICKED."? AND A NEW GUY VERSUS SPIDER-MAN? WHAT WERE YA SMOKIN'?
THEN YOU SCREWED UP ON ANOTHER NEW GUY, THAT FREAK THAT CAME OUT OF THAT COCOON THING LAST MONTH.**
* IT HAPPENED IN FCBD SPIDER-MAN SWING SHIFT.
** THAT WAS IN #553.
I DIDN'T LOSE A DIME ON THAT ONE.
YOU DIDN'T MAKE A DIME, EITHER. HAD TO GIVE ALL THAT MONEY BACK. COULDN'T EVEN ROLL IT ONTO ANOTHER BET. REMEMBER WHEN THE THING FOUGHT THE HULK?
WHICH TIME?
HERE WE GO AGAIN...
THE TIME THERE WAS ALMOST 300 LARGE RIDING ON IT, BACK WHEN 300 LARGE WAS REALLY LARGE! RESULT? STALEMATE.
DID I GIVE THE MONEY BACK? HELL NO!
I PARLAYED IT ONTO THAT DEAL WITH THE WIZARD AND I CLEANED UP!
LAST TIME YOU TOLD IT, IT WAS WITH THE SANDMAN.
WIZARD, SANDMAN, TRAPSTER...IT WAS ONE OF 'EM.
THE POINT IS, I TURNED A FLAT BET INTO A WINNER. AND IT COVERED THE DOWN PAYMENT ON THIS HOUSE.
MY MOTHER PAID FOR THIS HOUSE, LESTER! YOU SPENT THAT MONEY ON THAT BMW YOU HAD TO HAVE! WE STILL HAVE THE HOUSE. BUT WHERE'S THAT CAR?
WRAPPED AROUND A TREE IN HOBOKEN AND JUNKED FOR PARTS IS WHERE!
DON'T RESPOND. PLEASE, DO NOT RESPOND...
-SNRRRK-

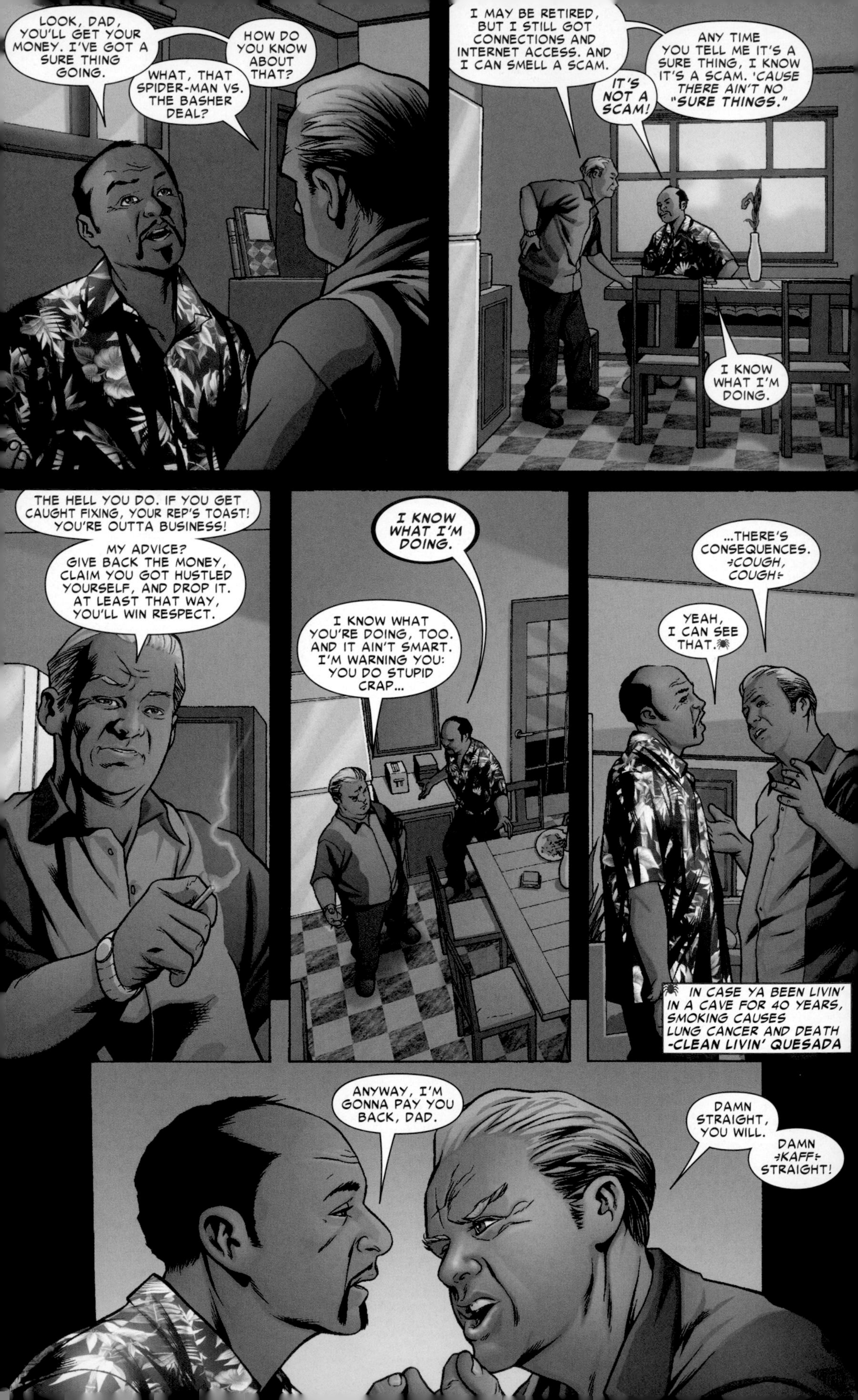
LOOK, DAD, YOU'LL GET YOUR MONEY. I'VE GOT A SURE THING GOING.
HOW DO YOU KNOW ABOUT THAT?
WHAT, THAT SPIDER-MAN VS. THE BASHER DEAL?
I MAY BE RETIRED, BUT I STILL GOT CONNECTIONS AND INTERNET ACCESS. AND I CAN SMELL A SCAM.
ANY TIME YOU TELL ME IT'S A SURE THING, I KNOW IT'S A SCAM. 'CAUSE THERE AIN'T NO "SURE THINGS."
IT'S NOT A SCAM!
I KNOW WHAT I'M DOING.
THE HELL YOU DO. IF YOU GET CAUGHT FIXING, YOUR REP'S TOAST! YOU'RE OUTTA BUSINESS!
MY ADVICE? GIVE BACK THE MONEY, CLAIM YOU GOT HUSTLED YOURSELF, AND DROP IT. AT LEAST THAT WAY, YOU'LL WIN RESPECT.
I KNOW WHAT I'M DOING.
I KNOW WHAT YOU'RE DOING, TOO. AND IT AIN'T SMART. I'M WARNING YOU: YOU DO STUPID CRAP...
...THERE'S CONSEQUENCES. COUGH, COUGH
YEAH, I CAN SEE THAT.
IN CASE YA BEEN LIVIN' IN A CAVE FOR 40 YEARS, SMOKING CAUSES LUNG CANCER AND DEATH -CLEAN LIVIN' QUESADA
ANYWAY, I'M GONNA PAY YOU BACK, DAD.
DAMN STRAIGHT, YOU WILL.
DAMN KAFF STRAIGHT!

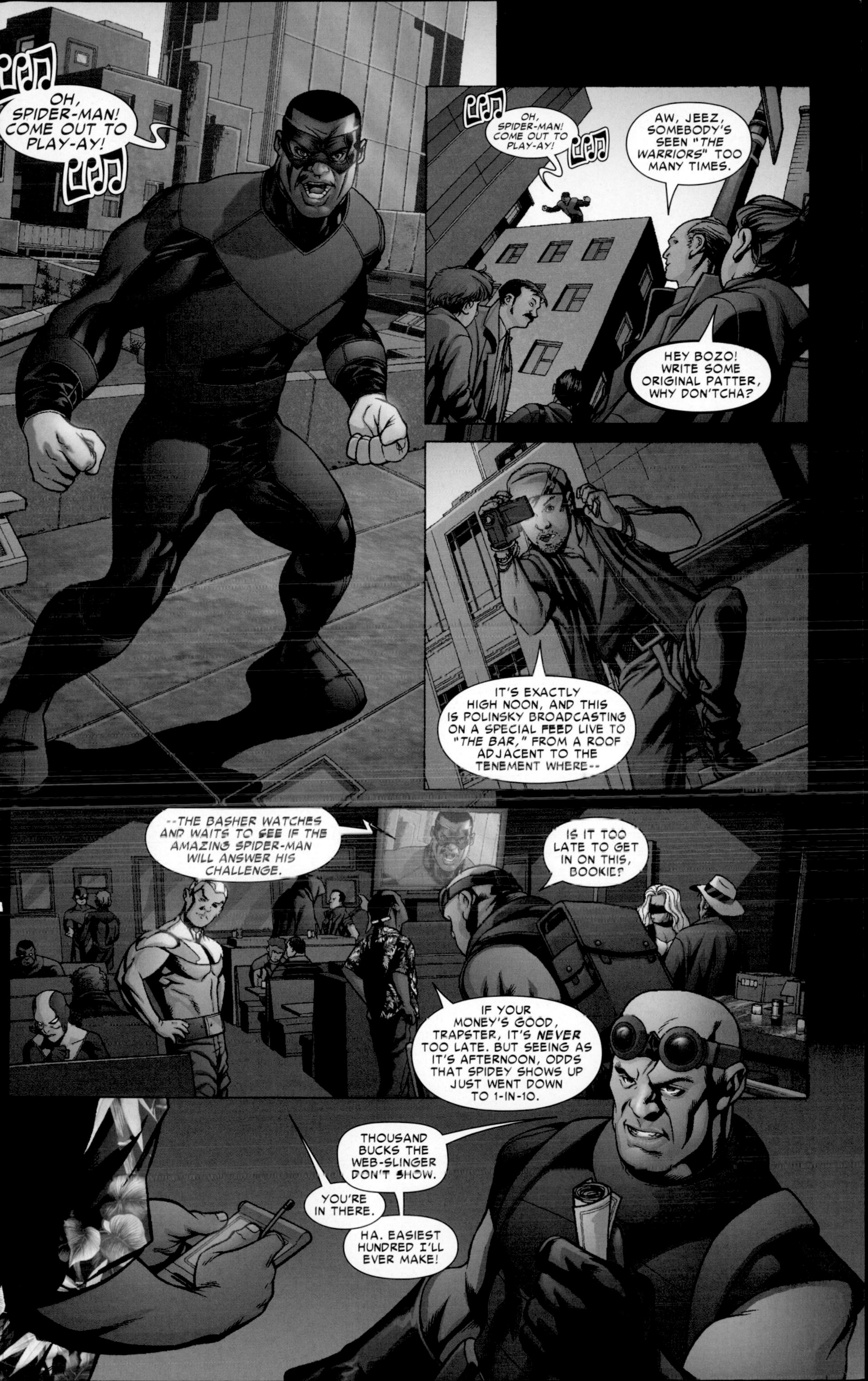
OH, SPIDER-MAN! COME OUT TO PLAY-AY!
OH, SPIDER-MAN! COME OUT TO PLAY-AY!
AW, JEEZ, SOMEBODY'S SEEN "THE WARRIORS" TOO MANY TIMES.
HEY BOZO! WRITE SOME ORIGINAL PATTER, WHY DON'TCHA?
IT'S EXACTLY HIGH NOON, AND THIS IS POLINSKY BROADCASTING ON A SPECIAL FEED LIVE TO "THE BAR," FROM A ROOF ADJACENT TO THE TENEMENT WHERE--
--THE BASHER WATCHES AND WAITS TO SEE IF THE AMAZING SPIDER-MAN WILL ANSWER HIS CHALLENGE.
IS IT TOO LATE TO GET IN ON THIS, BOOKIE?
IF YOUR MONEY'S GOOD, TRAPSTER, IT'S NEVER TOO LATE. BUT SEEING AS IT'S AFTERNOON, ODDS THAT SPIDEY SHOWS UP JUST WENT DOWN TO 1-IN-10.
THOUSAND BUCKS THE WEB-SLINGER DON'T SHOW.
YOU'RE IN THERE.
HA. EASIEST HUNDRED I'LL EVER MAKE!

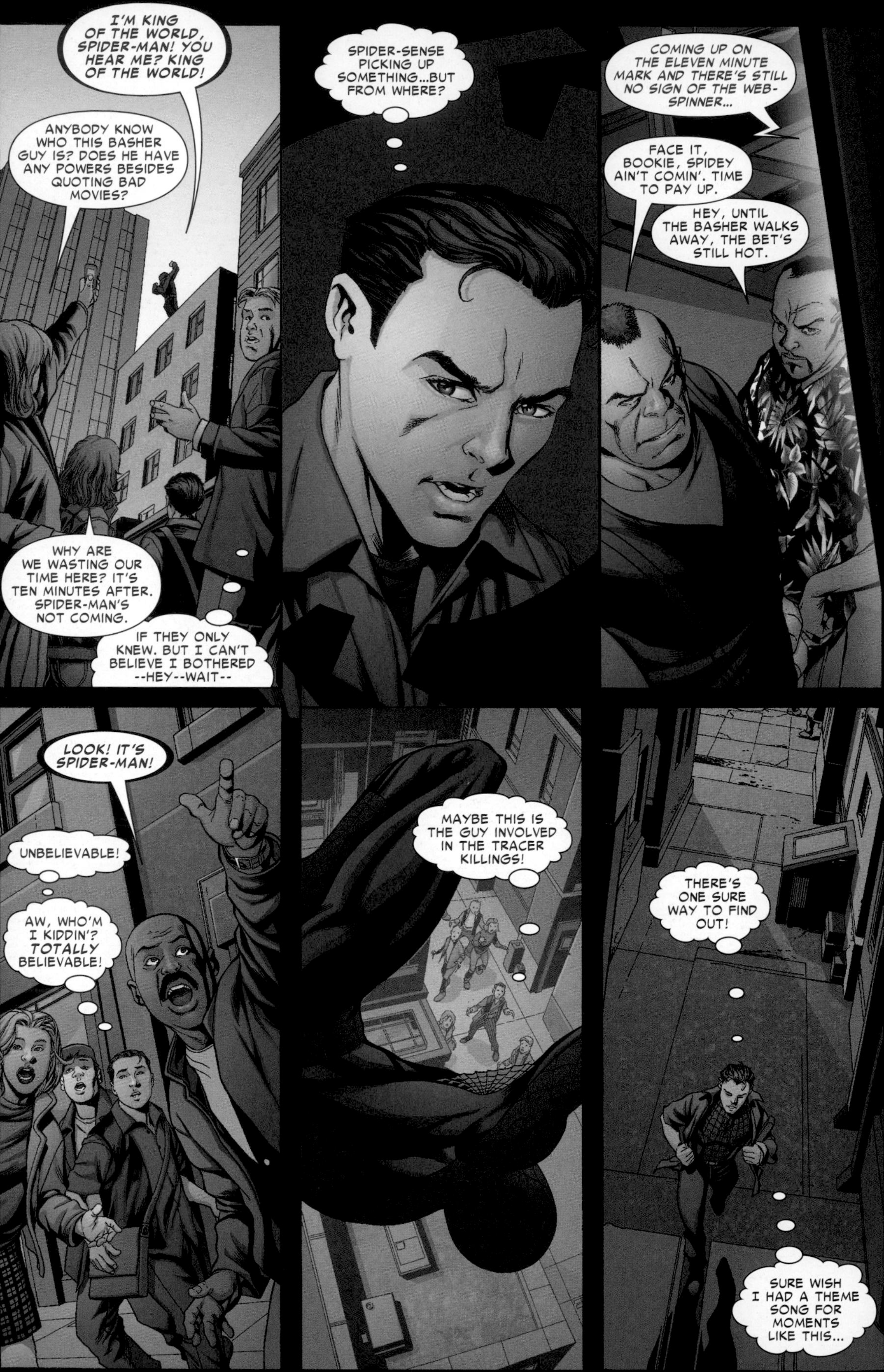
I'M KING OF THE WORLD, SPIDER-MAN! YOU HEAR ME? KING OF THE WORLD!
ANYBODY KNOW WHO THIS BASHER GUY IS? DOES HE HAVE ANY POWERS BESIDES QUOTING BAD MOVIES?
WHY ARE WE WASTING OUR TIME HERE? IT'S TEN MINUTES AFTER. SPIDER-MAN'S NOT COMING.
IF THEY ONLY KNEW. BUT I CAN'T BELIEVE I BOTHERED --HEY--WAIT--
SPIDER-SENSE PICKING UP SOMETHING...BUT FROM WHERE?
COMING UP ON THE ELEVEN MINUTE MARK AND THERE'S STILL NO SIGN OF THE WEB-SPINNER...
FACE IT, BOOKIE, SPIDEY AIN'T COMIN'. TIME TO PAY UP.
HEY, UNTIL THE BASHER WALKS AWAY, THE BET'S STILL HOT.
LOOK! IT'S SPIDER-MAN!
UNBELIEVABLE!
AW, WHO'M I KIDDIN'? TOTALLY BELIEVABLE!
MAYBE THIS IS THE GUY INVOLVED IN THE TRACER KILLINGS!
THERE'S ONE SURE WAY TO FIND OUT!
SURE WISH I HAD A THEME SONG FOR MOMENTS LIKE THIS...

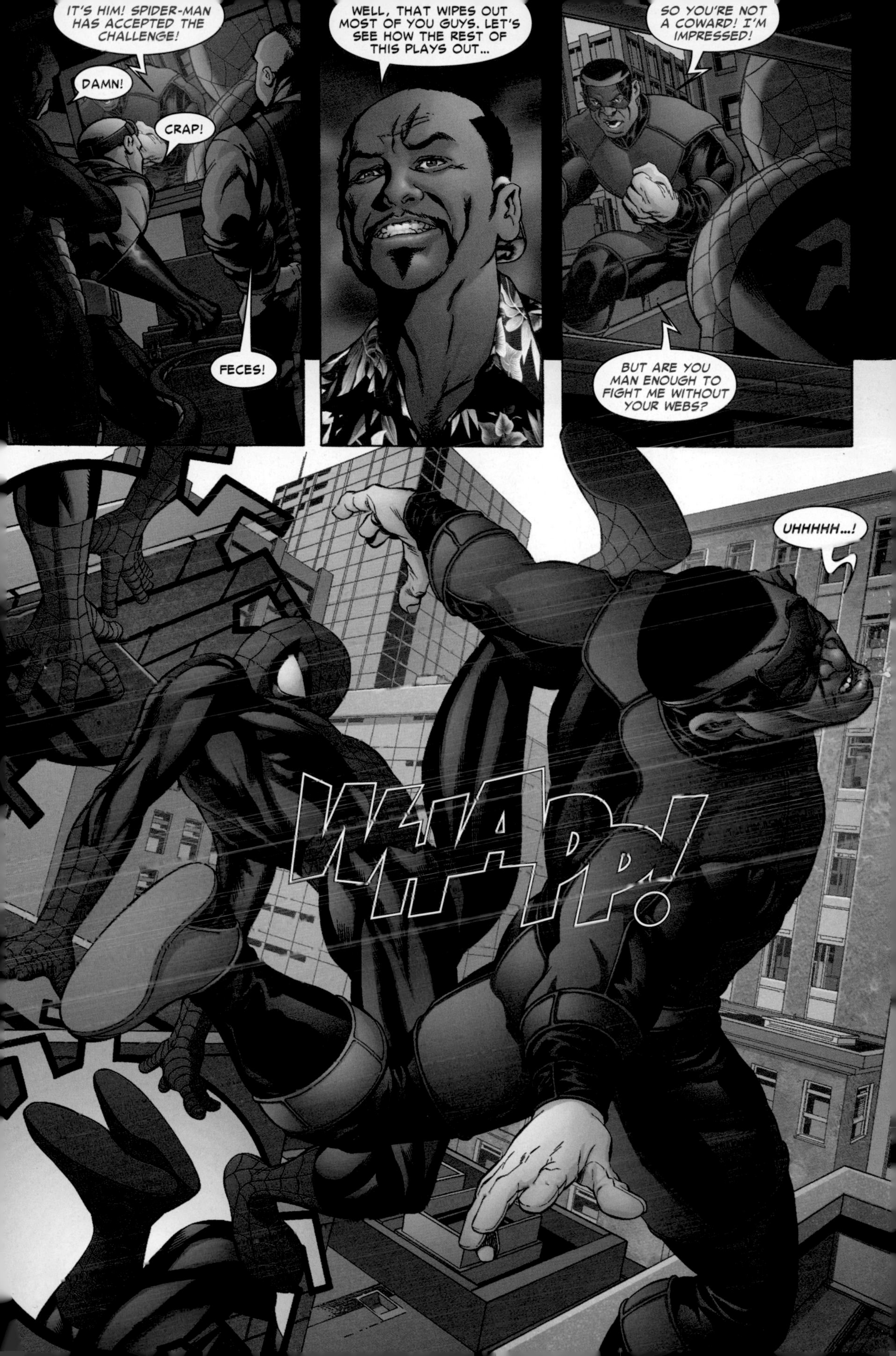
IT'S HIM! SPIDER-MAN HAS ACCEPTED THE CHALLENGE!
DAMN!
CRAP!
FECES!
WELL, THAT WIPES OUT MOST OF YOU GUYS. LET'S SEE HOW THE REST OF THIS PLAYS OUT...
SO YOU'RE NOT A COWARD! I'M IMPRESSED!
BUT ARE YOU MAN ENOUGH TO FIGHT ME WITHOUT YOUR WEBS?
WHAP!
UHHHHH...!

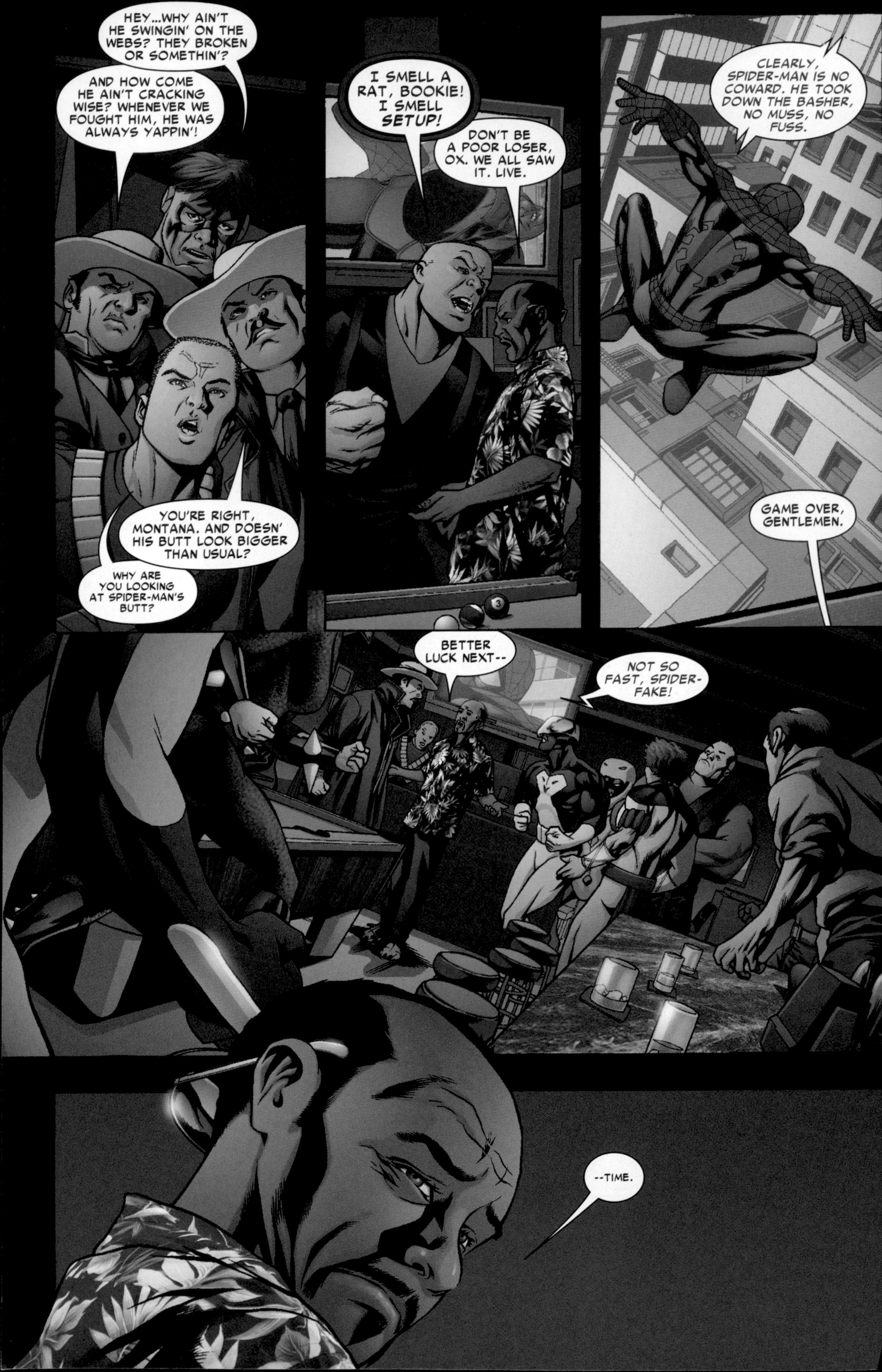
HEY...WHY AIN'T HE SWINGIN' ON THE WEBS? THEY BROKEN OR SOMETHIN'?
AND HOW COME HE AIN'T CRACKING WISE? WHENEVER WE FOUGHT HIM, HE WAS ALWAYS YAPPIN'!
YOU'RE RIGHT, MONTANA. AND DOESN' HIS BUTT LOOK BIGGER THAN USUAL?
WHY ARE YOU LOOKING AT SPIDER-MAN'S BUTT?
I SMELL A RAT, BOOKIE! I SMELL SETUP!
DON'T BE A POOR LOSER, OX. WE ALL SAW IT. LIVE.
CLEARLY, SPIDER-MAN IS NO COWARD. HE TOOK DOWN THE BASHER, NO MUSS, NO FUSS.
GAME OVER, GENTLEMEN.
BETTER LUCK NEXT--
NOT SO FAST, SPIDER-FAKE!
--TIME.

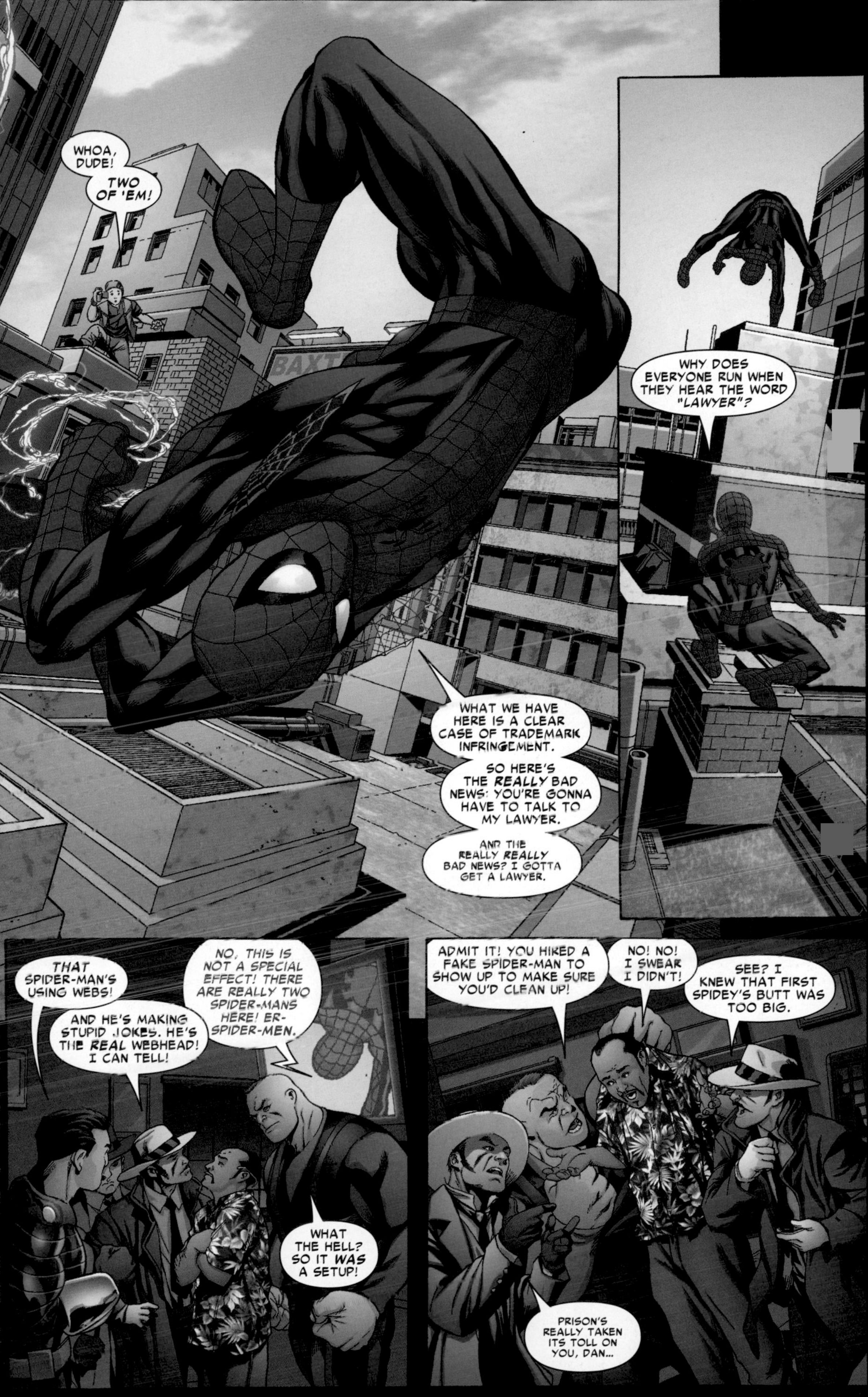
WHOA, DUDE!
TWO OF 'EM!
WHAT WE HAVE HERE IS A CLEAR CASE OF TRADEMARK INFRINGEMENT.
SO HERE'S THE REALLY BAD NEWS: YOU'RE GONNA HAVE TO TALK TO MY LAWYER.
AND THE REALLY REALLY BAD NEWS? I GOTTA GET A LAWYER.
WHY DOES EVERYONE RUN WHEN THEY HEAR THE WORD "LAWYER"?
THAT SPIDER-MAN'S USING WEBS!
AND HE'S MAKING STUPID JOKES. HE'S THE REAL WEBHEAD! I CAN TELL!
NO, THIS IS NOT A SPECIAL EFFECT! THERE ARE REALLY TWO SPIDER-MANS HERE! ER-SPIDER-MEN.
WHAT THE HELL? SO IT WAS A SETUP!
ADMIT IT! YOU HIRED A FAKE SPIDER-MAN TO SHOW UP TO MAKE SURE YOU'D CLEAN UP!
NO! NO! I SWEAR I DIDN'T!
SEE? I KNEW THAT FIRST SPIDEY'S BUTT WAS TOO BIG.
PRISON'S REALLY TAKEN ITS TOLL ON YOU, DAN...

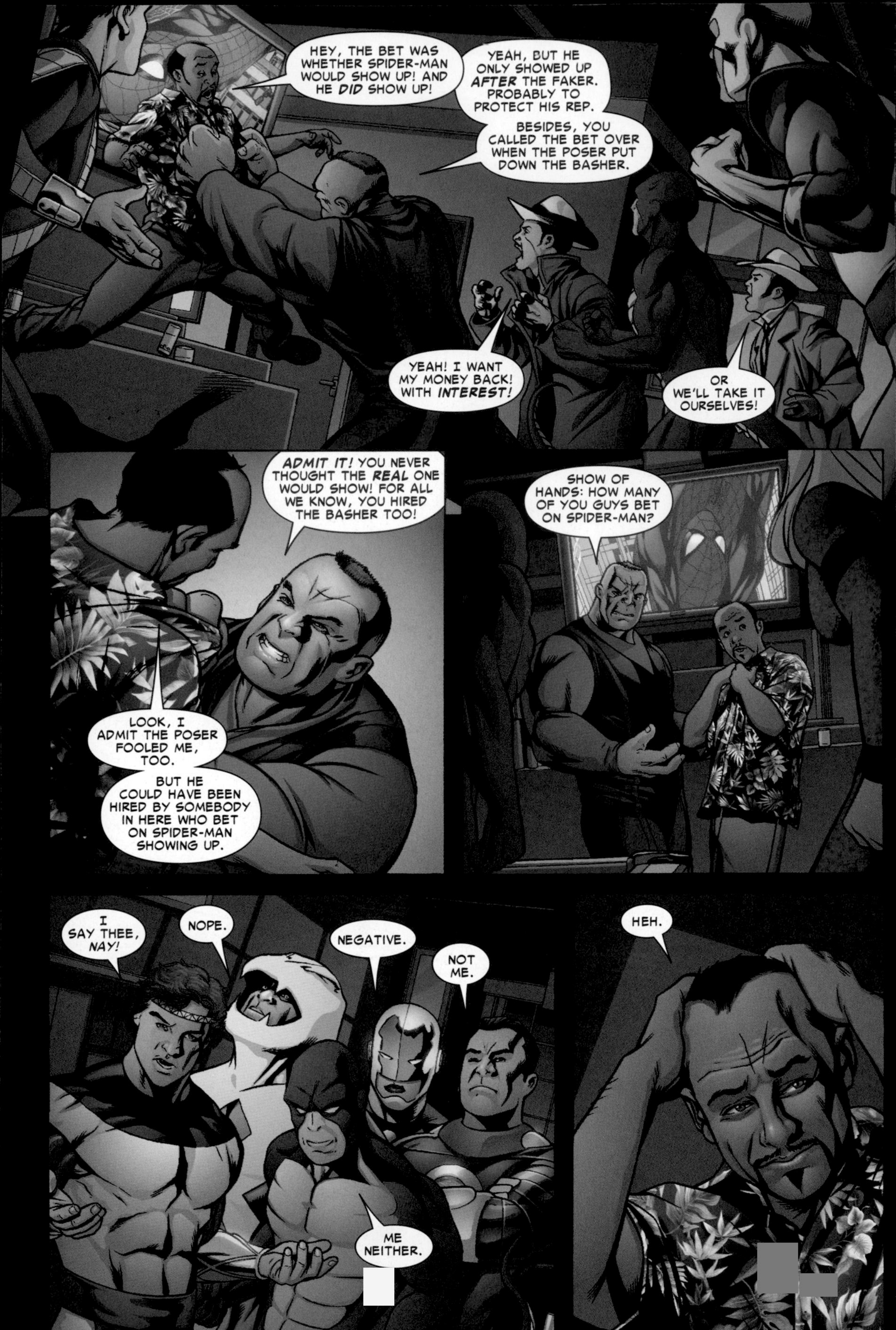
HEY, THE BET WAS WHETHER SPIDER-MAN WOULD SHOW UP! AND HE *DID* SHOW UP!
YEAH, BUT HE ONLY SHOWED UP *AFTER* THE FAKER. PROBABLY TO PROTECT HIS REP.
BESIDES, YOU CALLED THE BET OVER WHEN THE POSER PUT DOWN THE BASHER.
YEAH! I WANT MY MONEY BACK! WITH *INTEREST!*
OR WE'LL TAKE IT OURSELVES!
ADMIT IT! YOU NEVER THOUGHT THE *REAL* ONE WOULD SHOW! FOR ALL WE KNOW, YOU HIRED THE BASHER TOO!
LOOK, I ADMIT THE POSER FOOLED ME, TOO.
BUT HE COULD HAVE BEEN HIRED BY SOMEBODY IN HERE WHO BET ON SPIDER-MAN SHOWING UP.
SHOW OF HANDS: HOW MANY OF YOU GUYS BET ON SPIDER-MAN?
I SAY THEE, *NAY!*
NOPE.
NEGATIVE.
NOT ME.
ME NEITHER.
HEH.

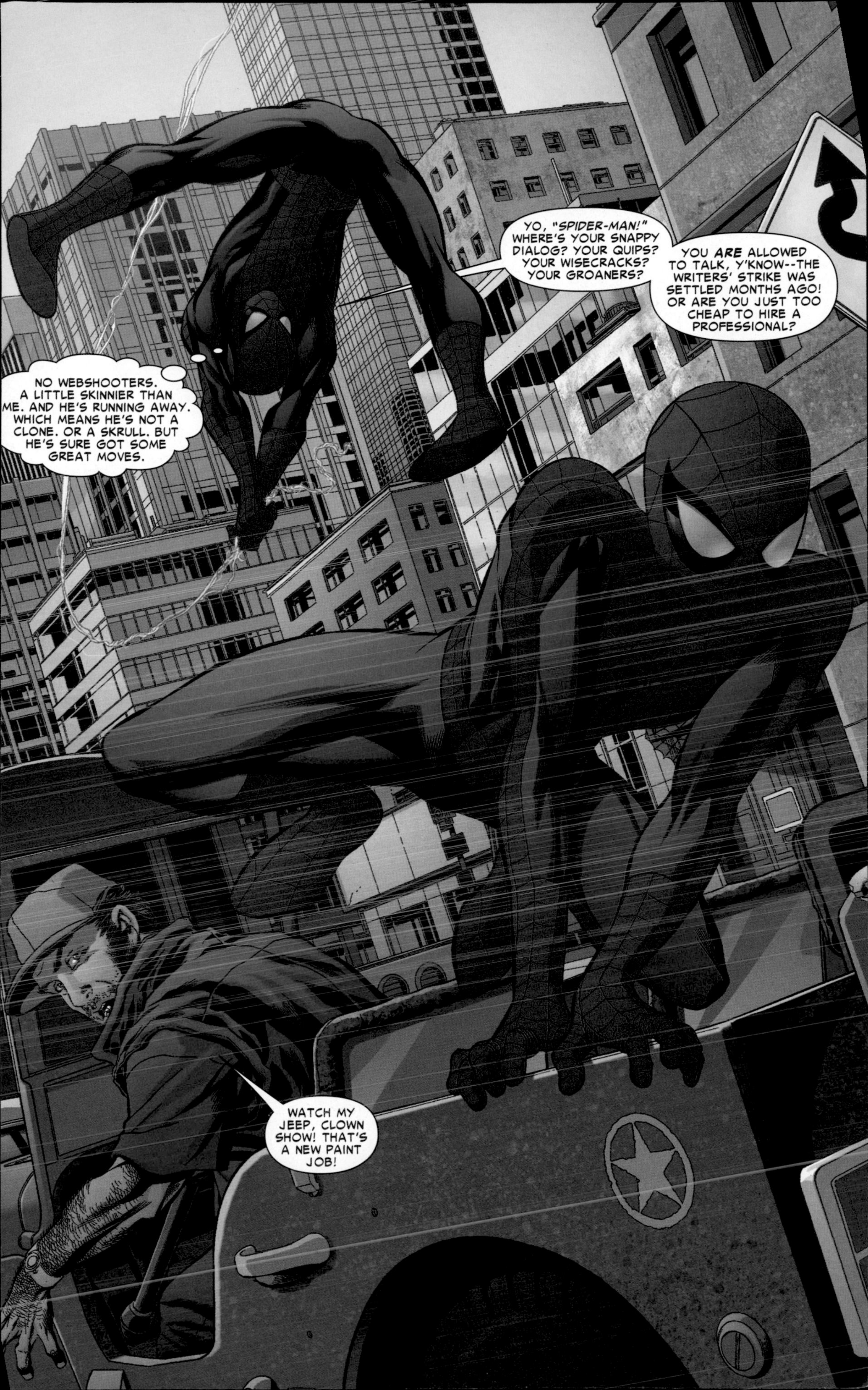
NO WEBSHOOTERS. A LITTLE SKINNIER THAN ME. AND HE'S RUNNING AWAY. WHICH MEANS HE'S NOT A CLONE. OR A SKRULL. BUT HE'S SURE GOT SOME GREAT MOVES.
YO, "SPIDER-MAN!" WHERE'S YOUR SNAPPY DIALOG? YOUR QUIPS? YOUR WISECRACKS? YOUR GROANERS?
YOU ARE ALLOWED TO TALK, Y'KNOW--THE WRITERS' STRIKE WAS SETTLED MONTHS AGO! OR ARE YOU JUST TOO CHEAP TO HIRE A PROFESSIONAL?
WATCH MY JEEP, CLOWN SHOW! THAT'S A NEW PAINT JOB!

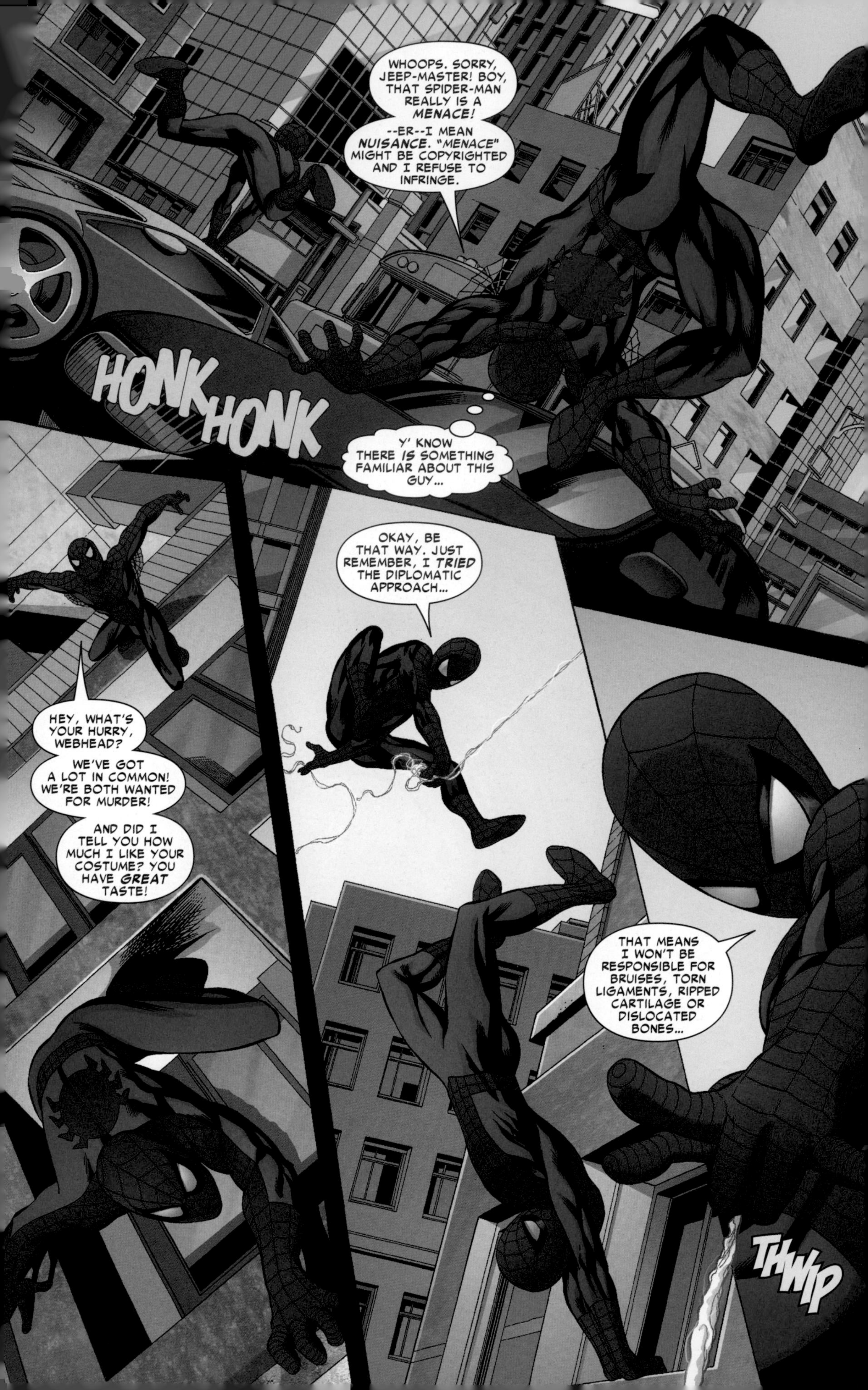

WHOOPS. SORRY, JEEP-MASTER! BOY, THAT SPIDER-MAN REALLY IS A *MENACE!*
--ER--I MEAN *NUISANCE.* "MENACE" MIGHT BE COPYRIGHTED AND I REFUSE TO INFRINGE.
HONK HONK
Y' KNOW THERE *IS* SOMETHING FAMILIAR ABOUT THIS GUY...
HEY, WHAT'S YOUR HURRY, WEBHEAD?
WE'VE GOT A LOT IN COMMON! WE'RE BOTH WANTED FOR MURDER!
AND DID I TELL YOU HOW MUCH I LIKE YOUR COSTUME? YOU HAVE *GREAT* TASTE!
OKAY, BE THAT WAY. JUST REMEMBER, I *TRIED* THE DIPLOMATIC APPROACH...
THAT MEANS I WON'T BE RESPONSIBLE FOR BRUISES, TORN LIGAMENTS, RIPPED CARTILAGE OR DISLOCATED BONES...
THWIP

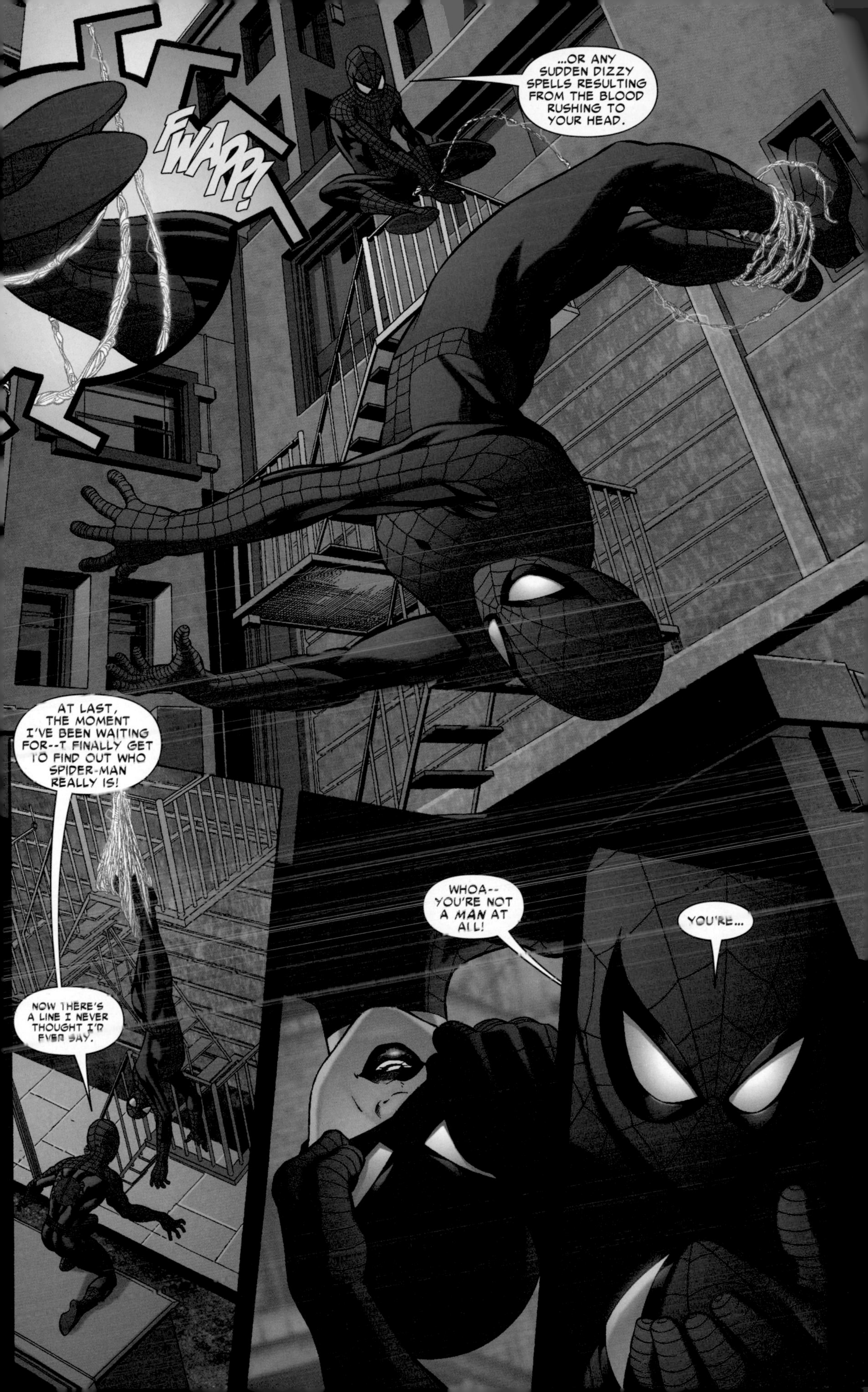
FWAPP!
...OR ANY SUDDEN DIZZY SPELLS RESULTING FROM THE BLOOD RUSHING TO YOUR HEAD.
AT LAST, THE MOMENT I'VE BEEN WAITING FOR--I FINALLY GET TO FIND OUT WHO SPIDER-MAN REALLY IS!
NOW THERE'S A LINE I NEVER THOUGHT I'D EVER SAY.
WHOA-- YOU'RE NOT A MAN AT ALL!
YOU'RE...

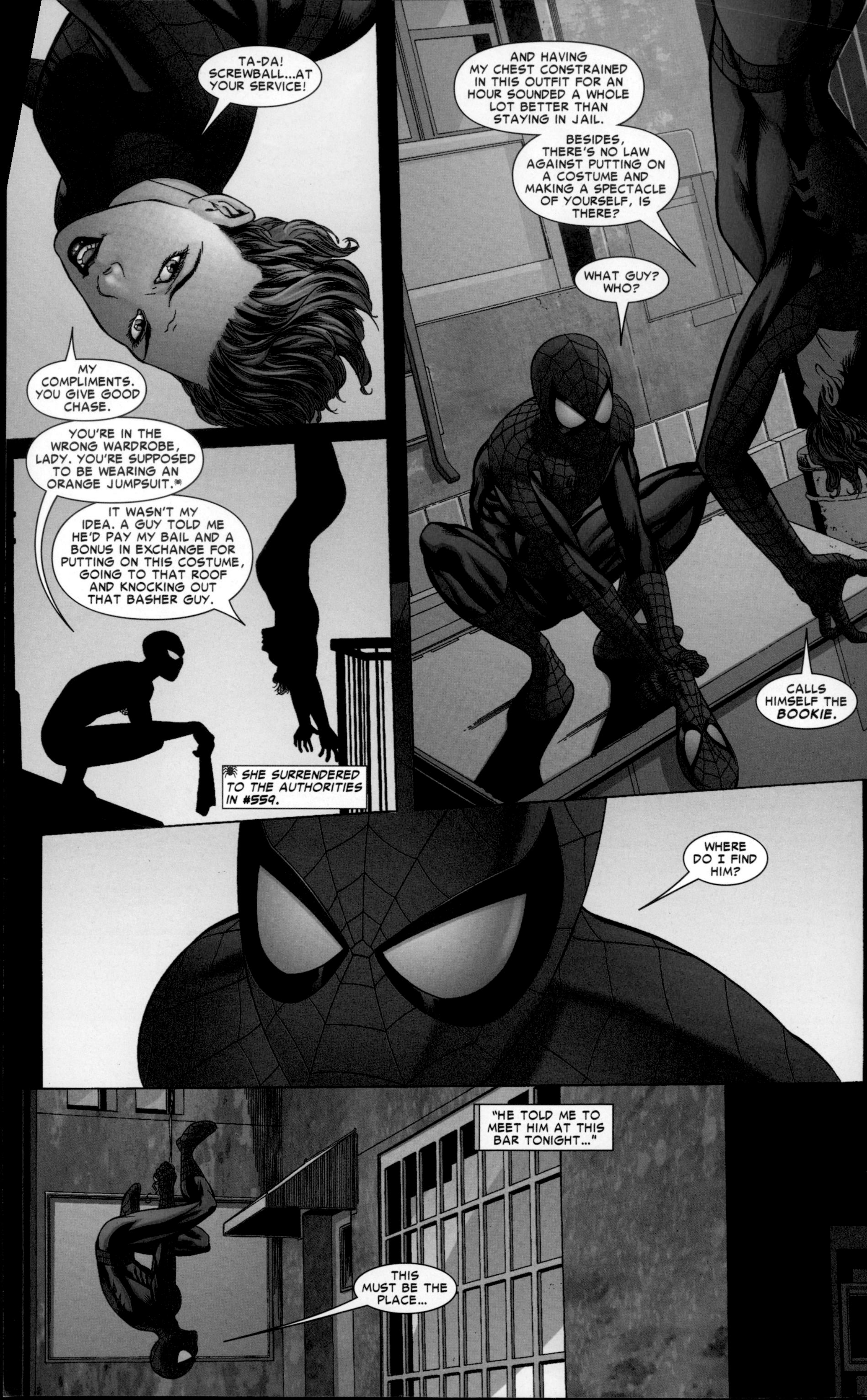
TA-DA! SCREWBALL...AT YOUR SERVICE!
MY COMPLIMENTS. YOU GIVE GOOD CHASE.
YOU'RE IN THE WRONG WARDROBE, LADY. YOU'RE SUPPOSED TO BE WEARING AN ORANGE JUMPSUIT.
IT WASN'T MY IDEA. A GUY TOLD ME HE'D PAY MY BAIL AND A BONUS IN EXCHANGE FOR PUTTING ON THIS COSTUME, GOING TO THAT ROOF AND KNOCKING OUT THAT BASHER GUY.
SHE SURRENDERED TO THE AUTHORITIES IN #559.
AND HAVING MY CHEST CONSTRAINED IN THIS OUTFIT FOR AN HOUR SOUNDED A WHOLE LOT BETTER THAN STAYING IN JAIL.
BESIDES, THERE'S NO LAW AGAINST PUTTING ON A COSTUME AND MAKING A SPECTACLE OF YOURSELF, IS THERE?
WHAT GUY? WHO?
CALLS HIMSELF THE BOOKIE.
WHERE DO I FIND HIM?
"HE TOLD ME TO MEET HIM AT THIS BAR TONIGHT..."
THIS MUST BE THE PLACE...

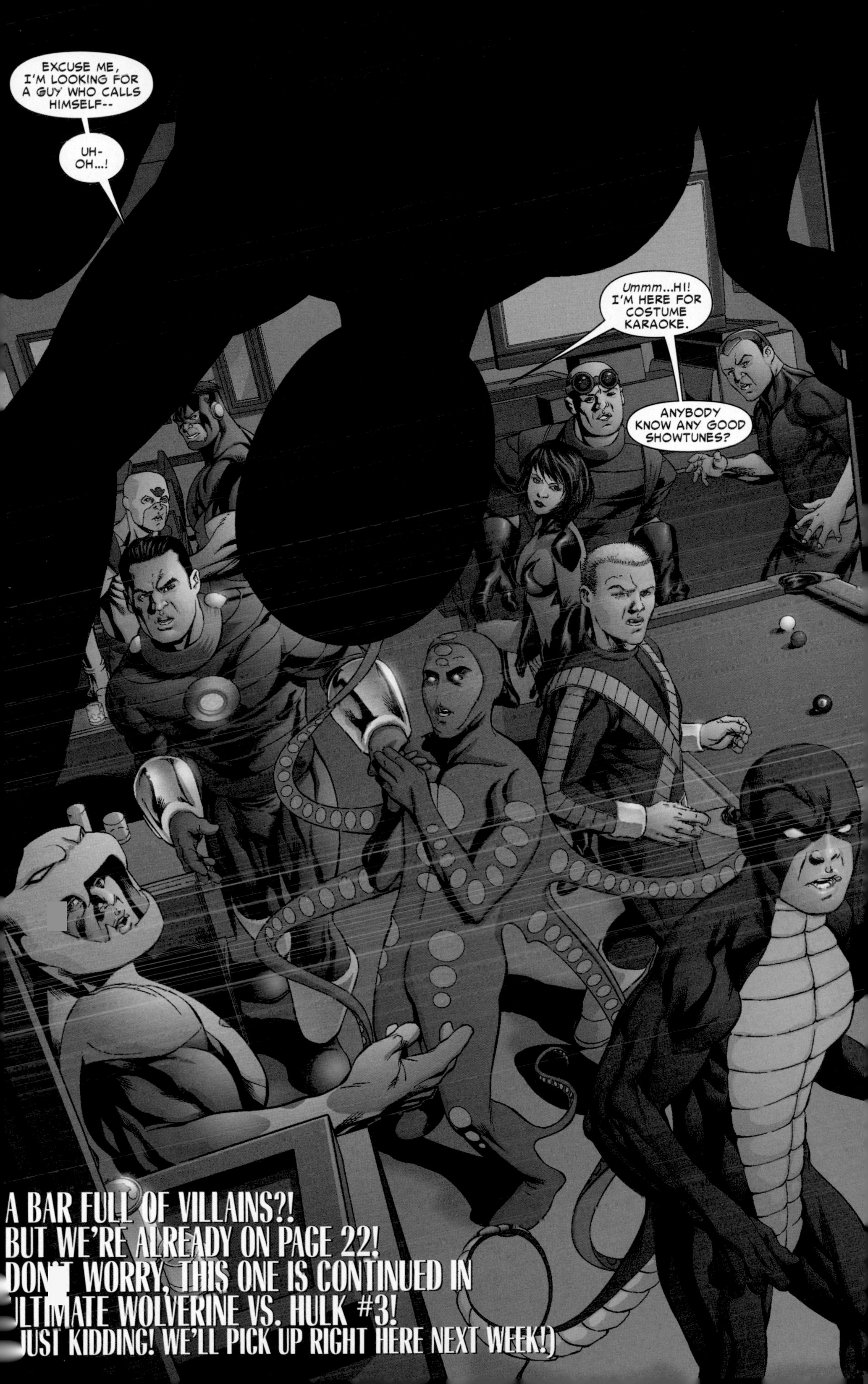
EXCUSE ME, I'M LOOKING FOR A GUY WHO CALLS HIMSELF--
UH-OH...!
Ummm...HI! I'M HERE FOR COSTUME KARAOKE.
ANYBODY KNOW ANY GOOD SHOWTUNES?
A BAR FULL OF VILLAINS?!
BUT WE'RE ALREADY ON PAGE 22!
DON'T WORRY, THIS ONE IS CONTINUED IN
LTIMATE WOLVERINE VS. HULK #3!
UST KIDDING! WE'LL PICK UP RIGHT HERE NEXT WEEK!)

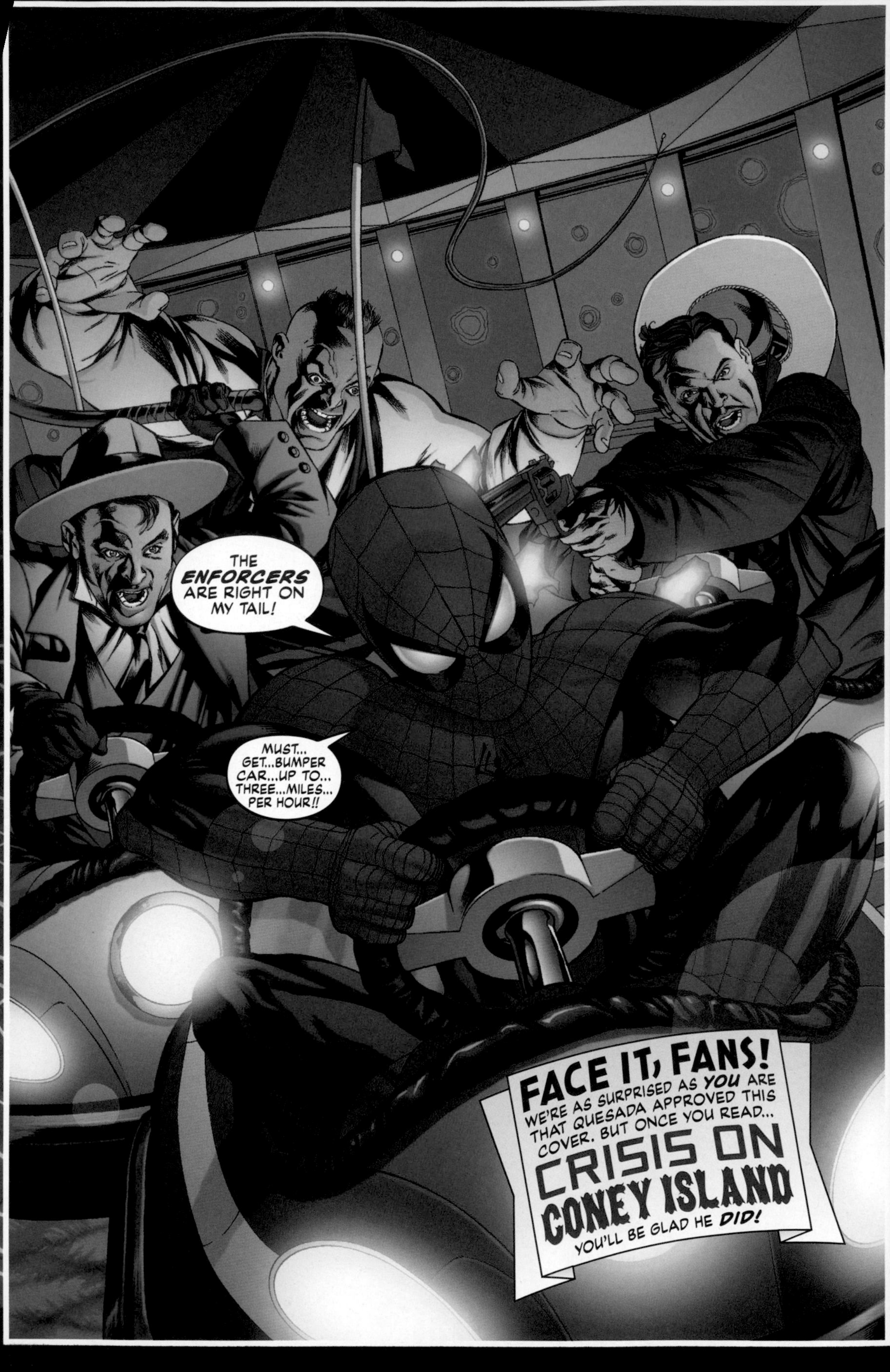
THE ENFORCERS ARE RIGHT ON MY TAIL!
MUST... GET...BUMPER CAR...UP TO... THREE...MILES... PER HOUR!!
FACE IT, FANS!
WE'RE AS SURPRISED AS YOU ARE THAT QUESADA APPROVED THIS COVER. BUT ONCE YOU READ...
CRISIS ON CONEY ISLAND
YOU'LL BE GLAD HE DID!

SO SPIDER-MAN WALKS INTO A BAR AND...

WHOA! I HAVEN'T SEEN THIS MANY VILLAINS, THUGS, AND LOWLIFES IN ONE PLACE SINCE I WATCHED C-SPAN'S COVERAGE OF CONGRESS YESTERDAY.

WHAM

GUYS, PLEASE! I KNOW YOU ALL CAN'T WAIT FOR ME TO GIVE YOU YOUR OWN OFFICIAL CUSTOMIZED SPIDER-MAN BRUISE MARKS, BUT ONE AT A TIME!

AND NO, KNOCKED-OUT TEETH ARE NOT COVERED BY CITY HEALTH INSURANCE.

BOB GALE WRITER	MIKE McKONE PENCILS	MARLO ALQUIZA INKS	JEROMY COX & ANTONIO FABELA COLORS
VC'S CORY PETIT LETTERS	TOM BRENNAN ASST. EDITOR	STEPHEN WACKER PUNCHLINE	
TOM BREVOORT EXECUTIVE EDITOR	JOE QUESADA EDITOR IN CHIEF	DAN BUCKLEY PUBLISHER	

GALE, GUGGENHEIM, SLOTT & WELLS
SPIDEY'S BRAINTRUST

THIRTY SECONDS AGO, SPIDER-MAN, ACTING ON A TIP, WALKED INTO "THE BAR WITH NO NAME" LOOKING FOR THE BOOKIE, WHO HAD HIRED SCREWBALL TO IMPERSONATE HIM. CLEARLY, SPIDEY IS ABOUT AS WELCOME HERE AS A LIVE RAT AT A TUPPERWARE PARTY.*

* BOB, NO ONE KNOWS WHAT A "TUPPERWARE PARTY" IS. -STEVE

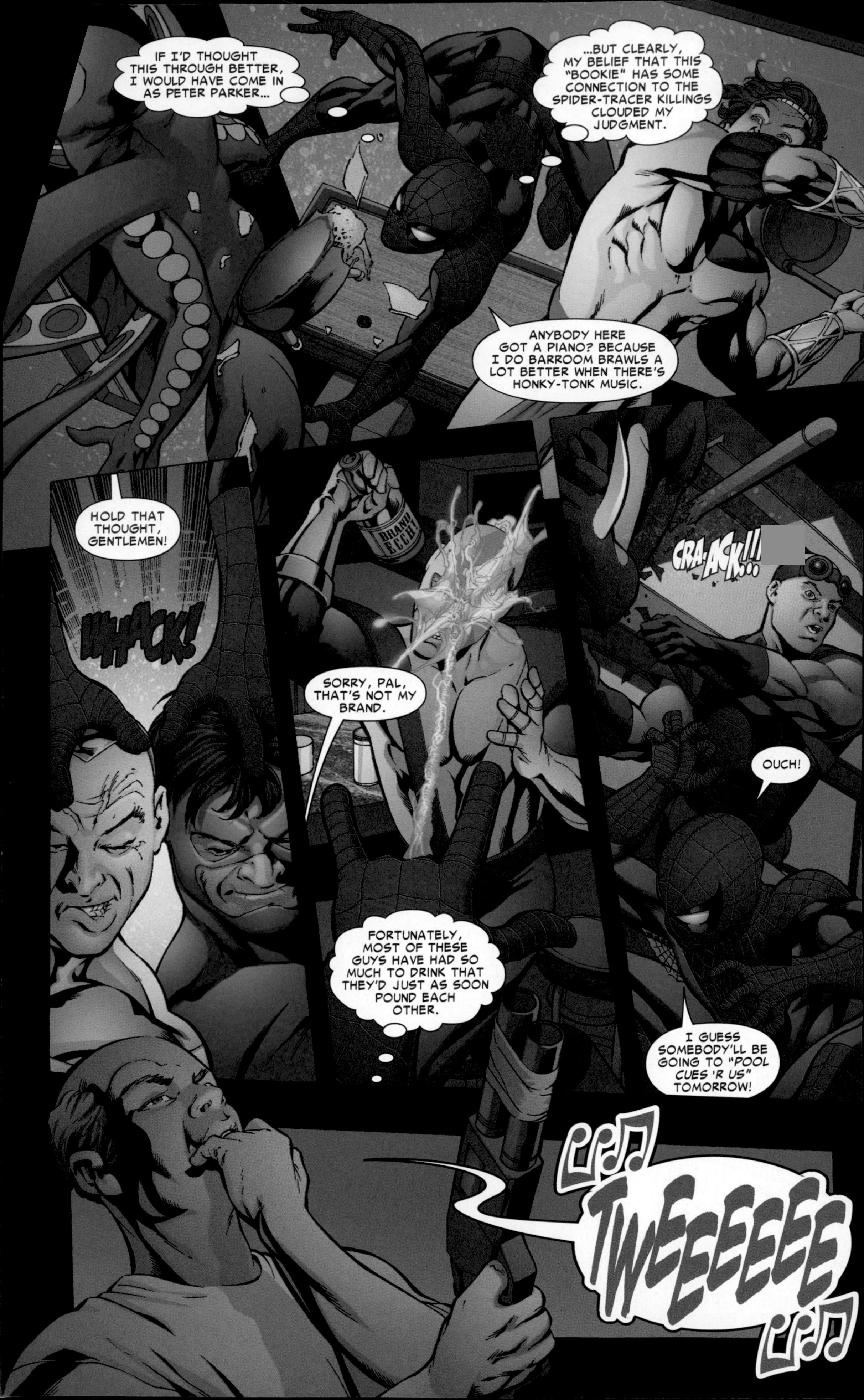
IF I'D THOUGHT THIS THROUGH BETTER, I WOULD HAVE COME IN AS PETER PARKER...
...BUT CLEARLY, MY BELIEF THAT THIS "BOOKIE" HAS SOME CONNECTION TO THE SPIDER-TRACER KILLINGS CLOUDED MY JUDGMENT.
ANYBODY HERE GOT A PIANO? BECAUSE I DO BARROOM BRAWLS A LOT BETTER WHEN THERE'S HONKY-TONK MUSIC.
HOLD THAT THOUGHT, GENTLEMEN!
WHACK!
BRAND ECCH!
SORRY, PAL, THAT'S NOT MY BRAND.
FORTUNATELY, MOST OF THESE GUYS HAVE HAD SO MUCH TO DRINK THAT THEY'D JUST AS SOON POUND EACH OTHER.
CRA-ACK!!!
OUCH!
I GUESS SOMEBODY'LL BE GOING TO "POOL CUES 'R US" TOMORROW!
TWEEEEEE

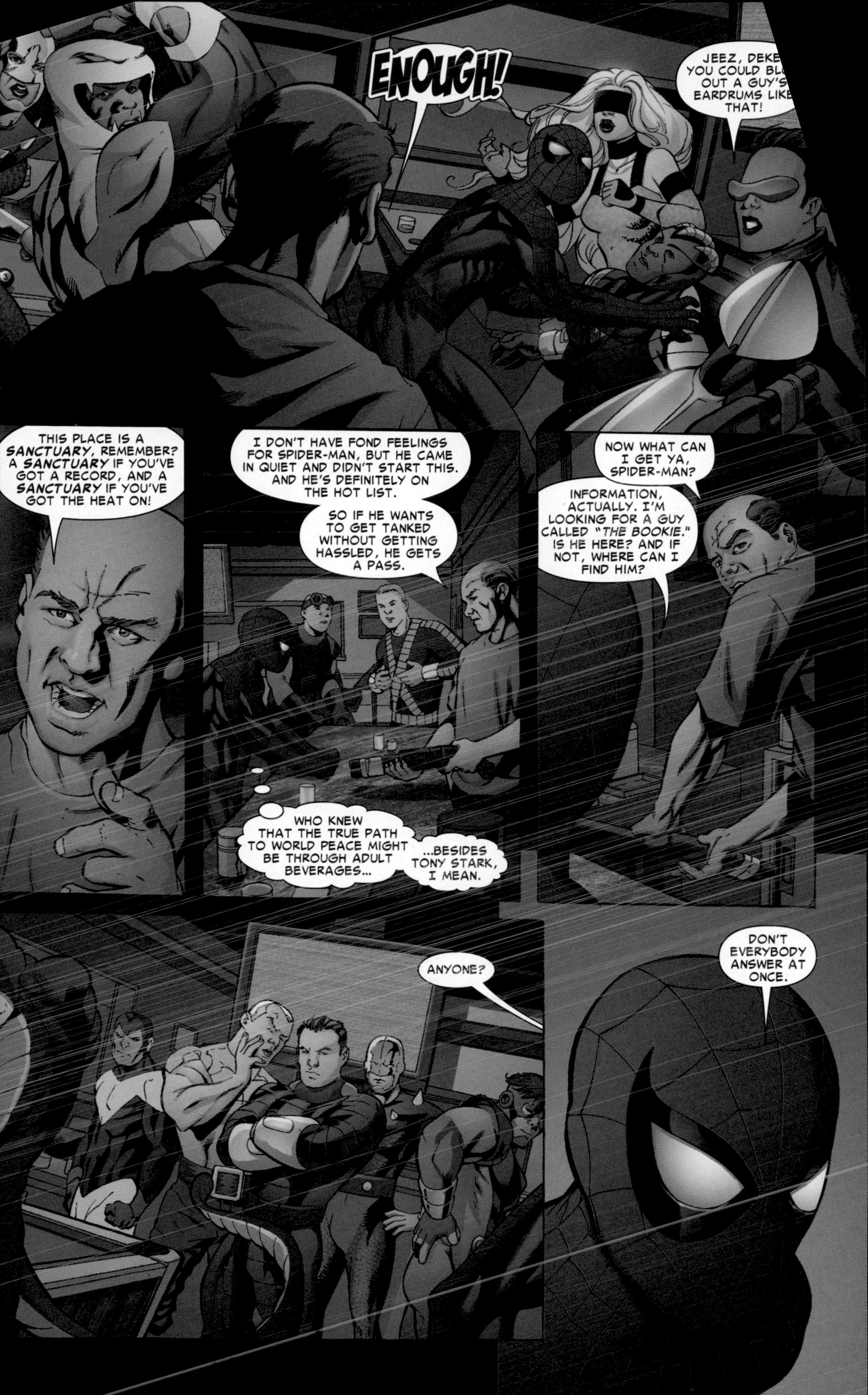
ENOUGH!
JEEZ, DEKE! YOU COULD BLOW OUT A GUY'S EARDRUMS LIKE THAT!
THIS PLACE IS A SANCTUARY, REMEMBER? A SANCTUARY IF YOU'VE GOT A RECORD, AND A SANCTUARY IF YOU'VE GOT THE HEAT ON!
I DON'T HAVE FOND FEELINGS FOR SPIDER-MAN, BUT HE CAME IN QUIET AND DIDN'T START THIS. AND HE'S DEFINITELY ON THE HOT LIST.
SO IF HE WANTS TO GET TANKED WITHOUT GETTING HASSLED, HE GETS A PASS.
WHO KNEW THAT THE TRUE PATH TO WORLD PEACE MIGHT BE THROUGH ADULT BEVERAGES...
...BESIDES TONY STARK, I MEAN.
NOW WHAT CAN I GET YA, SPIDER-MAN?
INFORMATION, ACTUALLY. I'M LOOKING FOR A GUY CALLED "THE BOOKIE." IS HE HERE? AND IF NOT, WHERE CAN I FIND HIM?
ANYONE?
DON'T EVERYBODY ANSWER AT ONCE.

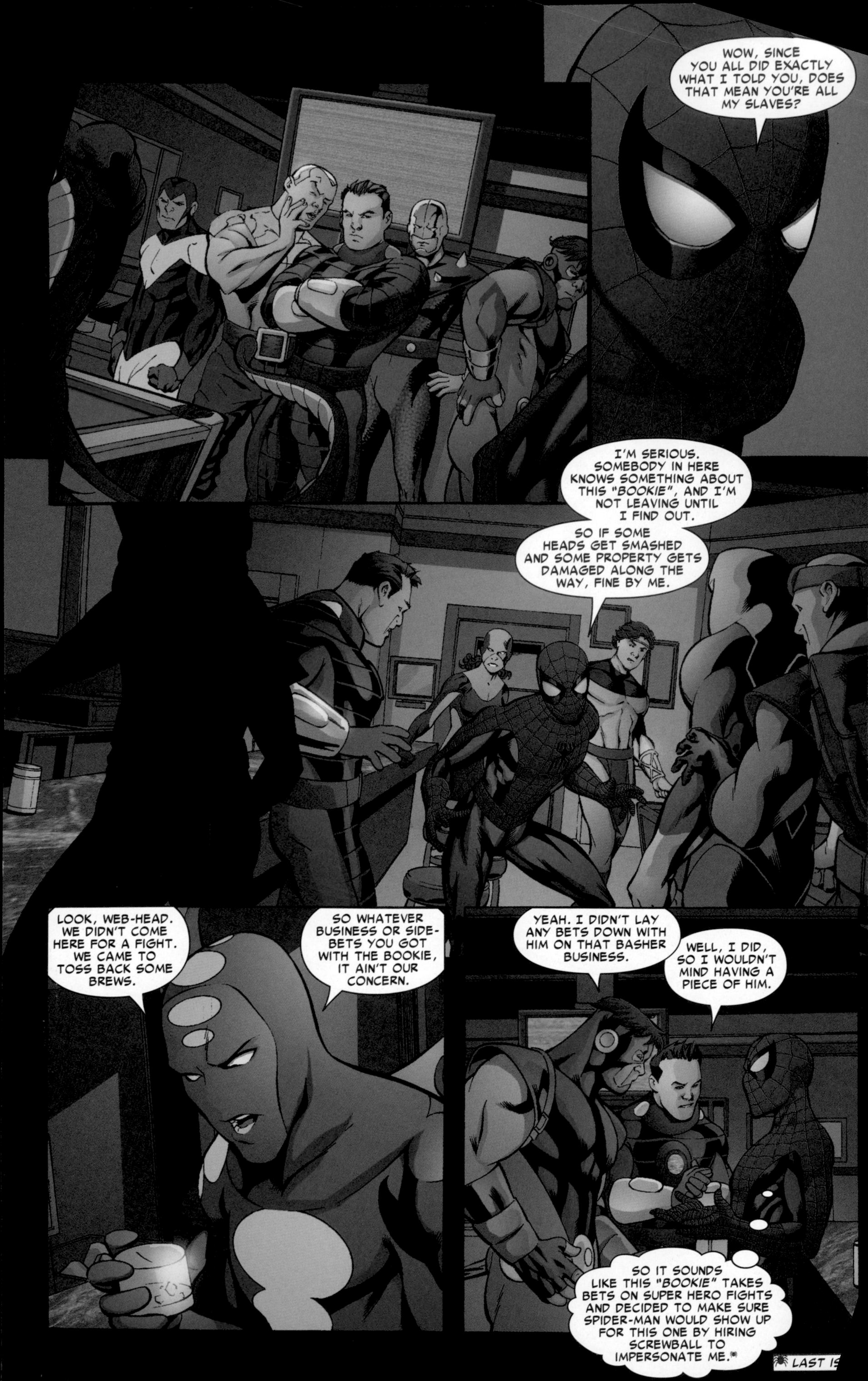
WOW, SINCE YOU ALL DID EXACTLY WHAT I TOLD YOU, DOES THAT MEAN YOU'RE ALL MY SLAVES?
I'M SERIOUS. SOMEBODY IN HERE KNOWS SOMETHING ABOUT THIS "BOOKIE", AND I'M NOT LEAVING UNTIL I FIND OUT.
SO IF SOME HEADS GET SMASHED AND SOME PROPERTY GETS DAMAGED ALONG THE WAY, FINE BY ME.
LOOK, WEB-HEAD. WE DIDN'T COME HERE FOR A FIGHT. WE CAME TO TOSS BACK SOME BREWS.
SO WHATEVER BUSINESS OR SIDE-BETS YOU GOT WITH THE BOOKIE, IT AIN'T OUR CONCERN.
YEAH. I DIDN'T LAY ANY BETS DOWN WITH HIM ON THAT BASHER BUSINESS.
WELL, I DID, SO I WOULDN'T MIND HAVING A PIECE OF HIM.
SO IT SOUNDS LIKE THIS "BOOKIE" TAKES BETS ON SUPER HERO FIGHTS AND DECIDED TO MAKE SURE SPIDER-MAN WOULD SHOW UP FOR THIS ONE BY HIRING SCREWBALL TO IMPERSONATE ME.*
LAST IS

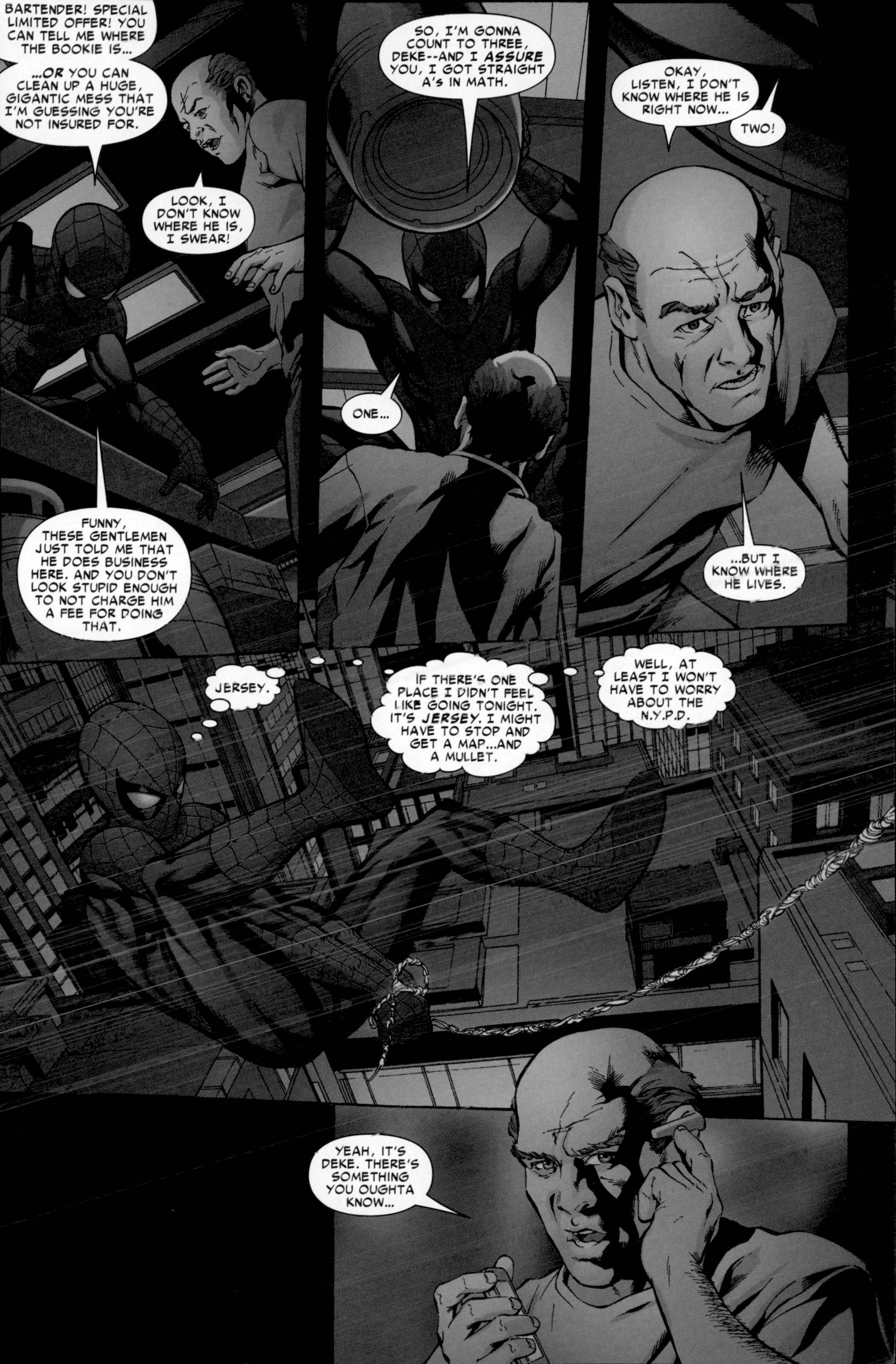
BARTENDER! SPECIAL LIMITED OFFER! YOU CAN TELL ME WHERE THE BOOKIE IS...
...OR YOU CAN CLEAN UP A HUGE, GIGANTIC MESS THAT I'M GUESSING YOU'RE NOT INSURED FOR.
LOOK, I DON'T KNOW WHERE HE IS, I SWEAR!
FUNNY, THESE GENTLEMEN JUST TOLD ME THAT HE DOES BUSINESS HERE. AND YOU DON'T LOOK STUPID ENOUGH TO NOT CHARGE HIM A FEE FOR DOING THAT.
SO, I'M GONNA COUNT TO THREE, DEKE--AND I ASSURE YOU, I GOT STRAIGHT A'S IN MATH.
ONE...
OKAY, LISTEN, I DON'T KNOW WHERE HE IS RIGHT NOW...
TWO!
...BUT I KNOW WHERE HE LIVES.
JERSEY.
IF THERE'S ONE PLACE I DIDN'T FEEL LIKE GOING TONIGHT, IT'S JERSEY. I MIGHT HAVE TO STOP AND GET A MAP...AND A MULLET.
WELL, AT LEAST I WON'T HAVE TO WORRY ABOUT THE N.Y.P.D.
YEAH, IT'S DEKE. THERE'S SOMETHING YOU OUGHTA KNOW...

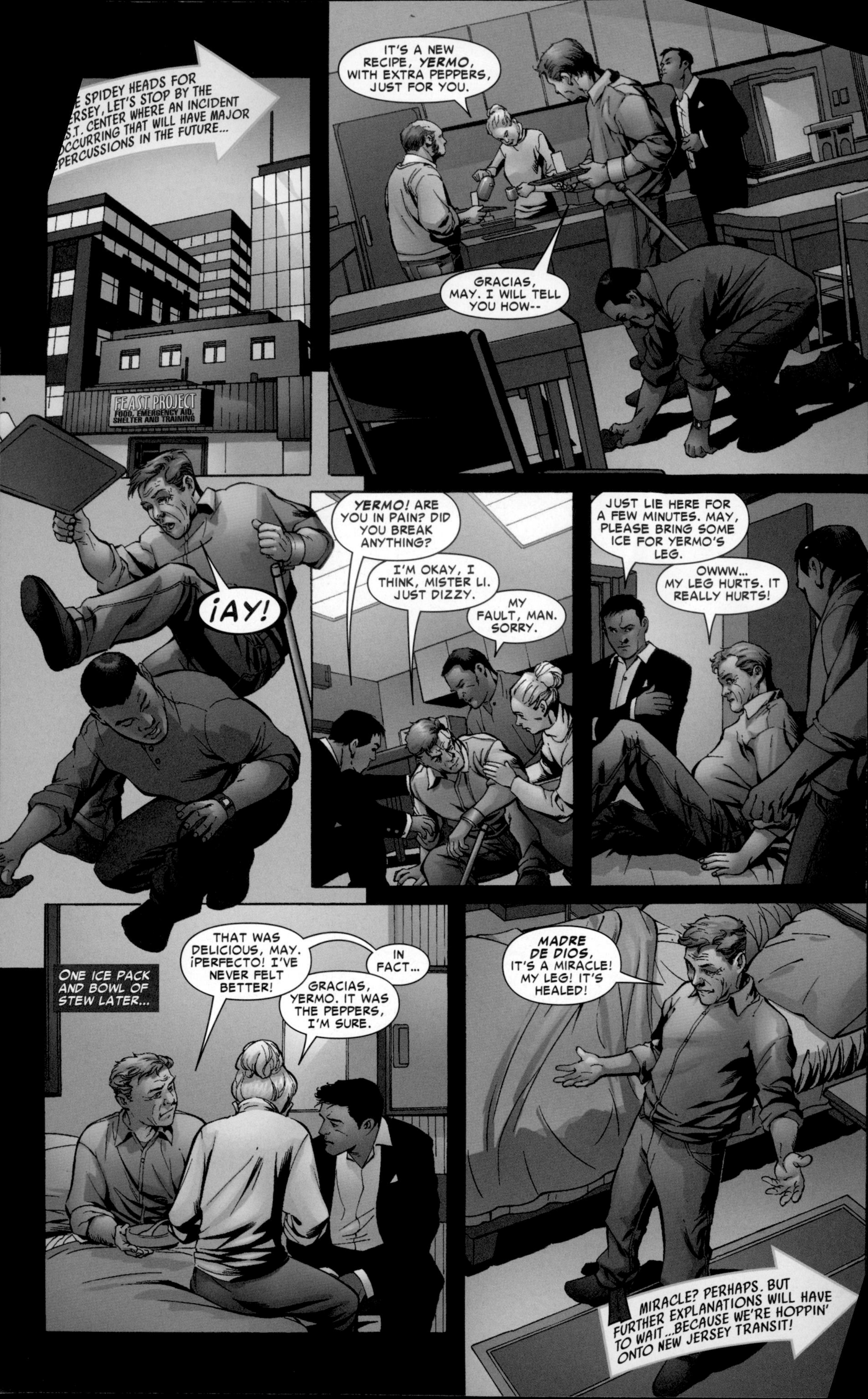
E SPIDEY HEADS FOR ERSEY, LET'S STOP BY THE S.T. CENTER WHERE AN INCIDENT OCCURRING THAT WILL HAVE MAJOR PERCUSSIONS IN THE FUTURE...
F.E.A.S.T. PROJECT FOOD, EMERGENCY AID, SHELTER AND TRAINING
IT'S A NEW RECIPE, YERMO, WITH EXTRA PEPPERS, JUST FOR YOU.
GRACIAS, MAY. I WILL TELL YOU HOW--
¡AY!
YERMO! ARE YOU IN PAIN? DID YOU BREAK ANYTHING?
I'M OKAY, I THINK, MISTER LI. JUST DIZZY.
MY FAULT, MAN. SORRY.
JUST LIE HERE FOR A FEW MINUTES. MAY, PLEASE BRING SOME ICE FOR YERMO'S LEG.
OWWW... MY LEG HURTS. IT REALLY HURTS!
ONE ICE PACK AND BOWL OF STEW LATER...
THAT WAS DELICIOUS, MAY. ¡PERFECTO! I'VE NEVER FELT BETTER!
IN FACT...
GRACIAS, YERMO. IT WAS THE PEPPERS, I'M SURE.
MADRE DE DIOS, IT'S A MIRACLE! MY LEG! IT'S HEALED!
MIRACLE? PERHAPS. BUT FURTHER EXPLANATIONS WILL HAVE TO WAIT...BECAUSE WE'RE HOPPIN' ONTO NEW JERSEY TRANSIT!

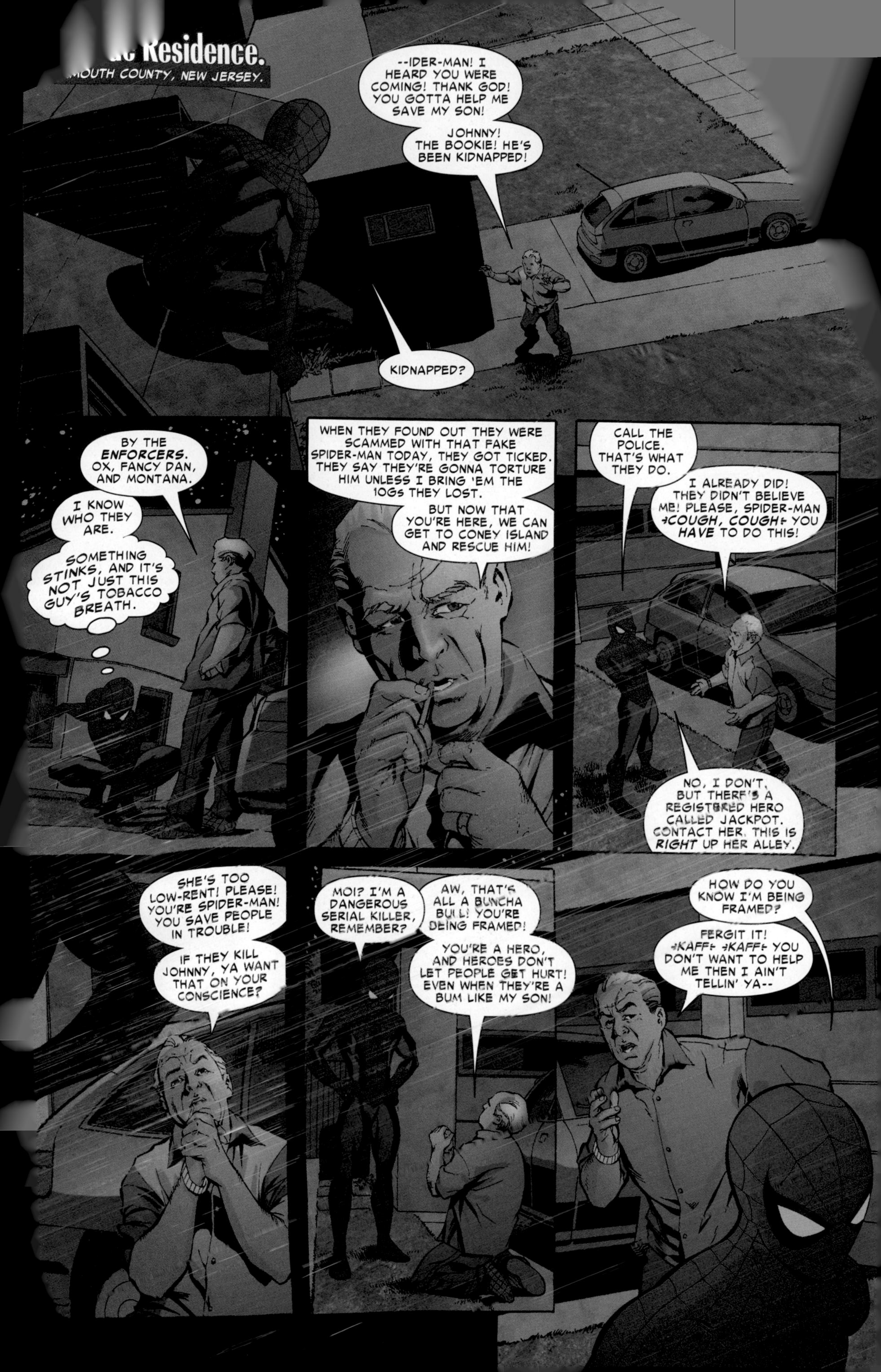

...Residence.
...MOUTH COUNTY, NEW JERSEY.
--IDER-MAN! I HEARD YOU WERE COMING! THANK GOD! YOU GOTTA HELP ME SAVE MY SON!
JOHNNY! THE BOOKIE! HE'S BEEN KIDNAPPED!
KIDNAPPED?
BY THE ENFORCERS. OX, FANCY DAN, AND MONTANA.
I KNOW WHO THEY ARE.
SOMETHING STINKS, AND IT'S NOT JUST THIS GUY'S TOBACCO BREATH.
WHEN THEY FOUND OUT THEY WERE SCAMMED WITH THAT FAKE SPIDER-MAN TODAY, THEY GOT TICKED. THEY SAY THEY'RE GONNA TORTURE HIM UNLESS I BRING 'EM THE 10Gs THEY LOST.
BUT NOW THAT YOU'RE HERE, WE CAN GET TO CONEY ISLAND AND RESCUE HIM!
CALL THE POLICE. THAT'S WHAT THEY DO.
I ALREADY DID! THEY DIDN'T BELIEVE ME! PLEASE, SPIDER-MAN -COUGH, COUGH- YOU HAVE TO DO THIS!
NO, I DON'T, BUT THERE'S A REGISTERED HERO CALLED JACKPOT. CONTACT HER. THIS IS RIGHT UP HER ALLEY.
SHE'S TOO LOW-RENT! PLEASE! YOU'RE SPIDER-MAN! YOU SAVE PEOPLE IN TROUBLE!
IF THEY KILL JOHNNY, YA WANT THAT ON YOUR CONSCIENCE?
MOI? I'M A DANGEROUS SERIAL KILLER, REMEMBER?
AW, THAT'S ALL A BUNCHA BULL! YOU'RE BEING FRAMED!
YOU'RE A HERO, AND HEROES DON'T LET PEOPLE GET HURT! EVEN WHEN THEY'RE A BUM LIKE MY SON!
HOW DO YOU KNOW I'M BEING FRAMED?
FERGIT IT! -KAFF- -KAFF- YOU DON'T WANT TO HELP ME THEN I AIN'T TELLIN' YA--

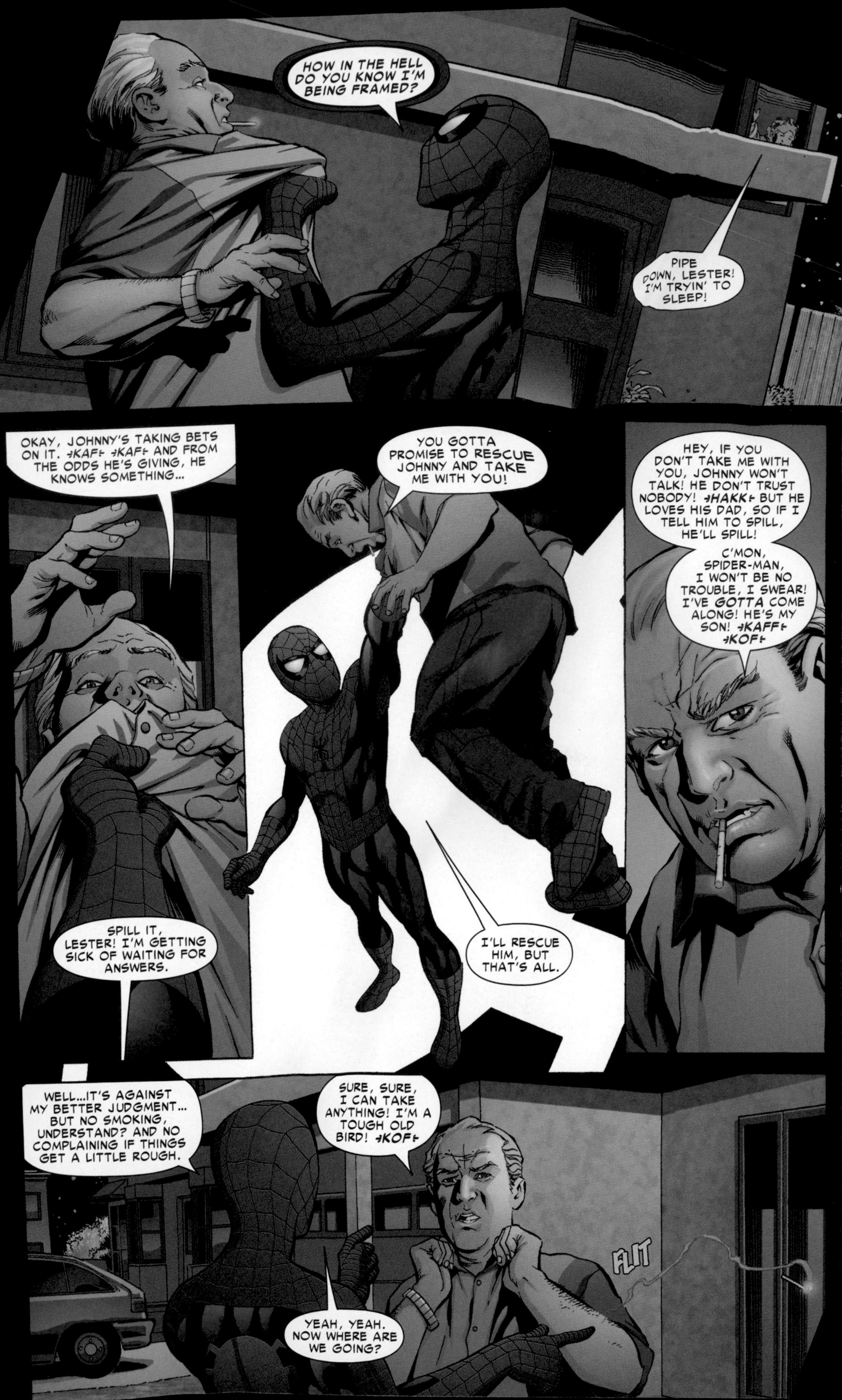

HOW IN THE HELL DO YOU KNOW I'M BEING FRAMED?
PIPE DOWN, LESTER! I'M TRYIN' TO SLEEP!
OKAY, JOHNNY'S TAKING BETS ON IT. *KAF* *KAF* AND FROM THE ODDS HE'S GIVING, HE KNOWS SOMETHING...
SPILL IT, LESTER! I'M GETTING SICK OF WAITING FOR ANSWERS.
YOU GOTTA PROMISE TO RESCUE JOHNNY AND TAKE ME WITH YOU!
I'LL RESCUE HIM, BUT THAT'S ALL.
HEY, IF YOU DON'T TAKE ME WITH YOU, JOHNNY WON'T TALK! HE DON'T TRUST NOBODY! *HAKK* BUT HE LOVES HIS DAD, SO IF I TELL HIM TO SPILL, HE'LL SPILL!
C'MON, SPIDER-MAN, I WON'T BE NO TROUBLE, I SWEAR! I'VE GOTTA COME ALONG! HE'S MY SON! *KAFF* *KOF*
WELL...IT'S AGAINST MY BETTER JUDGMENT... BUT NO SMOKING, UNDERSTAND? AND NO COMPLAINING IF THINGS GET A LITTLE ROUGH.
SURE, SURE, I CAN TAKE ANYTHING! I'M A TOUGH OLD BIRD! *KOF*
FLIT
YEAH, YEAH. NOW WHERE ARE WE GOING?

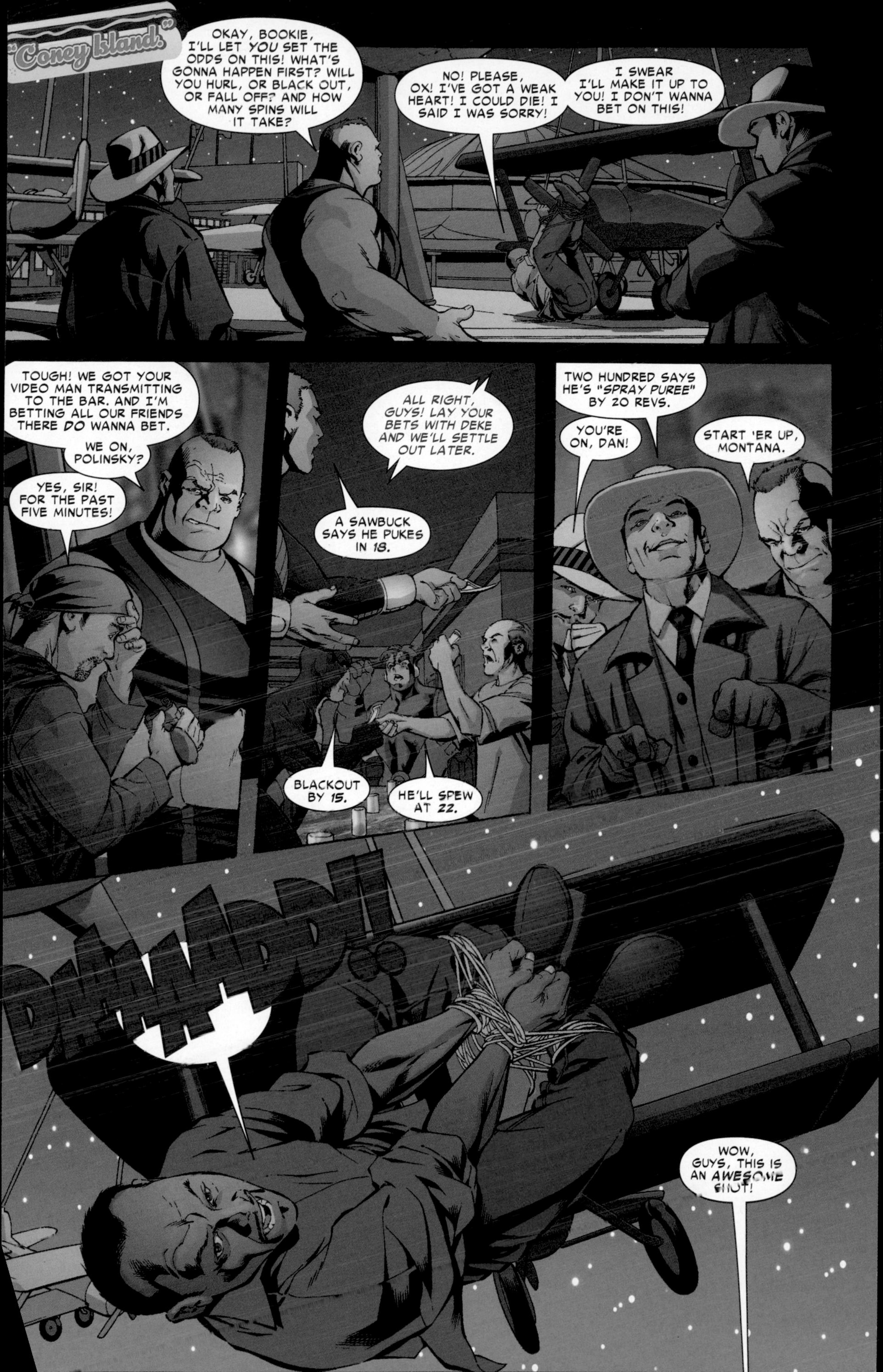
"Coney Island."
OKAY, BOOKIE, I'LL LET YOU SET THE ODDS ON THIS! WHAT'S GONNA HAPPEN FIRST? WILL YOU HURL, OR BLACK OUT, OR FALL OFF? AND HOW MANY SPINS WILL IT TAKE?
NO! PLEASE, OX! I'VE GOT A WEAK HEART! I COULD DIE! I SAID I WAS SORRY!
I SWEAR I'LL MAKE IT UP TO YOU! I DON'T WANNA BET ON THIS!
TOUGH! WE GOT YOUR VIDEO MAN TRANSMITTING TO THE BAR. AND I'M BETTING ALL OUR FRIENDS THERE DO WANNA BET.
WE ON, POLINSKY?
YES, SIR! FOR THE PAST FIVE MINUTES!
ALL RIGHT, GUYS! LAY YOUR BETS WITH DEKE AND WE'LL SETTLE OUT LATER.
A SAWBUCK SAYS HE PUKES IN 18.
BLACKOUT BY 15.
HE'LL SPEW AT 22.
TWO HUNDRED SAYS HE'S "SPRAY PUREE" BY 20 REVS.
YOU'RE ON, DAN!
START 'ER UP, MONTANA.
DAAAAAD!!
WOW, GUYS, THIS IS AN AWESOME SHOT!

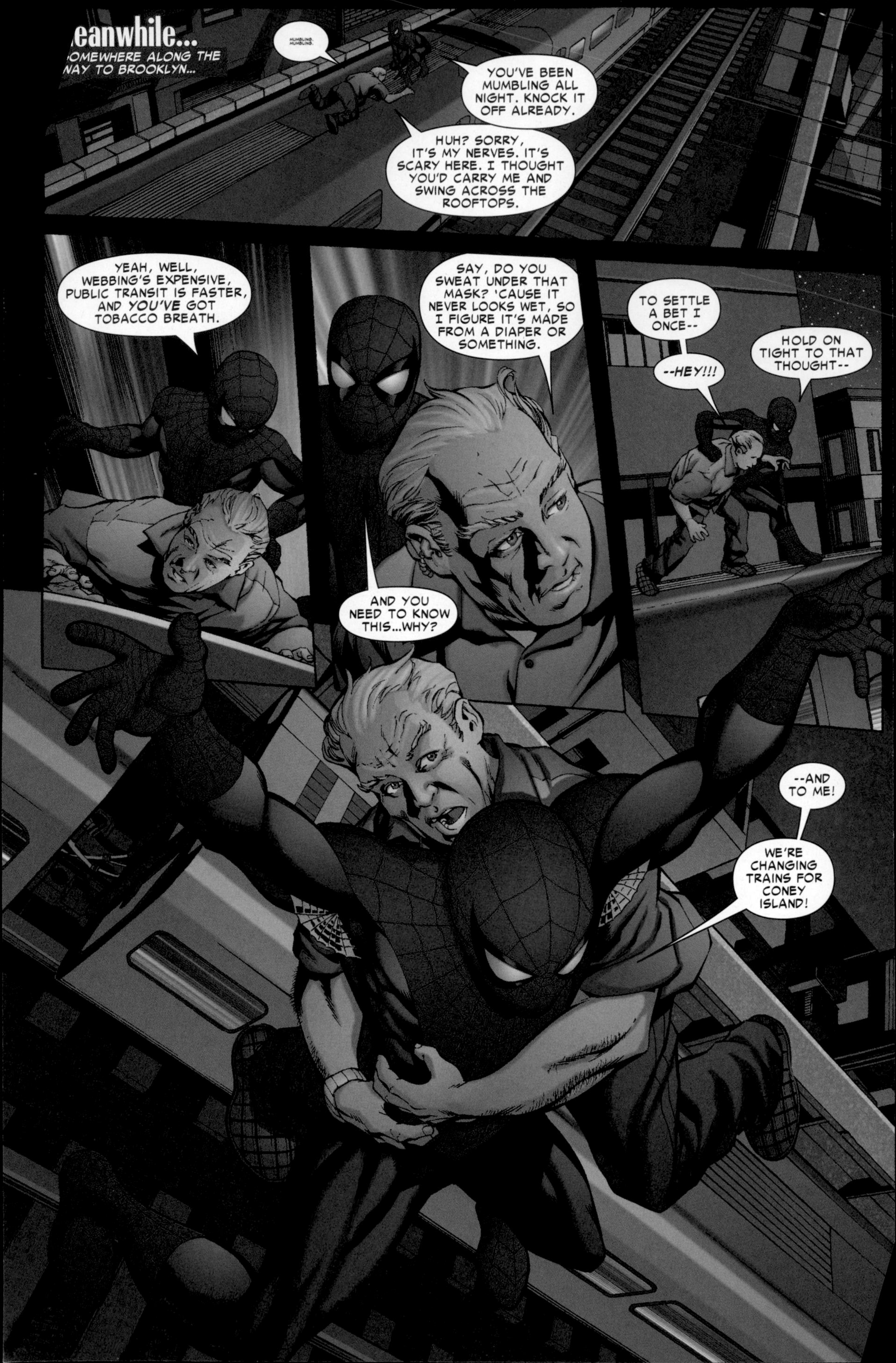
eanwhile...
OMEWHERE ALONG THE NAY TO BROOKLYN...
MUMBLING. MUMBLING.
YOU'VE BEEN MUMBLING ALL NIGHT. KNOCK IT OFF ALREADY.
HUH? SORRY, IT'S MY NERVES. IT'S SCARY HERE. I THOUGHT YOU'D CARRY ME AND SWING ACROSS THE ROOFTOPS.
YEAH, WELL, WEBBING'S EXPENSIVE, PUBLIC TRANSIT IS FASTER, AND *YOU'VE* GOT TOBACCO BREATH.
SAY, DO YOU SWEAT UNDER THAT MASK? 'CAUSE IT NEVER LOOKS WET, SO I FIGURE IT'S MADE FROM A DIAPER OR SOMETHING.
AND YOU NEED TO KNOW THIS...WHY?
TO SETTLE A BET I ONCE--
--HEY!!!
HOLD ON TIGHT TO THAT THOUGHT--
--AND TO ME!
WE'RE CHANGING TRAINS FOR CONEY ISLAND!

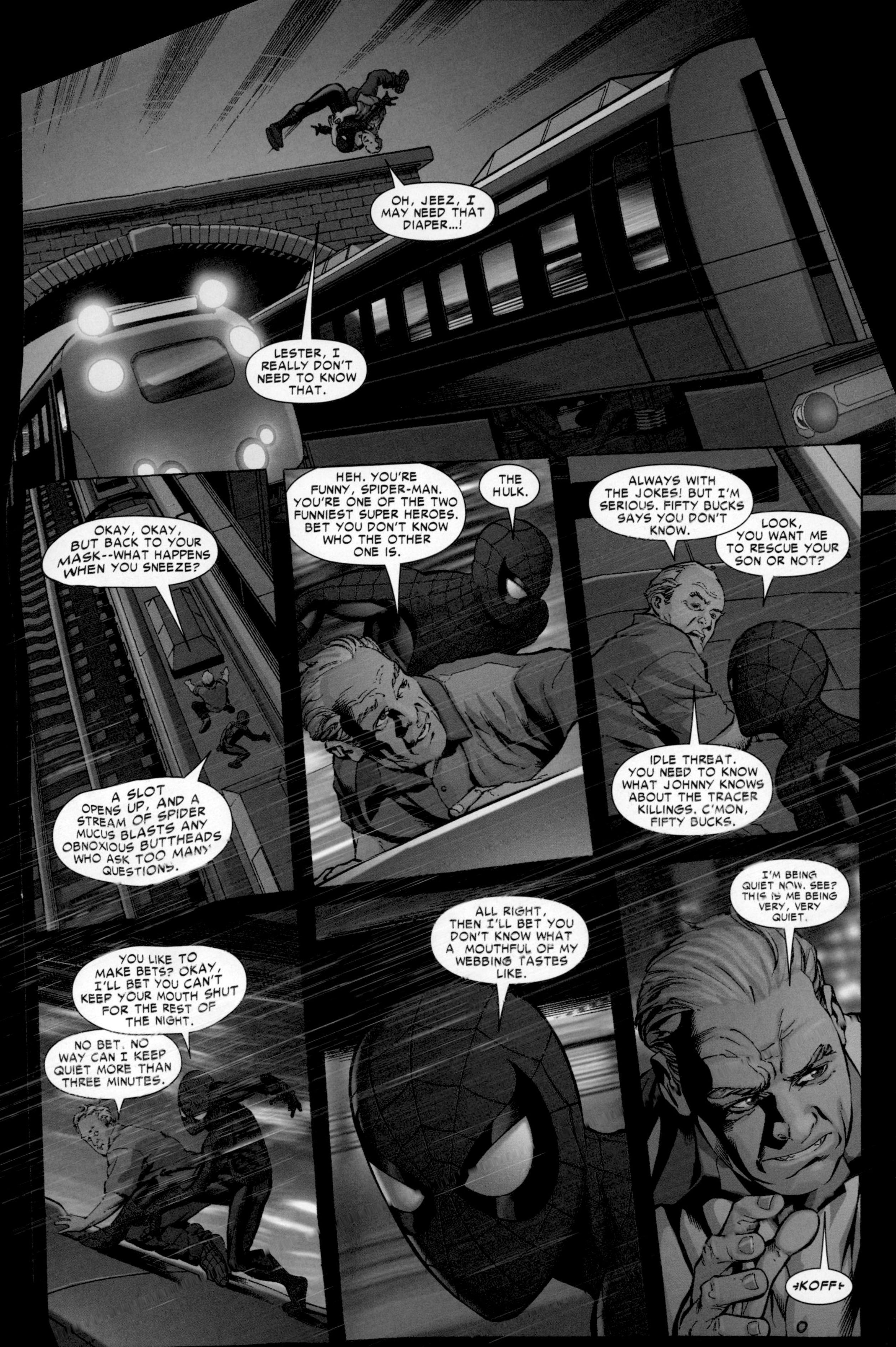
OH, JEEZ, I MAY NEED THAT DIAPER...!
LESTER, I REALLY DON'T NEED TO KNOW THAT.
OKAY, OKAY, BUT BACK TO YOUR MASK--WHAT HAPPENS WHEN YOU SNEEZE?
A SLOT OPENS UP, AND A STREAM OF SPIDER MUCUS BLASTS ANY OBNOXIOUS BUTTHEADS WHO ASK TOO MANY QUESTIONS.
HEH. YOU'RE FUNNY, SPIDER-MAN. YOU'RE ONE OF THE TWO FUNNIEST SUPER HEROES. BET YOU DON'T KNOW WHO THE OTHER ONE IS.
THE HULK.
ALWAYS WITH THE JOKES! BUT I'M SERIOUS. FIFTY BUCKS SAYS YOU DON'T KNOW.
LOOK, YOU WANT ME TO RESCUE YOUR SON OR NOT?
IDLE THREAT. YOU NEED TO KNOW WHAT JOHNNY KNOWS ABOUT THE TRACER KILLINGS. C'MON, FIFTY BUCKS.
YOU LIKE TO MAKE BETS? OKAY, I'LL BET YOU CAN'T KEEP YOUR MOUTH SHUT FOR THE REST OF THE NIGHT.
NO BET. NO WAY CAN I KEEP QUIET MORE THAN THREE MINUTES.
ALL RIGHT, THEN I'LL BET YOU DON'T KNOW WHAT A MOUTHFUL OF MY WEBBING TASTES LIKE.
I'M BEING QUIET NOW. SEE? THIS IS ME BEING VERY, VERY QUIET.
KOFF

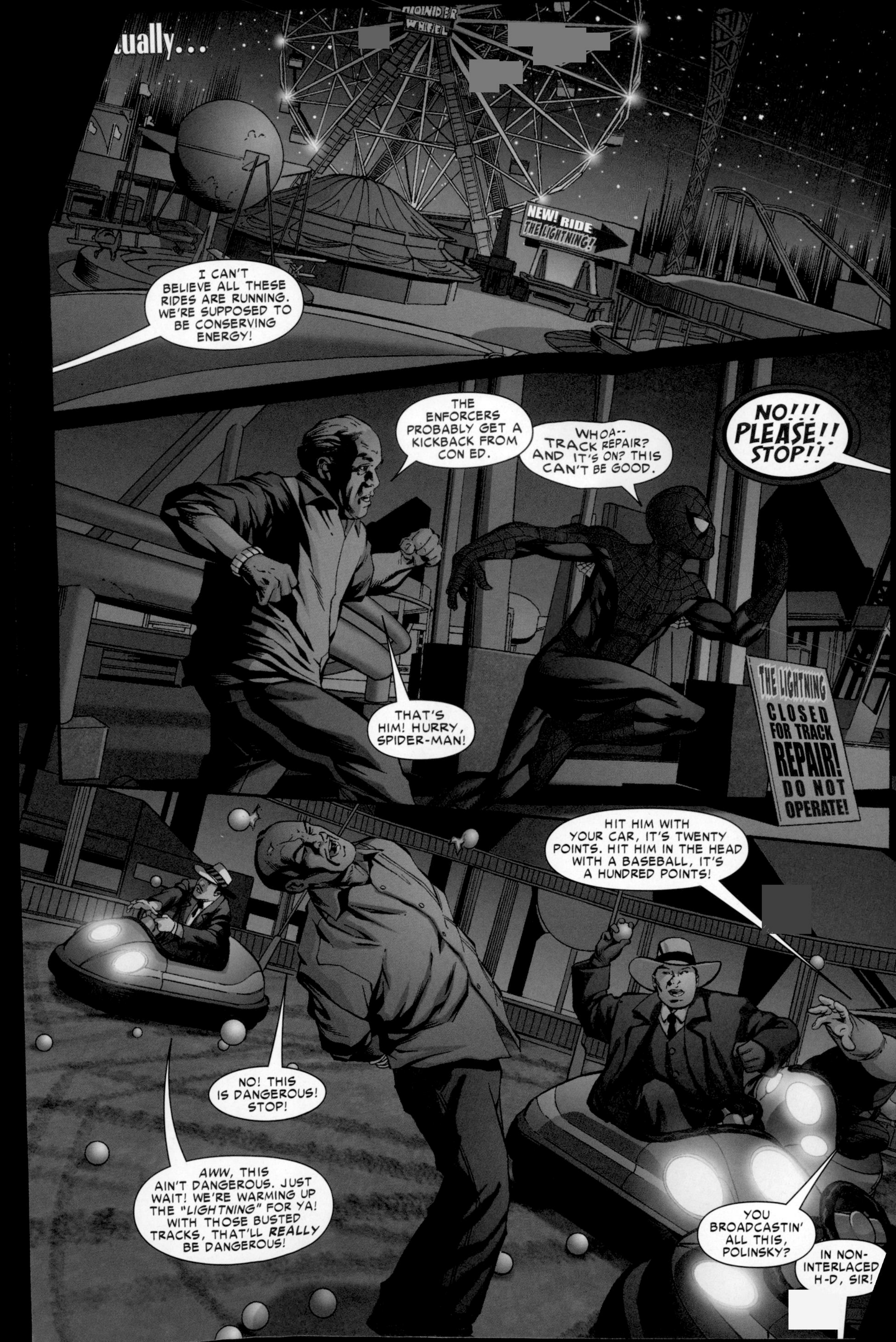

tually...
NEW! RIDE THE LIGHTNING!
I CAN'T BELIEVE ALL THESE RIDES ARE RUNNING. WE'RE SUPPOSED TO BE CONSERVING ENERGY!
THE ENFORCERS PROBABLY GET A KICKBACK FROM CON ED.
WHOA-- TRACK REPAIR? AND IT'S ON? THIS CAN'T BE GOOD.
NO!!! PLEASE!! STOP!!
THE LIGHTNING CLOSED FOR TRACK REPAIR! DO NOT OPERATE!
THAT'S HIM! HURRY, SPIDER-MAN!
HIT HIM WITH YOUR CAR, IT'S TWENTY POINTS. HIT HIM IN THE HEAD WITH A BASEBALL, IT'S A HUNDRED POINTS!
NO! THIS IS DANGEROUS! STOP!
AWW, THIS AIN'T DANGEROUS. JUST WAIT! WE'RE WARMING UP THE "LIGHTNING" FOR YA! WITH THOSE BUSTED TRACKS, THAT'LL REALLY BE DANGEROUS!
YOU BROADCASTIN' ALL THIS, POLINSKY?
IN NON-INTERLACED H-D, SIR!

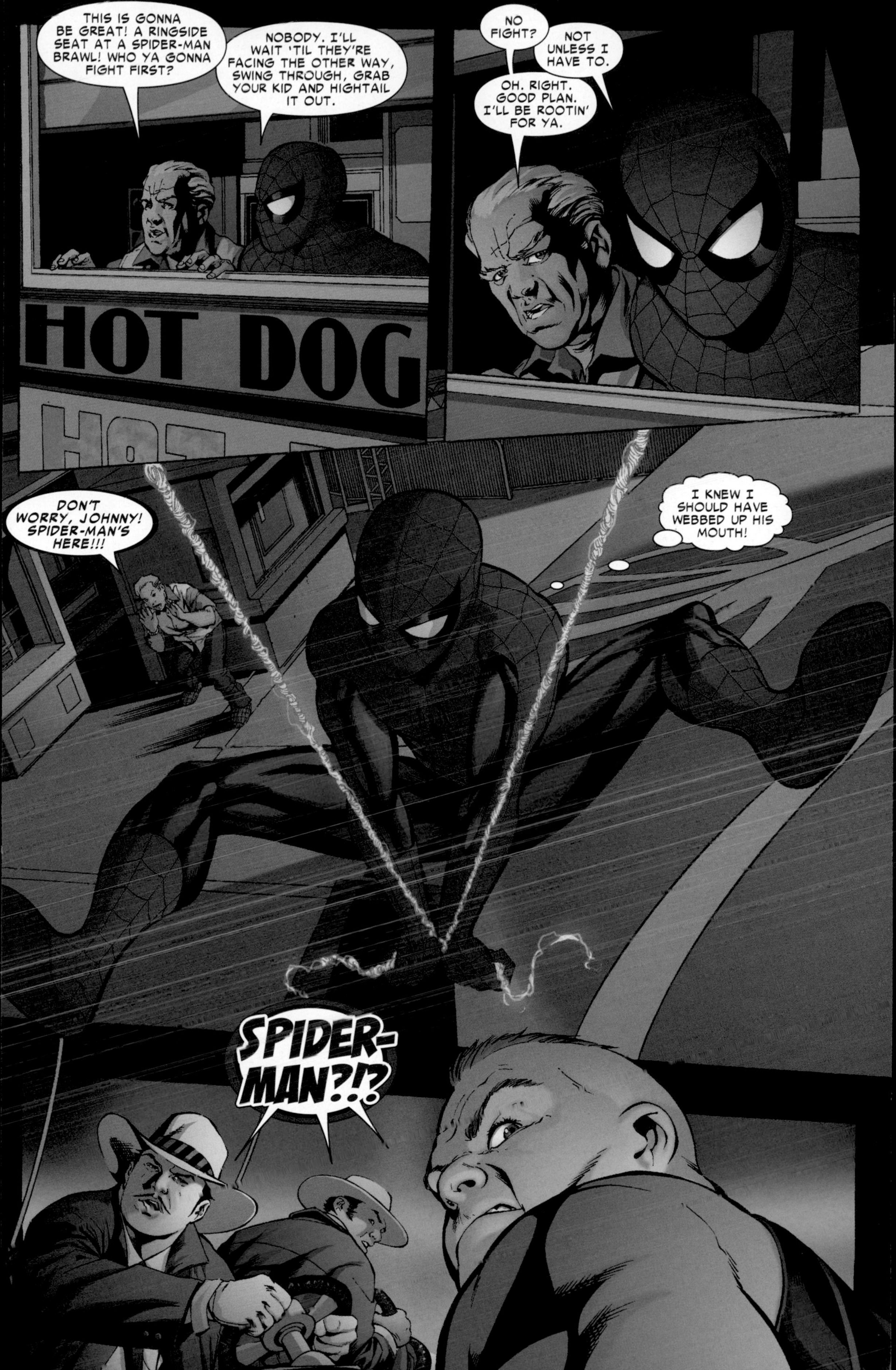
THIS IS GONNA BE GREAT! A RINGSIDE SEAT AT A SPIDER-MAN BRAWL! WHO YA GONNA FIGHT FIRST?
NOBODY. I'LL WAIT 'TIL THEY'RE FACING THE OTHER WAY, SWING THROUGH, GRAB YOUR KID AND HIGHTAIL IT OUT.
HOT DOG
NO FIGHT?
NOT UNLESS I HAVE TO.
OH. RIGHT. GOOD PLAN. I'LL BE ROOTIN' FOR YA.
DON'T WORRY, JOHNNY! SPIDER-MAN'S HERE!!!
I KNEW I SHOULD HAVE WEBBED UP HIS MOUTH!
SPIDER-MAN?!?

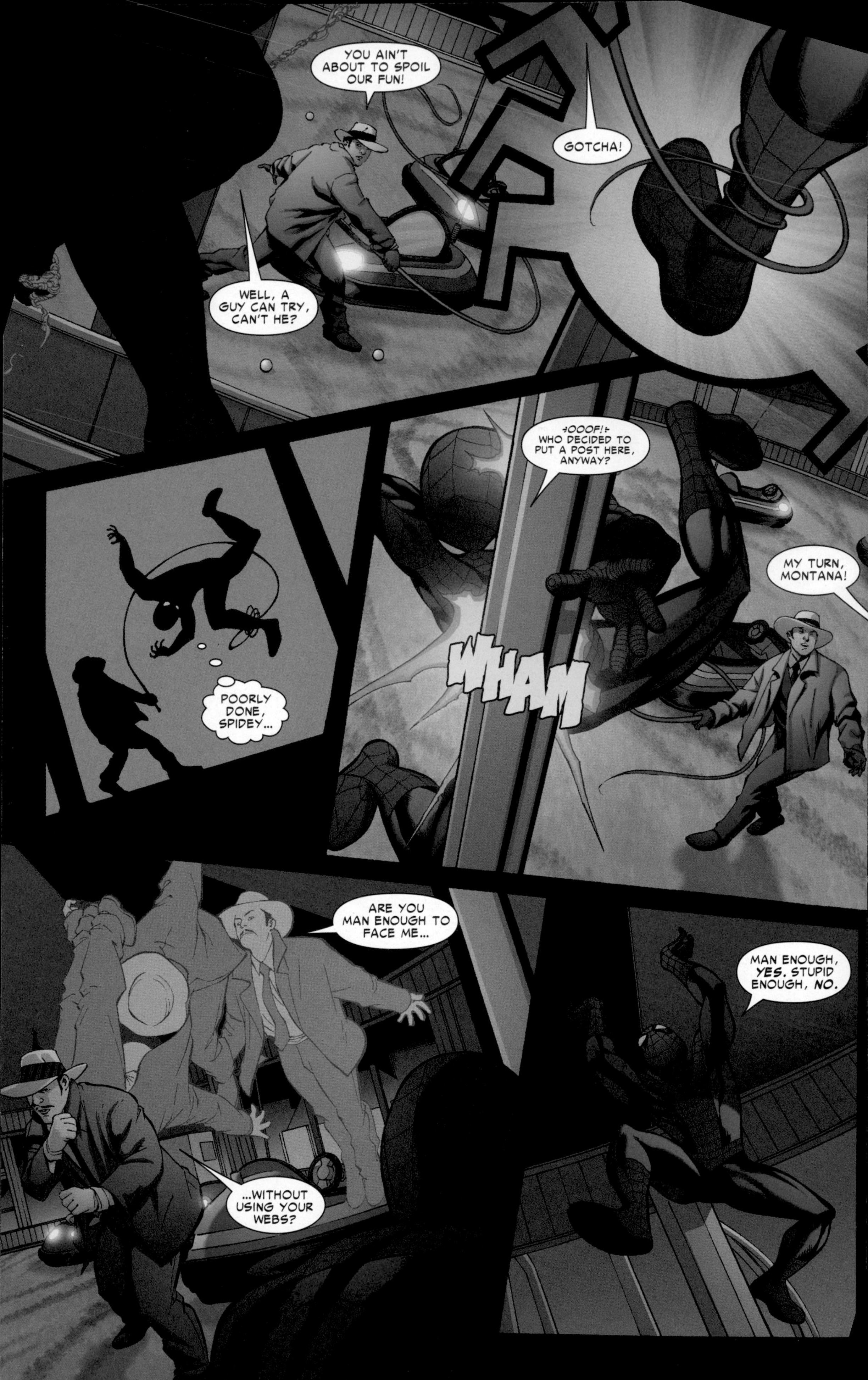

YOU AIN'T ABOUT TO SPOIL OUR FUN!
GOTCHA!
WELL, A GUY CAN TRY, CAN'T HE?
OOOF! WHO DECIDED TO PUT A POST HERE, ANYWAY?
MY TURN, MONTANA!
WHAM
POORLY DONE, SPIDEY...
ARE YOU MAN ENOUGH TO FACE ME...
...WITHOUT USING YOUR WEBS?
MAN ENOUGH, **YES.** STUPID ENOUGH, **NO.**

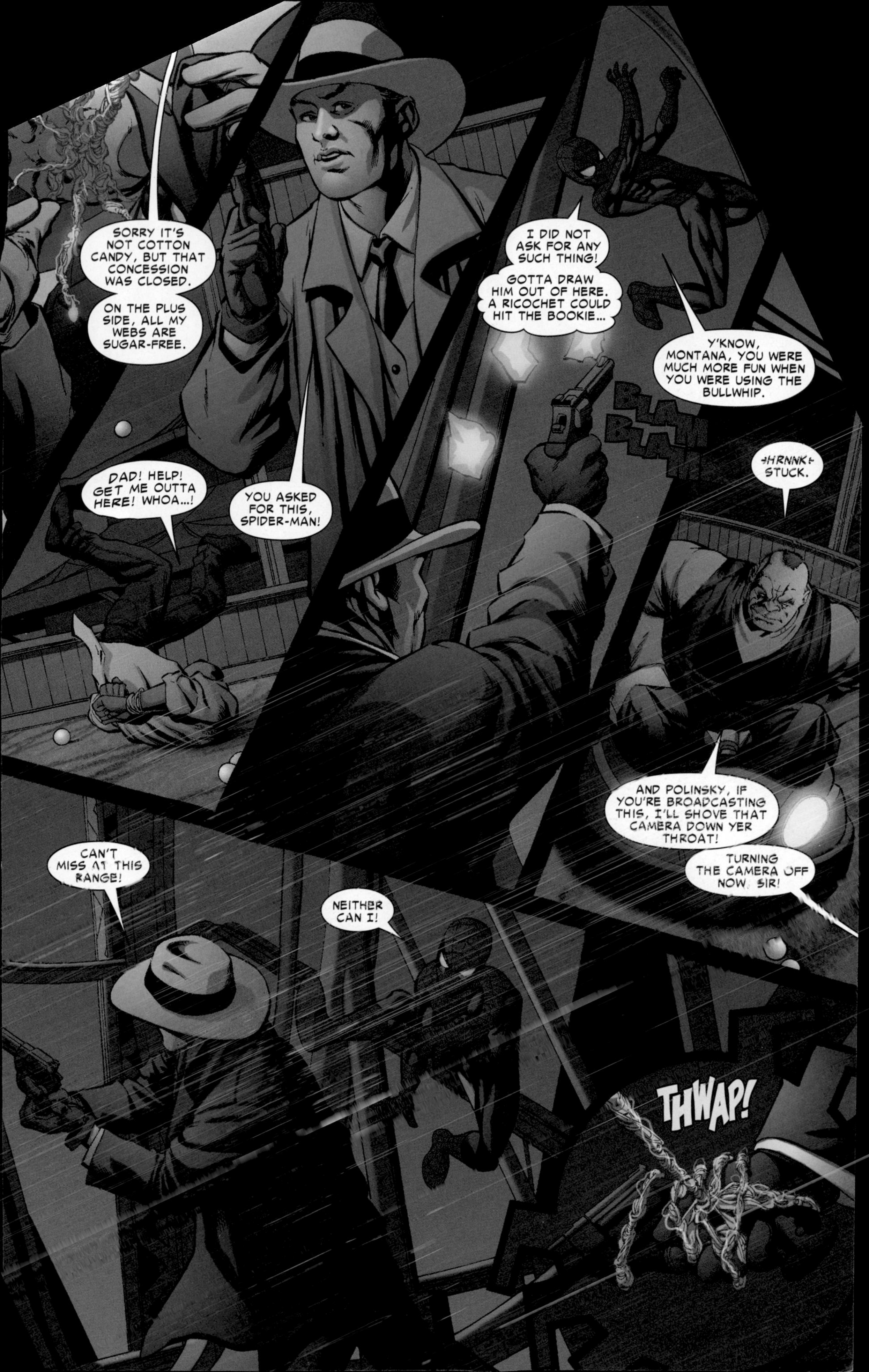
SORRY IT'S NOT COTTON CANDY, BUT THAT CONCESSION WAS CLOSED.
ON THE PLUS SIDE, ALL MY WEBS ARE SUGAR-FREE.
DAD! HELP! GET ME OUTTA HERE! WHOA...!
YOU ASKED FOR THIS, SPIDER-MAN!
I DID NOT ASK FOR ANY SUCH THING!
GOTTA DRAW HIM OUT OF HERE. A RICOCHET COULD HIT THE BOOKIE...
Y'KNOW, MONTANA, YOU WERE MUCH MORE FUN WHEN YOU WERE USING THE BULLWHIP.
BLAM BLAM
HRNNK STUCK.
AND POLINSKY, IF YOU'RE BROADCASTING THIS, I'LL SHOVE THAT CAMERA DOWN YER THROAT!
TURNING THE CAMERA OFF NOW, SIR!
CAN'T MISS AT THIS RANGE!
NEITHER CAN I!
THWAP!

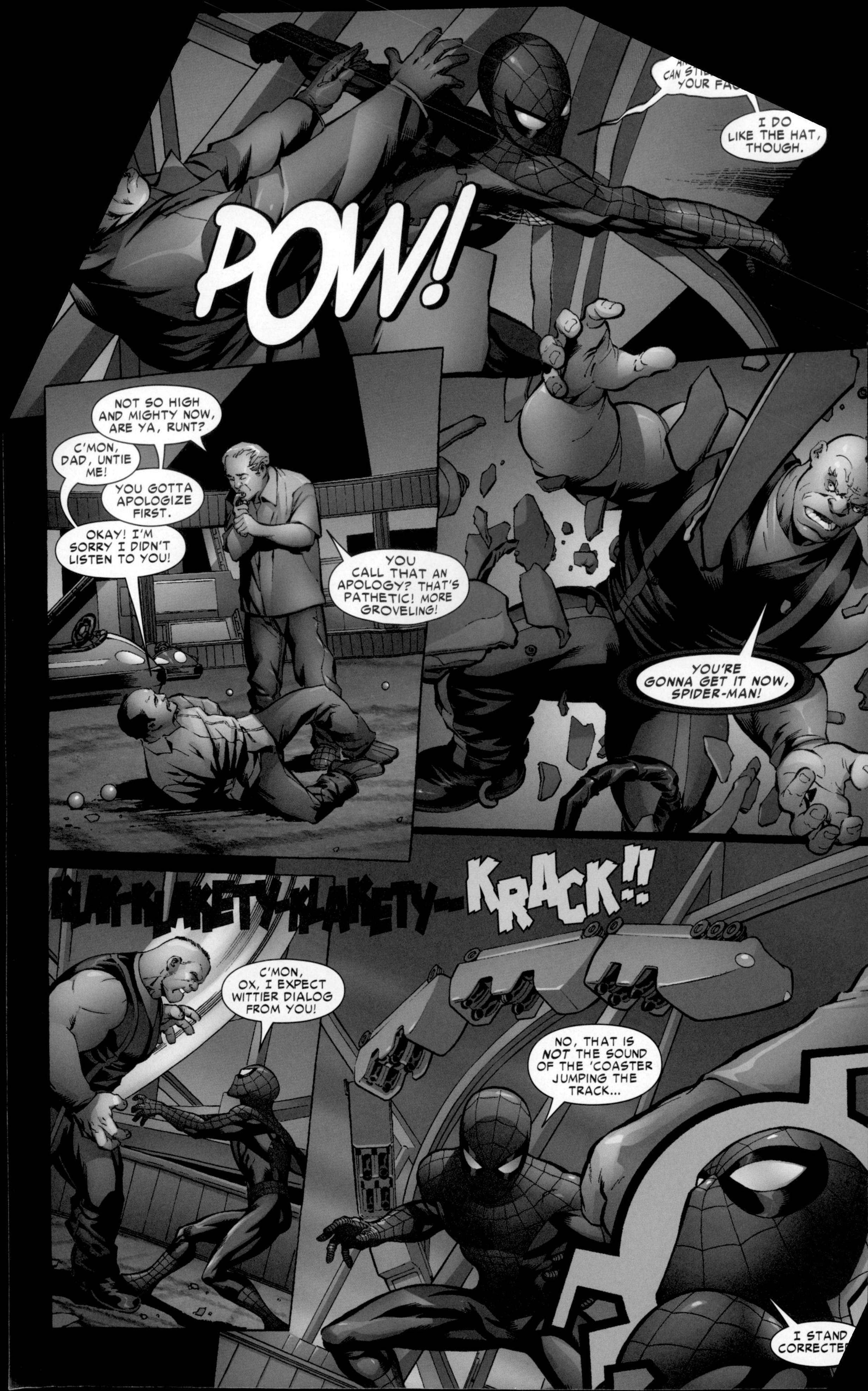
I DO LIKE THE HAT, THOUGH.
POW!
NOT SO HIGH AND MIGHTY NOW, ARE YA, RUNT?
C'MON, DAD, UNTIE ME!
YOU GOTTA APOLOGIZE FIRST.
OKAY! I'M SORRY I DIDN'T LISTEN TO YOU!
YOU CALL THAT AN APOLOGY? THAT'S PATHETIC! MORE GROVELING!
YOU'RE GONNA GET IT NOW, SPIDER-MAN!
KLAK-KLAKETY-KLAKETY-KRACK!!
C'MON, OX, I EXPECT WITTIER DIALOG FROM YOU!
NO, THAT IS NOT THE SOUND OF THE 'COASTER JUMPING THE TRACK...
I STAND

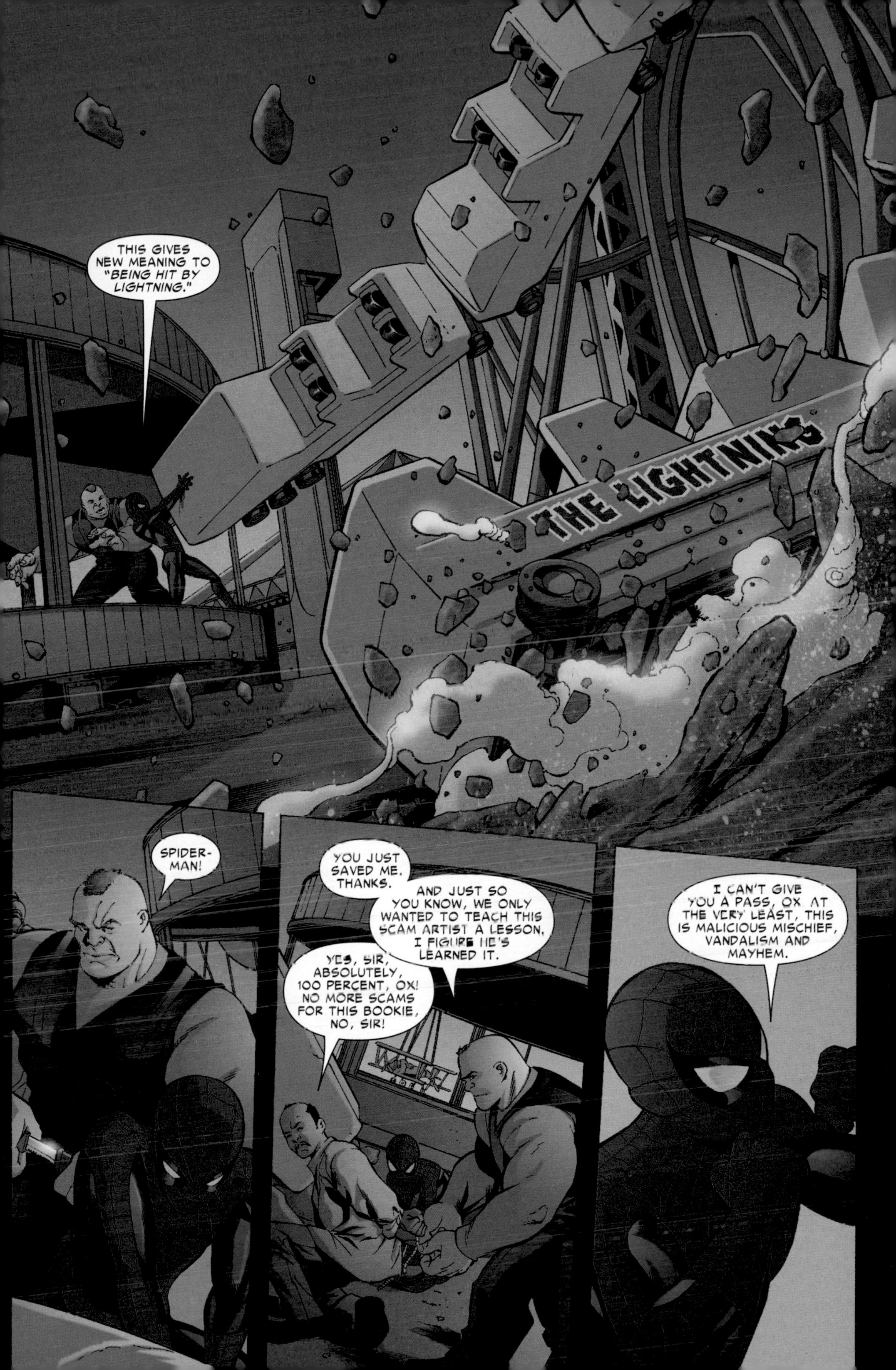
THIS GIVES NEW MEANING TO "BEING HIT BY LIGHTNING."
THE LIGHTNING
SPIDER-MAN!
YOU JUST SAVED ME. THANKS.
AND JUST SO YOU KNOW, WE ONLY WANTED TO TEACH THIS SCAM ARTIST A LESSON. I FIGURE HE'S LEARNED IT.
YES, SIR, ABSOLUTELY, 100 PERCENT, OX! NO MORE SCAMS FOR THIS BOOKIE, NO, SIR!
I CAN'T GIVE YOU A PASS, OX. AT THE VERY LEAST, THIS IS MALICIOUS MISCHIEF, VANDALISM AND MAYHEM.

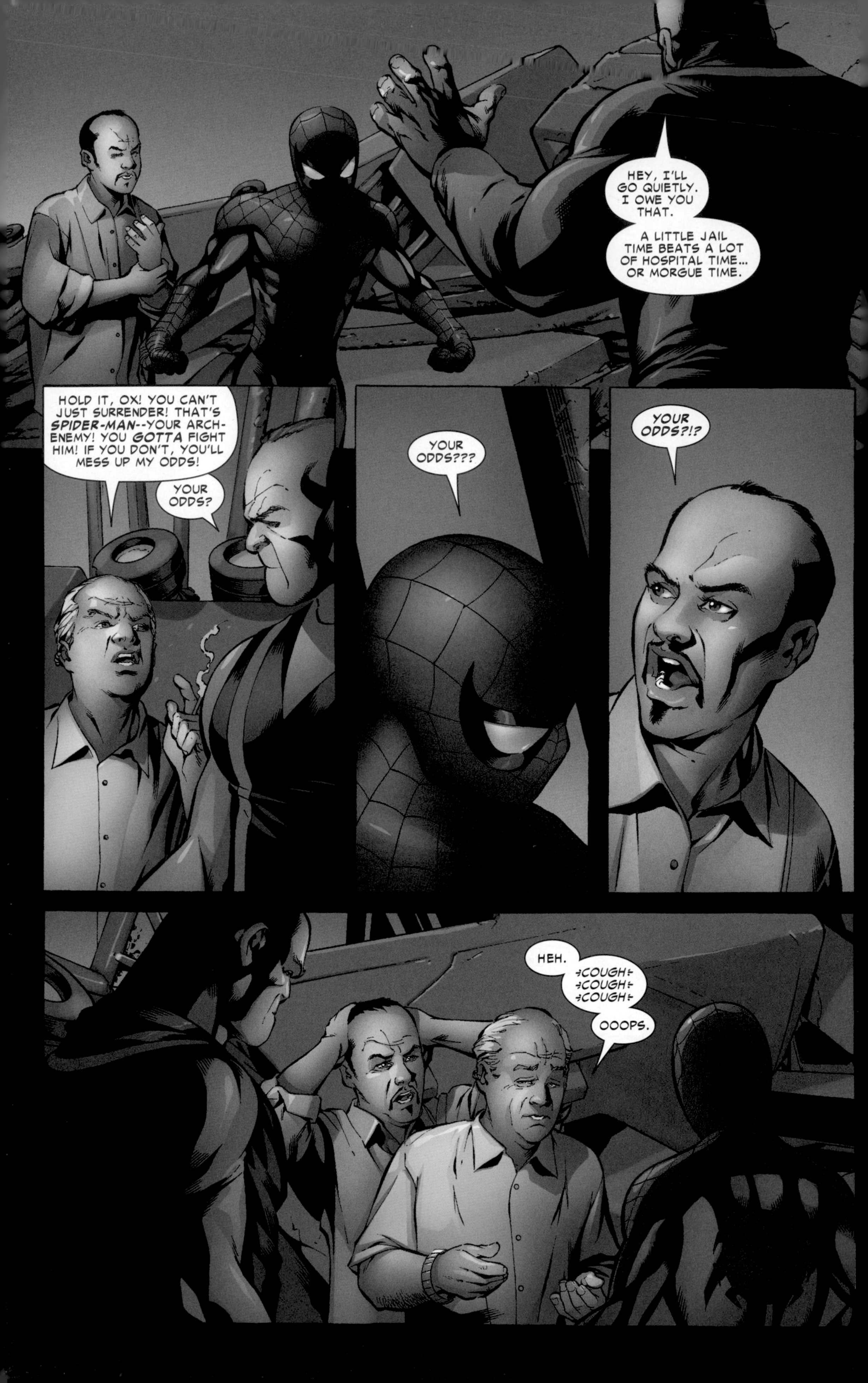

HEY, I'LL GO QUIETLY. I OWE YOU THAT.
A LITTLE JAIL TIME BEATS A LOT OF HOSPITAL TIME... OR MORGUE TIME.
HOLD IT, OX! YOU CAN'T JUST SURRENDER! THAT'S SPIDER-MAN--YOUR ARCH-ENEMY! YOU GOTTA FIGHT HIM! IF YOU DON'T, YOU'LL MESS UP MY ODDS!
YOUR ODDS?
YOUR ODDS???
YOUR ODDS?!?
HEH.
COUGH COUGH COUGH
OOOPS.

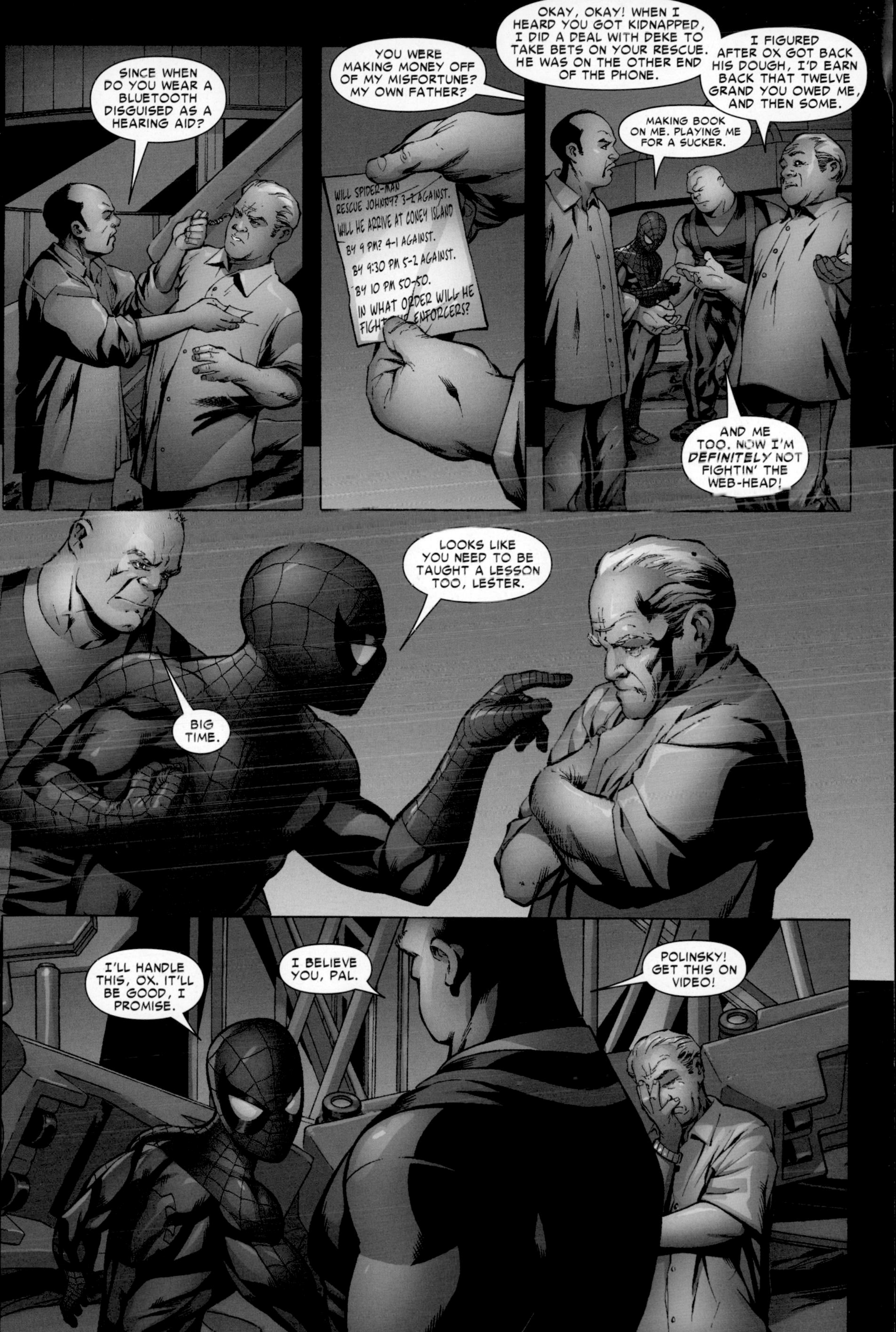
SINCE WHEN DO YOU WEAR A BLUETOOTH DISGUISED AS A HEARING AID?
YOU WERE MAKING MONEY OFF OF MY MISFORTUNE? MY OWN FATHER?
WILL SPIDER-MAN RESCUE JOHNNY? 3-2 AGAINST.
WILL HE ARRIVE AT CONEY ISLAND
BY 9 PM? 4-1 AGAINST.
BY 9:30 PM 5-2 AGAINST.
BY 10 PM 50-50.
IN WHAT ORDER WILL HE
ENFORCERS?
OKAY, OKAY! WHEN I HEARD YOU GOT KIDNAPPED, I DID A DEAL WITH DEKE TO TAKE BETS ON YOUR RESCUE. HE WAS ON THE OTHER END OF THE PHONE.
I FIGURED AFTER OX GOT BACK HIS DOUGH, I'D EARN BACK THAT TWELVE GRAND YOU OWED ME, AND THEN SOME.
MAKING BOOK ON ME. PLAYING ME FOR A SUCKER.
AND ME TOO. NOW I'M *DEFINITELY* NOT FIGHTIN' THE WEB-HEAD!
LOOKS LIKE YOU NEED TO BE TAUGHT A LESSON TOO, LESTER.
BIG TIME.
I'LL HANDLE THIS, OX. IT'LL BE GOOD, I PROMISE.
I BELIEVE YOU, PAL.
POLINSKY! GET THIS ON VIDEO!

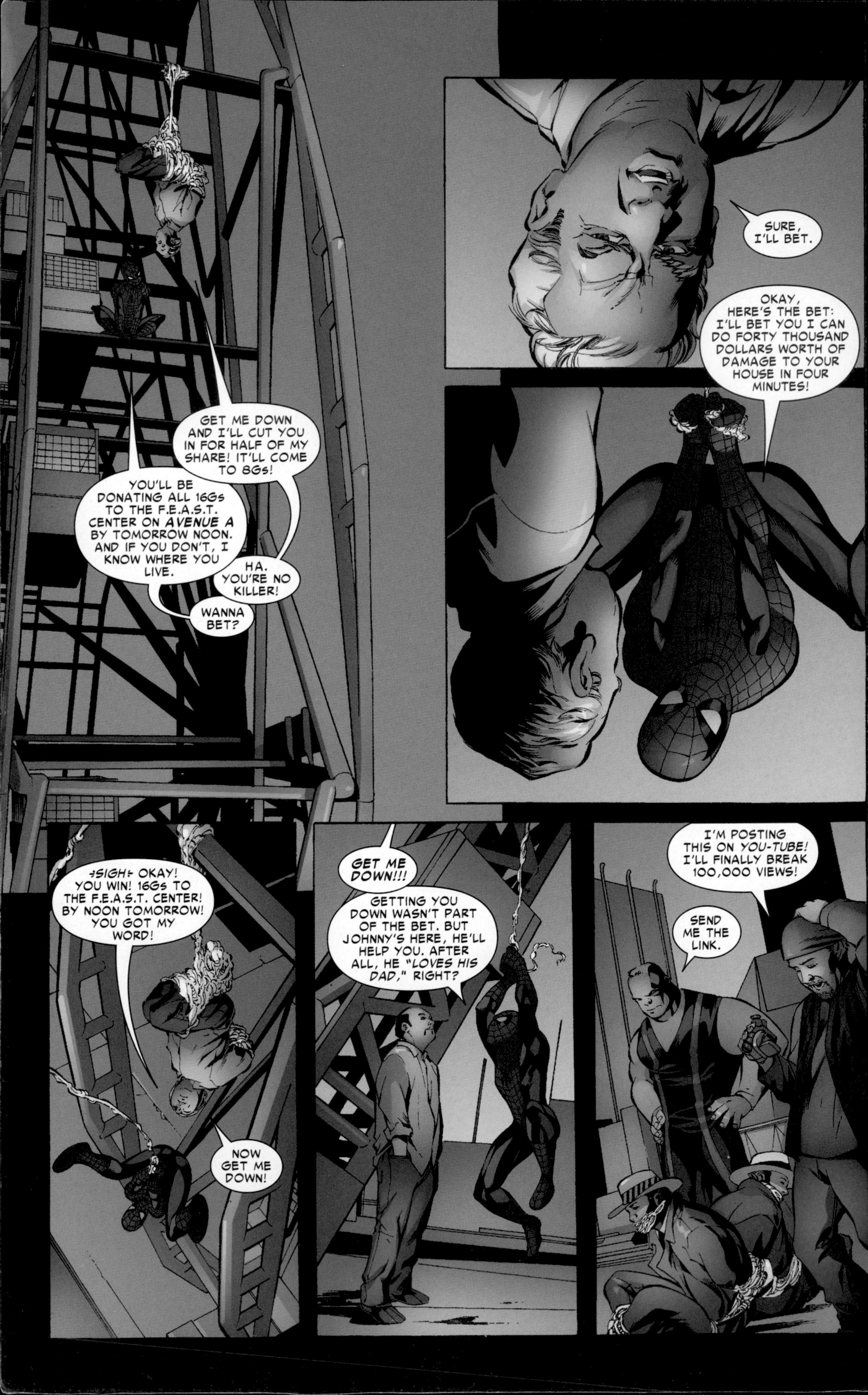

GET ME DOWN AND I'LL CUT YOU IN FOR HALF OF MY SHARE! IT'LL COME TO 8Gs!
YOU'LL BE DONATING ALL 16Gs TO THE F.E.A.S.T. CENTER ON *AVENUE A* BY TOMORROW NOON. AND IF YOU DON'T, I KNOW WHERE YOU LIVE.
HA. YOU'RE NO KILLER!
WANNA BET?
SURE, I'LL BET.
OKAY, HERE'S THE BET: I'LL BET YOU I CAN DO FORTY THOUSAND DOLLARS WORTH OF DAMAGE TO YOUR HOUSE IN FOUR MINUTES!
SIGH OKAY! YOU WIN! 16Gs TO THE F.E.A.S.T. CENTER! BY NOON TOMORROW! YOU GOT MY WORD!
NOW GET ME DOWN!
GET ME DOWN!!!
GETTING YOU DOWN WASN'T PART OF THE BET. BUT JOHNNY'S HERE, HE'LL HELP YOU. AFTER ALL, HE *"LOVES HIS DAD,"* RIGHT?
I'M POSTING THIS ON *YOU-TUBE!* I'LL FINALLY BREAK 100,000 VIEWS!
SEND ME THE LINK.

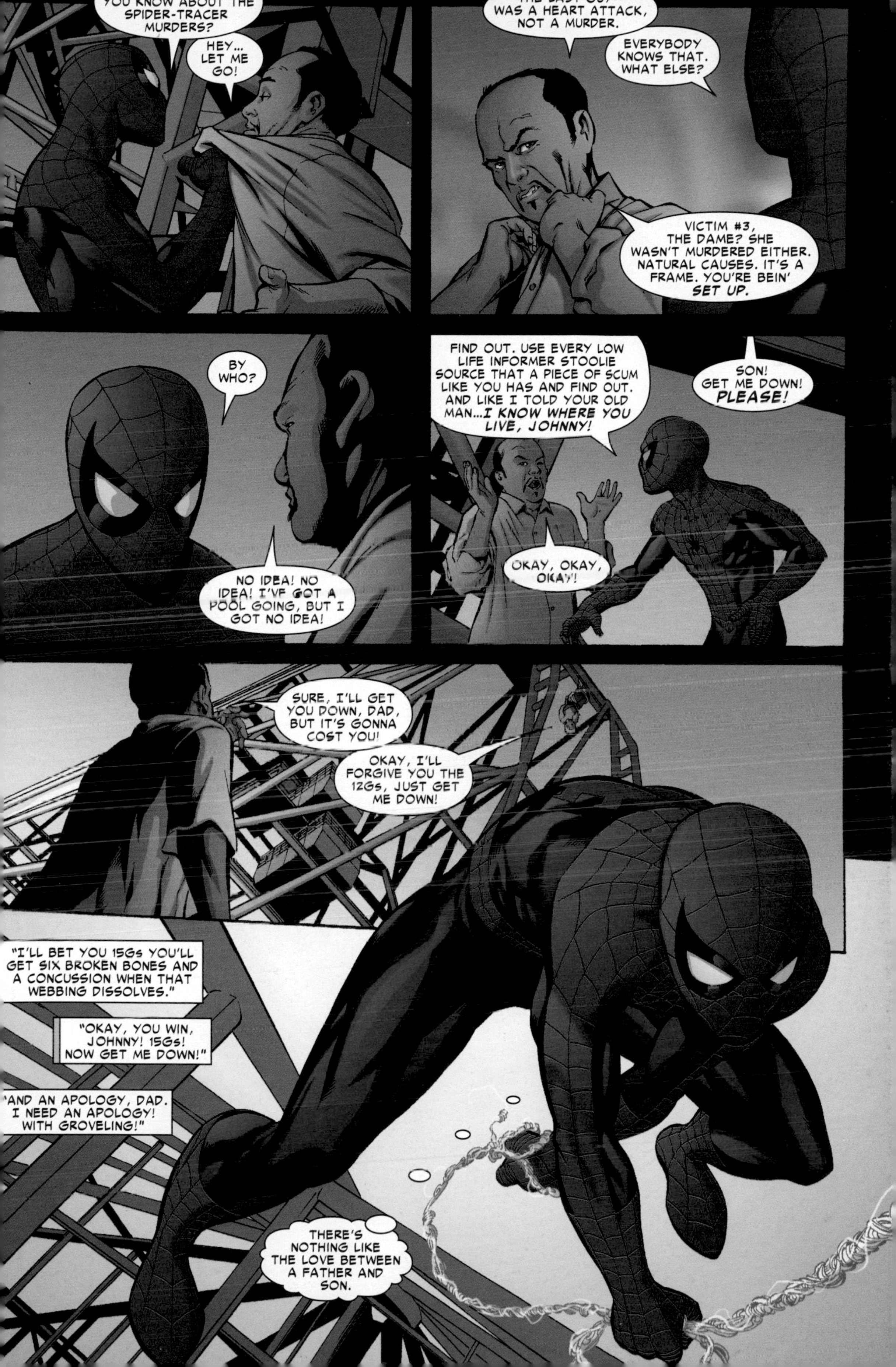
NOW TALK, LOWLIFE! WHAT DO YOU KNOW ABOUT THE SPIDER-TRACER MURDERS?
HEY... LET ME GO!
THE LAST GUY-- WAS A HEART ATTACK, NOT A MURDER.
EVERYBODY KNOWS THAT. WHAT ELSE?
VICTIM #3, THE DAME? SHE WASN'T MURDERED EITHER. NATURAL CAUSES. IT'S A FRAME. YOU'RE BEIN' SET UP.
BY WHO?
NO IDEA! NO IDEA! I'VE GOT A POOL GOING, BUT I GOT NO IDEA!
FIND OUT. USE EVERY LOW LIFE INFORMER STOOLIE SOURCE THAT A PIECE OF SCUM LIKE YOU HAS AND FIND OUT. AND LIKE I TOLD YOUR OLD MAN... I KNOW WHERE YOU LIVE, JOHNNY!
SON! GET ME DOWN! PLEASE!
OKAY, OKAY, OKAY!
SURE, I'LL GET YOU DOWN, DAD, BUT IT'S GONNA COST YOU!
OKAY, I'LL FORGIVE YOU THE 12Gs, JUST GET ME DOWN!
"I'LL BET YOU 15Gs YOU'LL GET SIX BROKEN BONES AND A CONCUSSION WHEN THAT WEBBING DISSOLVES."
"OKAY, YOU WIN, JOHNNY! 15Gs! NOW GET ME DOWN!"
"AND AN APOLOGY, DAD. I NEED AN APOLOGY! WITH GROVELING!"
THERE'S NOTHING LIKE THE LOVE BETWEEN A FATHER AND SON.

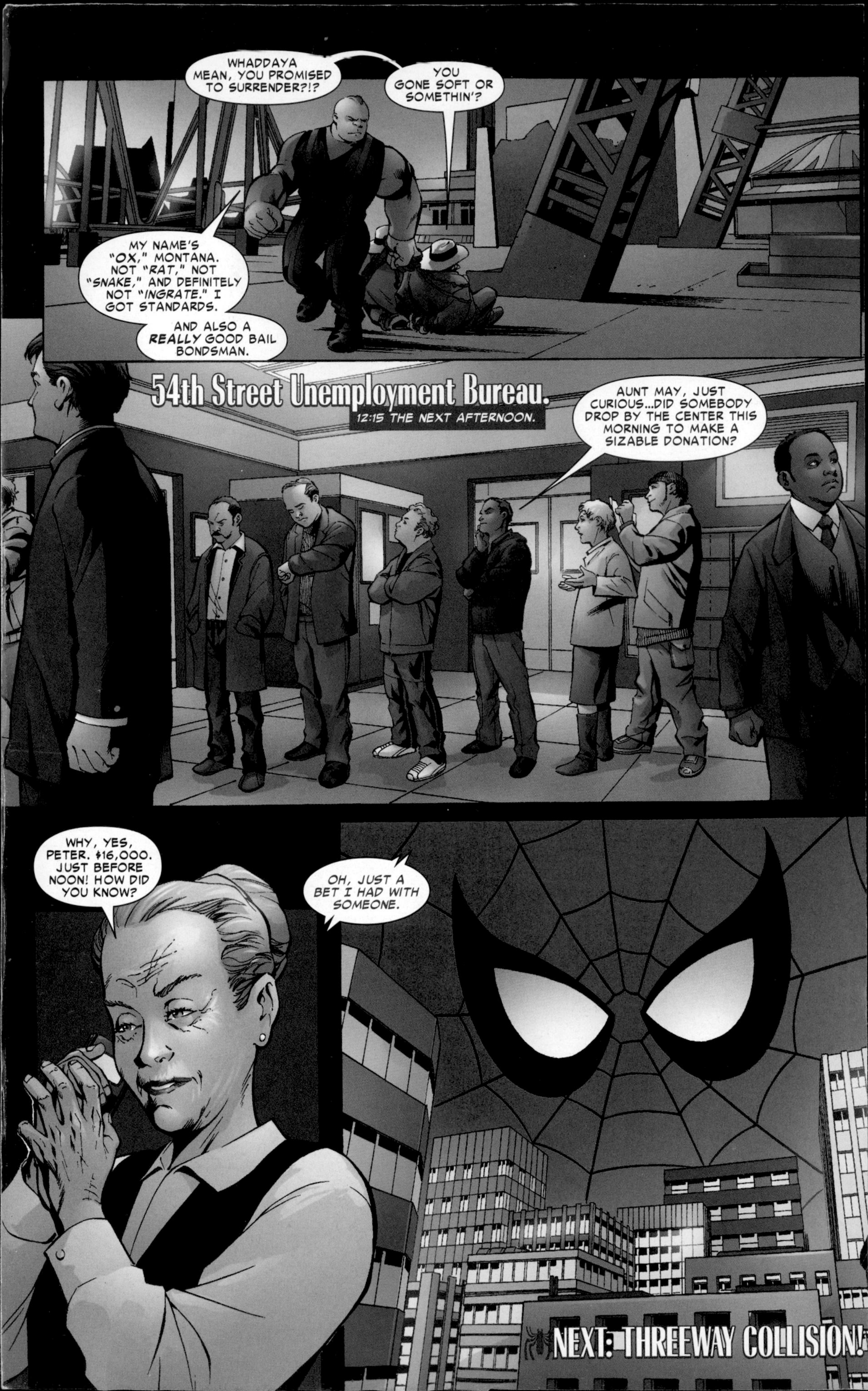
WHADDAYA MEAN, YOU PROMISED TO SURRENDER?!?
YOU GONE SOFT OR SOMETHIN'?
MY NAME'S "OX," MONTANA. NOT "RAT," NOT "SNAKE," AND DEFINITELY NOT "INGRATE." I GOT STANDARDS.
AND ALSO A REALLY GOOD BAIL BONDSMAN.
54th Street Unemployment Bureau.
12:15 THE NEXT AFTERNOON.
AUNT MAY, JUST CURIOUS...DID SOMEBODY DROP BY THE CENTER THIS MORNING TO MAKE A SIZABLE DONATION?
WHY, YES, PETER. $16,000. JUST BEFORE NOON! HOW DID YOU KNOW?
OH, JUST A BET I HAD WITH SOMEONE.
NEXT: THREEWAY COLLISION!